'*Creative Engagement in Psychoanalytic P,*
what is being called the "ontological" turn in psychoanalysis. Henry Markman, in a series of powerful clinically focused papers, shows how the transformation in the analyst, the risk to be opened and altered by emotional contact with an analysand, has extraordinary clinical potential and power. It is not what we know, it is what we allow ourselves to experience. This is psychoanalysis, lived in body and mind, in fantasy and in subtle unconscious transmissions across the analytic dyad. Brave and inspiring.'

Adrienne Harris, *NYU and the New School for Social Research*

'Henry Markman offers psychoanalysts a unique gift. Courageously, with remarkable generosity, openness, and sensitivity, he recounts his personal journey of becoming and being an analyst. This is a crucial contribution to finding ways to treat traumatized states in our patients. In multiple vignettes Markman vividly illustrates his intimate mutual and personal creative engagement, unfolding his unique and never-ending search for authentic involvement with the patient, without, for a moment, relinquishing his theoretical knowledge and analytic responsibility. It is a moving account of the rich vitality of the analyst's work. This book is fearlessly creative, profoundly important.'

Hayuta Gurevich, *Israeli Psychoanalytic Society*

'Henry Markman conceives the analyst's participation as a creative form of companionship. He finds the way to reach his patients' living core, engaging creatively the Body-Mind and exploring embodied participation as unique to each analytic dyad. Inspired by different theoretical sources like Ferenczi, Winnicott, and the South American Field theorists, *Creative Engagement in Psychoanalytic Practice* introduces the reader, with a personal and direct style, to the true spontaneous spirit of contemporary psychoanalysis. This book is essential reading for all the professionals who consider making emotional contact with the patient an irreplaceable priority.'

Riccardo Lombardi, *Italian Psychoanalytic Society*

Creative Engagement in Psychoanalytic Practice

Creative Engagement in Psychoanalytic Practice fills the gaps in current clinical training and theory by highlighting the importance of the analyst's unique voice, creativity, and embodied awareness in authentically being with and relating to patients. In this original and personal account, Henry Markman provides an integrated approach toward analytic work that focuses on engaged embodied dialogue between analyst and patient, where emotional states are shared in an open circuit of communication as the route to self-discovery and growth. The involvement of the analyst's singular and spontaneous self is crucial.

In integrated and illuminating chapters, Markman emphasizes the therapeutic importance of the analyst's embodied presence and openness, improvisational accompaniment, and love within the analytic framework. Vivid clinical vignettes illustrate the emotional work of the analyst that is necessary to be openly engaged in a mutual yet asymmetric relationship. From over 30 years of clinical practice and teaching, Markman has synthesized a variety of contemporary theories in an approachable and alive way.

This book will appeal to psychoanalytically oriented clinicians, ranging from those beginning training to the most seasoned practitioners.

Henry Markman is a psychoanalyst in private practice in Berkeley, CA. He is also a Training and Supervising Analyst at the San Francisco Center for Psychoanalysis.

Relational Perspectives Book Series

The Relational Perspectives Book Series (RPBS) publishes books that grow out of or contribute to the relational tradition in contemporary psychoanalysis. The term *relational psychoanalysis* was first used by Greenberg and Mitchell[1] to bridge the traditions of interpersonal relations, as developed within interpersonal psychoanalysis and object relations, as developed within contemporary British theory. But, under the seminal work of the late Stephen A. Mitchell, the term *relational psychoanalysis* grew and began to accrue to itself many other influences and developments. Various tributaries—interpersonal psychoanalysis, object relations theory, self psychology, empirical infancy research, feminism, queer theory, sociocultural studies, and elements of contemporary Freudian and Kleinian thought—flow into this tradition, which understands relational configurations between self and others, both real and fantasied, as the primary subject of psychoanalytic investigation.

We refer to the relational tradition, rather than to a relational school, to highlight that we are identifying a trend, a tendency within contemporary psychoanalysis, not a more formally organized or coherent school or system of beliefs. Our use of the term *relational* signifies a dimension of theory and practice that has become salient across the wide spectrum of contemporary psychoanalysis. Now under the editorial supervision of Adrienne Harris, Steven Kuchuck, and Eyal Rozmarin, the Relational Perspectives Book Series originated in 1990 under the editorial eye of the late Stephen A. Mitchell. Mitchell was the most prolific and influential of the originators of the relational tradition. Committed to dialogue among psychoanalysts, he abhorred the authoritarianism that dictated adherence to a rigid set of beliefs or technical restrictions. He championed open discussion, comparative and integrative approaches, and promoted new voices across the generations. Mitchell was later joined by the late Lewis Aron, also a visionary and influential writer, teacher, and leading thinker in relational psychoanalysis.

Included in the Relational Perspectives Book Series are authors and works that come from within the relational tradition, those that extend and develop that tradition, and works that critique relational approaches or compare and contrast them with alternative points of view. The series includes our most distinguished senior psychoanalysts, along with younger contributors who bring fresh vision. Our aim is to enable a deepening of relational thinking while reaching across disciplinary and social boundaries in order to foster an inclusive and international literature.

A full list of titles in this series is available at https://www.routledge.com/Relational-Perspectives-Book-Series/book-series/LEARPBS.

Note

1 Greenberg, J. & Mitchell, S. (1983). *Object relations in psychoanalytic theory*. Cambridge, MA: Harvard University Press.

Creative Engagement in Psychoanalytic Practice

Henry Markman

Routledge
Taylor & Francis Group

LONDON AND NEW YORK

First published 2022
by Routledge
2 Park Square, Milton Park, Abingdon, Oxon OX14 4RN

and by Routledge
605 Third Avenue, New York, NY 10158

Routledge is an imprint of the Taylor & Francis Group, an informa business

British Library Cataloguing-in-Publication Data
A catalogue record for this book is available from the British Library

Library of Congress Cataloguing-in-Publication Data
Names: Markman, Henry, author.
Title: Creative engagement in psychoanalytic practice / Henry Markman.
Description: Milton Park, Abingdon, Oxon; New York, NY: Routledge, 2022. | Includes bibliographical references and index.
Identifiers: LCCN 2021022049 | ISBN 9781032077246 (hardback) | ISBN 9781032077239 (paperback) | ISBN 9781003208518 (ebook)
Subjects: LCSH: Psychotherapist and patient. | Creative thinking.
Classification: LCC RC480.8 M367 2022 | DDC 616.89/14--dc23
LC record available at https://lccn.loc.gov/2021022049

ISBN: 978-1-032-07724-6 (hbk)
ISBN: 978-1-032-07723-9 (pbk)
ISBN: 978-1-003-20851-8 (ebk)

DOI: 10.4324/9781003208518

Typeset in Times New Roman
by MPS Limited, Dehradun

For Laura, Noah, and Sam

Contents

Acknowledgments

A growing life is one in dialogue with others. This project could not have been conceived and brought to life without many supportive and inspiring people. Conversations with them nourished my efforts and challenged me to think more, imagine more, reach for more—and strive for greater clarity, honesty, directness, and humility. It is with great pleasure and gratitude that I acknowledge their contributions now.

Several supervisors and mentors are mentioned in the introduction. I would like to thank them here: Stan Goodman, the late Betty Joseph, Owen Renik, and Hayuta Gurevich.

My thanks go to the Center for the Advancement of Psychoanalytic Studies group for lively discussions of clinical work and a space to discuss various, at times controversial, approaches and ideas. I especially want to thank Alexandra Harrison for our conversations about the "the music and dance" of therapy, and Steve Ablon for giving me a sense of how a child analyst listens to adult work. Joseph Fernando and Dwarky Rao patiently and critically listened as I developed some of the ideas in this book. Their love of dialogue is a gift.

I want to thank the "Semi-Baked" writing group for stirring and nurturing the writing process in me. Ric Almond, Terry Becker, Marilyn Caston, Joe Caston, Daphne de Marneffe, Dianne Elise, Sam Gerson, Peter Goldberg, Barbara Hauser, Laura Klein, Deborah Melman, Shelley Nathans, Rachael Peltz, Carolyn Wilson, Tsipora Peskin, and the late Harvey Peskin heard early versions of several chapters and helped shape the final presentation. I am grateful for Dianne Elise's encouragement and example of the writing and publishing process. Peter Goldberg's work on the body, music, and the analyst's necessary active role has had a strong influence on my thinking. Sam Gerson and I have exchanged psychoanalytical ideas going back 30 years. He is a present, gentle (though not uncritical) interlocutor. Along the way, when I mentioned a yet-to-be-realized desire to write, Sam encouraged me in meaningful ways that moved me forward. Mitch Wilson is a powerful thinker and generous friend, one who inhabits a very broad swath of psychoanalytic literature and history. This had made our teaching together and conversations a richly rewarding and usefully challenging learning experience. Terrance Becker and I share a love of psychoanalysis as it is practiced, eliciting help from each other to discern difficult clinical situations over the years. In our conversations, we often discuss curative factors in analysis and his insistence on the importance of the analyst's personal involvement, even love, in helping others.

I want to thank John Di Martini, David Socholitzky, and Susan Yamaguchi for reading and responding to the first chapters of the book. And Sandy Bemesderfer, Steve Baum, Robert Eskuchen, Ben Goldstone, and Suzanne Klein for their careful read of Chapter 7

Elizabeth Hersh read early versions of the chapters and the final manuscript. She encouraged me to bring out personal qualities in my writing.

I also want to thank Patricia Marra for bringing her skills as a psychoanalytic thinker and copy-editor to the task of pruning and clarifying my writing, for the better.

My friend and colleague Jim Dimon carefully read and responded to the entire manuscript. At times, he understood better than I did what I wanted to do and say. His sensitivity to language and style, and his deep knowledge of psychoanalytic ideas were invaluable to me.

I gratefully acknowledge my patients, from whom I learned the most important things about doing this work. I grew as a person in this process with them and because of them. It is really a privilege to be given their trust and honesty and to witness their courage and growth.

Finally, deep gratitude beyond words goes to my family—my wife Laura Klein, and our sons Noah and Sam. They have been loving companions on this journey. Laura, also a psychoanalyst, has read every word in the book. I depend on her perfect pitch to hear what is authentic (or not) in my written voice. She has an uncanny, no-nonsense way to get to the heart of the matter. Her sensitive input allowed me to find and maintain my voice in the writing.

Chapter 5 is based on "Embodied attunement and participation", *Journal of the American Psychoanalytic Association, 68*(5), 807–834. Used with permission from SAGE Publications, Inc. 5017801989610

Chapter 6 is based on "Accompaniment in jazz and psychoanalysis", *Psychoanalytic Dialogues, 30* (4), 432–447. Used with permission from Taylor & Francis Group, 5021350710905

Chapter 7 is based on "One-sided analysis is no longer possible": the relevance of "mutual analysis" in our current world, *fort da,* XXVII (1), Spring 2021. Used with permission from the Northern California Society for Psychoanalytic Psychology (NCSPP).

Introduction

Life itself consists in phases in which the organism falls out of step with the march of surrounding things and then recovers unison with it ... And, in the *growing life*, the recovery is never mere return to a prior state, for it is enriched by the state of disparity and resistance through which it has successfully passed.

— John Dewey, *Art as Experience*, 1934

For over 30 years of psychoanalytic practice and teaching, as I moved through various sorts of clinical experiences, I began to consider more and more my analytic way of being with and relating to another in my care. As I taught therapists and analysts during my career, I tried to convey this sensibility to them. I call this over-arching clinical approach "creative engagement"—an approach intended for both psychoanalytic therapists and psychoanalysts.

There are various experiences in psychoanalysis[1] that lead to change in our patients: they come to understand their emotional conflicts and the source of their distress; they feel recognized, supported, and cared for; they find companionship and a space to explore and experiment, to discover more of who they are. The therapeutic foundation of these experiences depends on our personal qualities of relating and participating. These qualities are expressed in the unique, authentic, and creative way we engage. This is the bedrock of our work—what we bring to the relationship in terms of our personal ways of being open and present, attuning and accompanying, and offering care. These creative efforts foster a potential

DOI: 10.4324/9781003208518-101

space where developments at a deep level can occur, between me and my patients.

I will focus in this book on the personal and emotional foundation of our work, emphasizing how I (and every analyst) creatively find—often struggles to find—distinctive therapeutic ways to relate to and meet each patient. We cannot be neutral. Our patients need us to bring in our full emotional, expressive, and authentic selves to the relationship. Who we are and how we are is an inherent part of the therapeutic process. It can at times be what impedes. We need to be in a constant process of self-sensing and self-knowing with each patient in order to track this. This self-sensing inevitably leads to disruption and growth. It also provides an ethical background to our work.

Fundamental clinical concepts make up a creatively engaged approach. These elements seem simple but are powerfully therapeutic and require hard emotional work. I have organized the book so that each chapter focuses on one of these elements that become the building blocks of a creatively engaged approach.

Chapter 1—"Creative engagement: an overture"—is a bird's eye view of creative engagement and its elements, which I illustrate with a detailed clinical case.

Chapter 2—"The development of analytic authenticity"—explores the nature and therapeutic importance of being authentically engaged and finding our own unique voice in our work. I use my analytic development to illustrate this, while also drawing on essential contributions from the literature.

Chapter 3—"Embodied presence: the analyst's home base"—introduces *presence* as our home base and the hub of our intended therapeutic actions and involvement. I will describe how to recognize the emotional and bodily qualities of presence in ourselves.

Chapter 4—"The analyst's emotional work of surrender and mourning"—describes the necessary, hard emotional work to attain openness and presence. Understanding and making use of our emotional experience and moving toward openness begin by taking up our own transferences to the patient and attachments to our ways of being and working that first need to be worked through.

Chapter 5—"Embodied attunement and participation"—follows the clinical consequences of viewing the analytic relationship as embodied. I look at the way we attune and engage in the bodily dimension of our work: the interactive, shared rhythms, tones, cadences, and gestures.

Chapter 6—"The analyst as improvisational accompanist"— continues to look at the clinical importance of embodiment. I illustrate with clinical and musical examples our efforts to find the right accompaniment found in our spontaneity and improvisation.

Chapter 7—"One-sided analysis is no longer possible": "mutual analysis" as the analysis of mutuality—considers the concept of mutuality as a vital clinical legacy of Ferenczi's clinical experiments. I argue for the ongoing relevance of the spirit of mutual analysis in our current clinical approach.

Chapter 8—"The radical uncertainty of psychoanalytic practice"— takes up our experience of (and resistance to) uncertainty in the session, as a central analytic sensibility and ethic. I draw on the metaphor of listening to dissonant music and the work of Bion and Berenstein.

Chapter 9—"Two modes of therapeutic time"—looks at modes of subjective time in analysis: "being-with-ness" and "now moments". The former, after Winnicott, describes a subjective timeless quality of un-impingement that we provide for the patient toward developing a stronger sense of self. The latter mode, after Stern, explores heightened passages of living that result from a disruption of the status quo and a reorganization of the relational dynamics and self-states in the patient and ourselves.

Chapter 10—"Moments of transformation and beauty"—further develops a model of mutual transformation. I bring in a developmental perspective and the language of aesthetics.

Chapter 11—"Process and non-process"—integrates the elements of creative engagement across the span of a treatment. I focus on the concept of *vinculo* and the "open circuit of communication", described by Pichon-Riviere, as the hallmark of the analytic process. I hypothesize "non-process" as a breakdown in communication, often caused by the analyst's inability to be open to receiving the patient's communication. I present specific forms of non-process and the way we can intervene to renew communication between ourselves and our patients.

Chapter 12—"Creative engagement in these times"—looks at the impact of COVID-19 on our work, and the enduring effort in us and our patients to communicate across many mediums. In this experience we find what is most essential in our work, and that our creative engagement fosters.

The chapters progress with each idea interlocking and depending on the others for its clinical meaning and depth. I have structured the book so that these key elements reappear in subsequent chapters, are progressively integrated with the newer concepts, and illustrated by additional clinical examples. Each time we refocus on a concept, it's enriched.

To describe the emotional level where things happen, where the particular personalities and vulnerabilities of each participant matter, I present many clinical examples. I feel this is the best way to show how I work, the emotional challenges that are involved, and the clinical ideas that guide me. Each chapter revolves around at least one vignette to illustrate the particular clinical idea I am developing. The clinical encounter is central; theory follows.

Freud, the Rat Man, and I

Recently, an experience brought home my evolution as an analyst and my shifting perspective that led to my current approach. I taught Freud's (1909) Rat Man Case to candidates for the first time in more than 25 years. Previously, as an early career psychoanalyst, I taught the paper to illustrate Freud's brilliant insights into the roots of obsessional neurosis—his depiction of the power of unconscious phantasy stirred by Oedipal rivalry. Freud's way of working with Ernst Lanzer (The Rat Man) was primarily didactic, explaining the cause of his suffering rooted in his phantasy wish to kill his father as an oedipal rival, and fearing retaliation. That Lanzer's father actually died when he was a late adolescent launched his obsessional symptoms—his phantasy was actualized. These ideas of Freud's were the main ones I originally taught, as Freud's heavy-handed clinical interpretive style was at odds with the then-current ideas of resistance interpretation. I could not find in the Rat Man an illustration of modern ideas of therapeutic action, so this dimension of the case—what really helped Lanzer—was not discussed.

When I taught the case again. I was interested in an important aspect of Freud's clinical engagement that I now found actually therapeutic. I saw the case with fresh eyes and a different emphasis and was taken by the alive relationship between Freud and Lanzer. I can only describe this relationship as a loving one.

Freud's analysis of Lanzer's oedipal conflicts seemed therapeutically important. Yet, I now believe Freud's interpretive power primarily rested on the nature of their personal relationship. Freud's way of being with Lanzer was truly his own, in the frame-changing, intimate conversation that he developed and fostered. Lanzer had to find in Freud a loving and attentive father, a robust father he could not kill (or be killed by in retaliation). It seemed to me that Freud sincerely loved Lanzer as a father loves his son—in the potential space the analytic conversation creates. He loved Lanzer in the support, affection, and careful attention he paid to him. Because of the relationship Freud offered, Lanzer could face the early loss of the father he dearly loved (and hated, perhaps killed in phantasy) and was finally able to mourn that loss. This crucial transformative element was not explicitly theorized in the text.[2]

This teaching experience showed me much about the road I traveled in finding my voice and my approach as an analyst (and teacher). I am not aligned to one particular psychoanalytic tradition. The ideas that make up creative engagement are an integrated blend of analytic theories and models I have found most helpful in doing this work—especially ideas that open up the personal, emotional dimension of the analytic interaction. This has been an ongoing pragmatic process for me, where I ask myself what this particular idea offers me concretely in my work (its "cash value" to use William James's [1907] metaphor for the pragmatic consequences of a particular idea). To assimilate these diverse influences, I have had to develop a personal language. And, I also searched for language to describe the indescribable in my experience with patients—states of mind and modes of communication, often primitive and resistant to symbolization.

This book is my effort to pass on my personal assimilation of what I find fundamental in this very specialized conversation Freud invented for one person to heal another. I am in an alive conversation with those who taught me along the way, in passing on what they believed most important to know in doing this work. And, I have been in conversations with colleagues and students that were lively, at times argumentative, almost always informative. Writers also join this chorus—as psychoanalysis is both an oral and a written tradition. This ongoing dialogue has been with me throughout my years of practice and teaching. It is the personal relationships in all these conversations that led to my emotional and intellectual growth—even if the relationship was with an analyst or writer I had never met or who worked before my time. The practice of psychoanalysis is a living thing, a *growing life*—to bring Dewey back in. These learning experiences altered and expanded, at times exploded my analytic mind, and pressed me to change and grow, enlarging what I could offer patients. Contradictory, at times disruptive, experience needed to be integrated along the way in becoming the analyst I am.

My psychoanalytic culture and teachers

I entered analytic training at an American Psychoanalytic Institute that taught the structural model—ego psychology—and the clinical approach of "classical technique". Classical technique is when the analyst functions more or less as a "mirror" (Freud's metaphor), primarily communicating through interpretation that is carefully dosed, starting at the surface to avoid piercing the patient's defenses. This method, in the right hands, shows great respect for the patient's autonomy, psychic reality, and vulnerability. The work is not rushed.

Although "technique" means a particular stance and way of communicating, I noticed that other, personal aspects of the analyst's way of being and relating also seemed therapeutic. I tried to pay attention to these qualities as well —even if these qualities were not talked about that much.

My first teachers and my training analyst had sensitive and strong personalities, and each had a unique therapeutic way of being present and embodying care. And their care came through. Some had very colorful personalities. This was all within a more or less "classical" tradition. I also knew that some analysts were described as working in ways that fell well outside the traditional guidelines—arguing with their patients, giving advice, and personally disclosing. I heard a story about a famous analyst who was heard yelling to his patient as she left his office, "You must not marry him!" These were thought to be the exceptions—at least when it became public. But what part did these exceptions play in helping or hindering patients, I wondered to myself?

I valued qualities my teachers (and analyst) embodied in their way of working—a capacity to listen carefully and patiently, opening up space for the patient to roam. The standard framework I was exposed to—even if not always followed—seemed to bring out some very good qualities in the analyst. One analyst wonderfully said, "We are all Watson to the patient's Holmes" meaning, "Let the patient teach us who they are and why they suffer. Don't be too smart in sorting them out". There was real humility and wisdom there. I believed my teachers practiced in ways that helped their patients well beyond how they conceptualized this, at least in conversation with me as a student. I wanted to know what did they emotionally bring to the conversation that helped?

My first teachers and analyst had a gift for non-judgmental openness, which allowed the patient to speak as freely as possible. They also brought deep insights about emotional conflicts into their conversation with their patients. My first analytic supervisor, Stan Goodman, was a wise man and a deep listener to the patient's unconscious desires and anxieties, communicated in their associations. Speech, I learned from Goodman, always says more, reveals more than its content, all the time. One needed to pay careful attention and listen carefully. And Goodman heard the underlying messages, even if, and often when, the patient did not. I came to appreciate how richly meaningful human speech is—the flow of words particularly. In attending now to the patient's speech, I often have Goodman's words in my mind: "The patient cannot change the subject"—psychic determinism expressed in an aphorism—because the unconscious is always speaking. The unconscious as it emerges in speech is a web of related, connected meanings, desires, and fears. I still listen in this way as part of my work, for the palpable unconscious expression in speech.

Goodman also taught me about interpretation, the transformative effect of putting experience into words. Putting things into words creates a new reality. I noticed that when my patients were free to associate out loud they encountered unknown parts of themselves— hidden wishes, desires, and fears. They surprised themselves with what they said to me and to themselves. And when I could name an emotion, state, or phantasy, it was as if the patient now had a mental handle to consider and interrogate and play with it. In language, something now existed that could be seen. As one patient said to me, "What have I been saying ... how are you hearing me?" This person understands that she is saying something that is below the surface, coming from elsewhere, out of her awareness, and she is expecting me to attend to that dimension. From Goodman, I aspired to listen as he did and find words, as he artfully did, for what had been unspokenly spoken. His credo was "less is more", meaning, instead of explaining, let the patient do something with what we say in their own way, sometimes expansively, sometimes anxiously and defensively.

Yet, what affected me as much was Goodman's *way* of attending—a warm, quiet, and thoughtful manner—with a tinge of irony about himself and the world. I wanted to emulate or at least find my own way to do what he did. It was ... something so difficult to name at the time, his *presence*. This is an important yet illusive concept, presence, and it took me years to find a good language to talk about it. I will devote a full chapter to its meaning and value. I never asked him about his way of being present and whether he considered it part of his technique or how he developed and maintained this—even *if* he developed it consciously. I think I did not venture there because aspects of my personality that obviously came into my work were not of interest to him—at least we didn't talk about it. The analyst's personality, it seemed, was not relevant, as long as it did not cloud good listening and get in the way of the patient. But what if it *helped?* My personality and his personality were important ingredients in engaging the patient, so it was strange we could not discuss it.

Owen Renik was another influential teacher early on in my development, very different from Goodman in two ways. Renik was interested in the subjectivity of the analyst and in clinical experimentation. He had a strong pragmatic streak. What works was more important to him than following the prescribed technique. Renik gave me the freedom to talk about my experiments with patients. He liked to think about the most effective way to make the point and help the patient develop. He would listen to my detailed process notes patiently, but clearly not in a fine-grained way. Instead of hearing the material as Goodman did, the unfurling of unconscious wishes and desires, he would say, tapping his fingers impatiently on his desk,

"Why isn't this guy dating? What is he doing in analysis to get over his fear of women?" These questions had a practical meaning: What was I doing to help the patient with the problem that brought him to analysis? How come listening and interpreting did not always lead to concrete gain? He used the metaphor of the painter's palette: "We're always looking for new colors to add to our analytic palette to use in order to reach the patient, to affect the patient". When I stumbled upon a new color, he was always supportive. I was coming to view my work as encompassing participation and activity in addition to listening and interpretation.

Renik viewed enactments as inevitable and knowable only in retrospect—making the analyst and patient's subjectivities essential parts of the process. This puts the analyst in a decentered, non-objective position that fits well with my experience being with patients.[3]

Then, early on, I entered a study group with Betty Joseph that lasted over 20 years. This had a defining influence on me but perhaps in ways not expected. Joseph thought it possible to use one's countertransference to avoid entanglements, or, at least, get untangled. She viewed projective identification as pressure on the analyst to enact. In practice, in listening to case after case, she noted the analyst's participation in enactments, yielding to the patient's projective identifications rather than understanding them. Interpretation for Joseph was the way, the only way, to interrupt and make meaning of enactments—once we stopped enacting, that is. This was important in my developing understanding of the analyst's emotional work. Like Renik, she recognized the inevitable nature of enacting. But her emphasis on the internal work of the analyst to recognize emotional states engendered by the relationship, *as it is happening*, was an extremely valuable insight. The analyst's work begins in self-awareness, in the here-and-now.

To bring this point home, process notes were presented in our study group with very little context. Our attention would then be directed to the present moment, not influenced by theory or history. As the group read the notes together, all of us, including Joseph (who did not read notes beforehand), encountered the analyst-patient dyad for the first time. This group experience was a model for an important kind of listening and receptivity, starting in the dark and gaining a view of the patient's world by what he or she *does* with the analyst.

But what felt most meaningful to me was Joseph's focus on what enactments do. Enactments protect the vulnerable part of the patient in need of contact and understanding in a dependent relationship with their analyst. As long as enactments occurred, the part of the self that needs the analyst's help remains inaccessible. Joseph was very skeptical of "good" interpretations in the classical Freudian or Kleinian sense. For her, enactments need to be interrupted by interpretation, and these inevitably come as a surprise to the patient. Joseph could sense when the patient unconsciously led the analyst to expectable interpretations that remained emotionally limited. Joseph wanted the analyst's interventions to grab the patient's attention in a deeper, emotionally disruptive, non-conscious way. No reconstructions, no comments about yesterday's session, no speculation about motivations, but a clear description (she called it a "running commentary") of what is going on now between patient and analyst, and what the patient unconsciously wants the analyst to feel and do.

Joseph's attention to what transpires in the moment-to-moment exchanges conveyed a fundamental loving care for the hurt or tortured part of the patient. She could say quite confrontative and disturbing things to the omnipotent part of patients because of her care for the vulnerable part of the patient and what she truly believed they needed. This care was fundamentally (fiercely?) communicated. This is a guiding principle in my work to this day.

One point to add here: Joseph's style was inimitable. What I mean is that her way of being, listening, engaging, was authentically hers. Again, there was something striking about her presence. To try to be like her in the work—I noticed this in myself—felt like imitation and not really embodied. I struggled to make use of her ideas while remaining myself.

I was unsettled though by two aspects of her approach that left out elements of the analytic relationship. First, there was a focus on the here-and-now that could narrow the analyst's view of the subjectivity of the patient. I remember a famous philosopher, who upon hearing a (Kleinian) clinical presentation, asked in jest, "Didn't anyone visit the patient? Aunts and uncles ... friends?" The point is that our patients live in a context of family, history, ethnicity, and culture, and these influences are important elements of who they are—and who *we* are.

There is another important dimension of analytic process that was missing for me in Joseph's clinical theory: the analyst contributes *independently* their own transferences and projective identifications to the relationship. When Michael Feldman came a few times to the group, I started reading his important articles. Solidly in the neo-Kleinian tradition, Feldman was subtly more radical,[4] I thought, by describing the way the analyst also uses projective identification to stabilize his (or her) sense of self. The analyst uses the patient as well.[5] Feldman also seemed less sure than Joseph of the analyst's position of knowing—perhaps as a result of his expanded, mutual view of projective identification.

An important development in my growth over the last several years comes from regular meetings with Israeli analyst Hayuta Gurevich, a clinician deeply committed to the tradition of Ferenczi and Winnicott. She embodies their spirit as a wonderful teacher of their ideas in clinically immediate ways. Gurevich's theoretical grounding and support helped me theorize the way I was working that I had not articulated before. Highly attuned to the impact of environmental failures in childhood—not experienced but dissociated—and how this inevitably shows up in the analytic relationship, she is attentive to our analytic failures in terms of our absence *in the sessions* as traumatic repetitions, and how to recognize and take responsibility for this. This allows the patient to experience—make present—these absences. I gained an understanding that my absences and misattunements, if acknowledged, make present for the patient what could not be experienced before.

So, in listening to my work, Gurevich emphasized the progressive aspects of the interaction that had often felt to me to be destructive and defensive. In her view, the patient will bring in, if the emotional environment is right, the most difficult, dissociated aspects of their traumatic history to be experienced that are made present in the relationship with the analyst. This view really enlarged my receptivity to moments between me and the patient that had previously felt hopeless or dead or maddening.

Gurevich also introduced me to Ferenczi's (Dupont, 1995) *Clinical Diaries*. His unique voice gives us a rich language for the very personal nature of our work and how to think about our contribution in a mutual way. Ferenczi is the father of intersubjectivity and decenteredness. You will hear Ferenczi's voice interwoven with mine throughout the book—which is one of Gurevich's gifts to me.

Clinical and personal experience

I have described the seminal teachers in my career in a linear, historical way. Now, I want to go back in time to recount a clinical experience coincident with my analytic training that dramatically changed the course of my work—though at the time I could not theorize this change.

Early on, I worked with adolescents as a significant part of my practice. Shortly after completing my psychiatric residency, I became the medical director of adolescent treatment programs in both hospital and day treatment settings, and half of my private practice consisted of adolescent patients. The unique kind of interaction and world that adolescents bring to therapy shaped my clinical sensibility from the get-go. With adolescents, I was more active, experimental, and playful—more "real"—and brought in a more alive and spontaneous part of me into the relationship.

From my work with adolescents, I wrote a paper (1997) describing a central element of adolescent treatment as "interactive play": the patient's playful use of the interaction in ways that invite the therapist to meet the patient at the point of his or her developmental crisis. I was starting to think about play happening beyond child therapy, into adolescent and adult work. I recognized the intrinsic therapeutic value of this play—a non-defensive action-dimension that had therapeutic value in its own right. I wrote that "viewing the interaction as play offers specific technical choices, and participating in the play is a constructive clinical activity which deepens the work... The analyst's attention is usefully drawn to ways the play progresses or is interfered with by his or her own behavior, as seen in the patient's response" (p. 191).

Adolescents have an acute sense of the therapist's attitudes and intentions, and are most willing to say something about it. Most can detect insincerity and inauthenticity immediately. Most do not tolerate neutrality and so force active engagement in interactive play. These young patients were searching for a sense of themselves in an environment that is responsive and that feels real to them. The importance of *authenticity* in the interaction is essential for a growing relationship. The climate adolescents create, the insistent felt realness of the interaction they forced and demanded, allowed me a much greater creative range than I had yet permitted myself in work with adults.

Many of the adolescents I saw came from traumatic (neglectful and abusive) backgrounds. In almost every case the teenager blamed themselves for what happened, and this manifested in self-destructive behavior of some sort. Or their sense of themselves was so unstable as a result of the lack of basic parental provisions that they relied on destructive ways to hold themselves together—often addictively with drugs and food and sex. I tried to help them face the agonizing reality of their experience of environmental failures. I tried to put their inner world into words to give them tools for reflecting on themselves and their object world and history. From this, I sharpened my view of the patient within an environmental context and not as an isolate. At that time, I was also clarifying my ideas about the development of the self and its response to impingements, as well as the varieties of the ways they cohere and self-regulate, or don't (i.e., as in dissociation).

Eventually, my experiences with adolescents changed how I worked with my adult patients. I became more playful. I also realized that what adolescent patients were striving for was not so different from that of my adult patients. Many adult patients do not have a strong sense of self and do not have an enduring feeling of well-being and internal safety. Space for them to discover this, often in playful interaction, taught me something I understood later: the idea of potential space and transitional phenomena as a path to self-establishment. In myself, I had a new feeling of freedom and aliveness in my work. I noticed that this spirit added rather than detracted from a deepening of intimacy and emotional growth with all my patients.

As an adolescent, my own personal experience in treatment was very convincing about how analysis works and the qualities the analyst brings that really matter. I was struggling and found a low-fee analytic candidate to help me sort things out. With him, I had unprecedented experiences of open receptivity—a non-judgmental invitation. This analysis progressed very slowly by outside measures, but it allowed me to search for and establish a firmer sense of myself in his unobtrusive presence. He eventually said many things to me, understandings that are with me to this day, but it was the way he allowed me to emerge that was most crucial. However clumsily and confusingly I expressed myself, he consistently met me with a warm, calm, and capacious presence. He allowed for the sort of regression that is therapeutic—he allowed for intense feelings of dependency for quite a while, before he eventually helped me understand what was happening and why. I had a wonderful freeing feeling that I did not have to attend to him or his expectations. This adolescent analysis brought me back into life in a fuller, freer way. I believe an important part of that transformation was that I strongly felt his loving care, and I felt a deep love for him as well.

The literature

In this section, I will highlight the most crucial, defining influences that relate to my evolution toward psychoanalytic creative engagement. The work of Freud and Klein and her school are foundational pillars of my understanding of psychoanalytic therapy. Their influence is a deep part of me that is expressed implicitly in my work. In this book, I emphasize subsequent writers who explicitly focus on what the analyst emotionally brings to the relationship. From the beginning of my career, I have looked for language and theory to help me articulate the ways I aspire to relate and be with my patients. I have also sought language that captured the more primitive, regressed states in my patients and the more inchoate moments of shared experience between us—especially the heightened intimate moments of transformation that can occur.

Following my formal analytic training, I immersed myself in reading theory new to me, though these ideas had been in the larger analytic world of ideas for some time. First, I studied Bion, whose electrifying work opened a door wide to new ways of working. The theories he developed and the clinical approach he prescribed felt like a new home for me. Here, I want to briefly highlight two areas of his thinking that profoundly affected me, and will discuss his work more thoroughly later in Chapter 8.

One strand of his theorizing, starting in *Experience in Groups* (1961), describes communication between people occurring at the proto-mental, non-verbal level, within an "emotional field"—a constant flow of emotional sharing that determines their experiences. This theory of an intersubjective dynamic field captured how I intuitively felt about the analytic conversation.

The second strand deals with Bion's clinical perspective in his so-called late work revolving around the role of receptivity (at-one-ment) and uncertainty ("negative capability"). His late metapsychology prioritizes experience over knowledge—Being not Knowing. These ideas all fit well and began to influence my way of being with patients. Overall, reading Bion inspired me to seek the hard emotional truth of the relationship.

Another major influence was my encounter with the American philosophical tradition of Pragmatism. Dewey's (1934) *Art as Experience* was a stirring revelation. From my understanding of this work, I could connect his idea of transformational aesthetic experience to moments of transformation in analysis, when patient and analyst enter a heightened passage of living together, when both undergo something that indelibly alters the status quo. A new way of being becomes possible. I will have more to say about his notion of transformational experiences and their relevance for psychoanalysis in Chapters 7 and 8.

Many of the people I treated have had difficulties in self-establishment, lacking a sense of aliveness and meaningfulness in their daily lives. These problems did not seem to arise from internal conflicts—at least not unconscious conflict around desires and phantasies—but from a lack of the capacity to feel a solid sense of self and to regulate themselves. When I studied Winnicott and Balint, it felt like a natural extension of the primitive world I encountered in my work with adolescents. Winnicott's poetic language was like finding words for experience without words. His key concepts—the true self, play, potential space, the facilitating environment, regression to dependence—gave me a way of holding onto and elaborating the clinical intuitions I had developed in my work to date. Winnicott's (1971, 1985) theory of creativity is a background to my views on creative engagement described in this book. I owe a great deal to Winnicott.

The most immediate and profound influence in terms of developing my analytic sensibility and way of engaging comes from Ferenczi's late work. His emphasis on the personal, passionate, and human ways of relating to patients infuses all I do. You will find his specific contributions discussed in Chapter 2 (authenticity) and Chapter 7 (mutuality), but his voice is everywhere. I owe a great debt to analysts in the American Relational Group (especially Adrienne Harris and Lou Aron) who elaborated the clinical implications of his ideas in the *Clinical Diary*.[6]

Finally, I have a longstanding interest in music, and feel analytic interactions to be musical, evoking rhythmic dances. So one researcher is close to my heart—Trevarthan. I was inspired to find in his work (Trevarthen & Malloch, 2002, 2009) the concept of "communicative musicality". This concept describes the way humans at birth, and through their life span, communicate in the medium of tone, rhythm, and cadence—an emotional conversation without words. Or put another way, these non-verbal experiences are the necessary substrate to make words feel real and matter.

Patients

Over time, as I opened myself more to my patients, I began to see more of what they saw in me, registering my impact on them positively and negatively. I settled into what felt like a more intimate and vulnerable dialogue with them. This experience was crucial to my development as a clinician. When patients continued to return to a focus on difficult aspects of my personality, including my particular defenses—especially at times of high interpersonal tension—it seemed far-fetched to attribute this only to their transferences. I could see that it usually was not easy for patients to share their very real critical observations, their feelings of anger and disappointment in me. They feared hurting me. They feared "interpretation" as a form of retaliation. And most importantly, they feared losing me as a caring presence.

I have been grateful to my patients for their courage and insight. But I have had to do some hard emotional work getting there. I had to recognize the way I used certain elements in the "analytic frame" to protect myself and kept me from what was most essential and immediate between us. I needed to let go of the protection of some elements of the analytic tradition and of my own characterological ways of keeping emotionally safe. I came to call this emotional work "surrender and mourning"—which I'll discuss more in Chapter 4. In surrendering and mourning, we struggle to let go of old, protective, repetitive attachments of our own, in order to take in the current emotional reality and be present and available for our patients. This is an ongoing process, which I discover anew with each patient.

As my patients sensed my openness, vulnerability, and limitations, they were freer to recognize defended, at times dissociated, parts of themselves as well. They felt more real in themselves in concert with a greater sense of realness between us. I've seen that these personal changes in the way I work had a favorable influence on my patients.

In this book, I am expressing my analytic sensibility and the ways I have developed and changed as a psychoanalyst. I will describe in the following chapters more about the theories I've valued, detailed descriptions of important clinical experiences I've had, and an account of the emotional work I've needed to do. This book is personal, reflecting the inherently personal nature of the work we do. From these experiences, I've found and tested ideas that helped me in my work and helped many of my patients. I offer these ideas in the same spirit, for you to test out to see if they will help you as well.

Notes

1 When I use the terms "psychoanalysis" and "analyst", I mean to include psychoanalytic therapy and psychoanalytically oriented therapists.

2 There is a rich literature on Freud's case of the Rat Man. The relevance for us here is Lipton's (1977, 1979) argument that Freud considered technique in a narrow sense that did not include the "personal relationship". This personal relationship was not theorized by Freud. It was simply his way of working, and thus it was not problematic to give Lanzer a meal. In this book, I consider those personal elements crucial to therapeutic action.

3 Renik (1993,1999, 2004) later made the implications of his intersubjective view clear in a number of influential papers. These papers allowed me to continue my conversation with him after my supervision.

4 See Markman (2010) for a discussion of Feldman's "subtle radicalism".

5 See Harris, A. & Kuchuck, S. (2015). *The legacy of Sandor Ferenczi: From ghost to ancestor.* Routledge.

6 See also Aron, L. (1996). *A meeting of the minds: Mutuality in psychoanalysis.* Routledge.

Chapter 1

Creative engagement: an overture

I must however make it clear that what I am asserting is that this technique is the only one suited to my individuality; I do not venture to deny that a physician quite differently constituted might find himself driven to adopt a different attitude to his patients and to the task before him.

Freud, Recommendations to Physicians Practicing Psychoanalysis, 1912

In this chapter, I introduce the overarching approach of creative engagement and touch on its essential elements. It is an overture, a broad view, that hits some main themes that subsequent chapters will take up in more depth. In order to give you a vivid sense of these ideas, I will illustrate what creative engagement looks like by a detailed clinical example.

As I mentioned in the introduction, this approach (echoing Freud above) is my way of working. In the next section, I will say something about how I found my way to this approach. I'm not claiming it is the best way but one that may be of use to you in grounding your practice in essential, emotional ways of being with and relating to your patients. I see my approach as a starting point, a ground floor in our work.

By "creative engagement", I mean the personal, originative, and non-formulaic ways we meet patients, emotionally connect, and create an environment for their emotional growth. We do this through improvisation, playfulness, and spontaneity. By "personal" I mean that we find unique ways to participate with each person—to attune, accompany, and strive for openness to receive what they

DOI: 10.4324/9781003208518-1

communicate in all registers (verbal, unsymbolized, and embodied). This is what Freud had in mind—personal as in singular to us. But I also mean it this way: we are *personally* involved in the relationship with our patients in an intimate way that matters. Our emotions and vulnerabilities are a part of the communication.

Our engagement aims to give another a safe place to express dissociated and repressed parts of their personality, to feel recognized and understood, and to find a (potential) space to creatively explore and experiment as well. My engagement is meant to foster an "open circuit of communication"[1] where emotional states are shared as the basic mode of communication, building common ground between us. This sharing is intrinsically therapeutic; it occurs in words and-or in enactments and action. In this open circuit, I am sensing the way I affect the patient while self-sensing my internal state—how patients are affecting me and my openness to them.

In engaging creatively I am also offering the patient an emotional experience to find their own creative ways of being and living and authentic self-expression, in the session and in their life. As Winnicott (1971) writes, creativity comes from an authentic and unique part of us. He emphasizes the feeling of surprise as a hallmark of being creative. I have found this to be so. But surprise can be both energizing and disruptive—for both participants—as we will see in the following clinical example and the many others that follow in this book.

"Coming from afar":[2] the first session with Edwin

Some time ago I received this message on my phone: "I'm in bad shape. I need to talk to you soon … I've never done this before, never turned to anyone", spoken in a desperate, deep, raspy voice. I imagined a frail, older man.

When I went to gather Edwin from the waiting a few days later, I was surprised to meet an energetic man in his early 40s, grinning widely at me. Excitedly bounding up the stairs to my office, his behavior was so at odds with his voice and message—his urgent call, and now, his giddy, coiled-up energy. He plunged into his narrative at a dizzying pace—the way he spoke carried with it an urgent appeal from a young and vulnerable part of him that touched me. This part of him seemed to say, "Don't hurt me—please like me and take care of me". Where was that appeal coming from in him?

There were other incongruities in the way Edwin communicated. Though he was born in a non-English speaking country, he spoke English perfectly. More than perfectly. I don't think I've encountered anyone with more command of the English language. His vocabulary, grammar, jargon, and vast literary allusions were astonishing. While describing bone-crushing depression, self-torment, and intrusive suicidal images, he seamlessly inserted quotes by Victor Jarra, Borges, and Neruda to get his emotions across. He lacked his own language for what was happening inside him. At one point I interrupted: "I'm sorry but these quotes are a bit distracting to me. Can you try to use your own words?" He looked blankly back at me, confused and at a loss how to comply with my request. He apparently had no words of his own for his emotional state. Instead, another literary allusion poured forth: "I guess I'm 'tangled up in blue'," he said with a smile.

At other moments when his emotional situation was not expressed through references to literature, movies, and music, he expressed himself vividly in pantomime by acting out emotions with grunts, exaggerated facial expressions, and extreme gestures. He had a real talent. His bodily expressions perfectly captured a particular emotion. This might be acting but there was a sincerity too, in trying to communicate something real the only way he knew how. Though he did not have words for his feelings, I viscerally felt them and tried to translate these gestures into words. The emotional impact of his gestures pulled me along, powerfully, like catching a wave that's too big for one's surfing skills. Hang on!

I had disturbing and conflicting reactions to Edwin: fascination, pleasure, irritation, confusion, and feelings of genuine warmth—especially when I sensed the frightened and vulnerable young boy peering out from behind the curtain of the performance going on stage. The disturbing part was that in spite of him telling me unbidden, ruminative images of shooting himself in the head (and the relief he would feel in going through this), I had no idea really *what* was torturing him so. I struggled to feel more directly into his suffering, a suffering without words or context. It was such a strange mixture of agony and theater—but theater with an urgent purpose. I worked to get to, in myself, the seriousness of the situation—to take him very seriously—because there was something slightly off and unreal about his way of speaking. There were moments when he conveyed terrible feelings through bodily expression. Then I fell in touch with something fearful and traumatic.

I told him that I could see he wanted to gain my interest and feel comfortable with me because he was frightened and desperately needed help. I said I wanted to help him. He calmed down a bit and was silent for the first time in our meeting. We then made plans to begin our work together at several times a week.

Entering into creative engagement with Edwin

At the moment I explicitly invite Edwin on this emotional journey, the passage and destination are uncertain, and my responsibility feels unmistakable and weighty. Though I am filled with all sorts of feelings and hypotheses, I am well aware how much I don't know and understand. Because of this uncertainty, crucial clinical issues come into greater relief, issues that need attention and that will pertain well beyond this first meeting. Edwin and I are each "coming from afar", to use Borgogno's (2014) phrase, from different, at times distant, worlds that are determined by childhood experiences, as well as socio-cultural and historical contexts. All of this shapes our unique ways of being. These differences count. There will hopefully be important areas of overlap, some basis of communication and understanding, but that will take time, and the way these overlaps occur is unconscious and unpredictable. When we first meet each other, the space between us is real and palpable and the possibility for learning is always at hand. This sense will (it is hoped) persist throughout the analytic relationship if the analyst and patient don't become trapped in habit, routine, and other forms of collapse or symbiosis that block evolution. It is a delicate balance to maintain, one of keeping space open while building emotional bridges between us.

Personal and clinical questions that energize and challenge my way of working follow from the sense of uncertainty and space between us. I've asked these same questions many times over the years. They gathered and formed my approach. They concern how I will embody the responsibility of inviting Edwin into a relationship of struggle and pain, tumult, perhaps mourning, and ultimately, I hope, greater freedom and a more meaningful and creative way of living. What will be the quality and range of my empathic imagination? Will I be able to make contact with the vulnerable, younger part of him in a meaningful way that matters? How willing will I be to face new, uncharted areas of my own personality that will inevitably come up? As this work may entail sharing an emotional world of trauma and dissociation, will this extend beyond the reach of what I can bear? When we inevitably become embroiled with each other in uncomfortable, conflictual interactions, in entangled transferences, how will we sort that out? Will we be able to?

Then clinical questions come up that pertain to my intention and actions. What ethos will guide me? What position of relating, caring, and responding will I adhere to? Where will I direct my attention and participation in a situation that is often indeterminate and in flux, in which there will be periods of uncertainty and confusion and discomfort and times of real interpersonal stress? How will I interpret and make use of my emotional to benefit the patient reactions—especially those that are disturbing? How will I respond to and make use of my failures?

From these questions that I have asked myself again and again with my patients, striving to a get deeper understanding each time, I arrived at "creative engagement" as my over-arching sensibility and way of analytic relating. How did I come to think of my work as creative engagement? In conceptualizing how I work, "technique" seemed distant from the emotional immediacy of encountering the world and mind of another and trying to understand, emotionally connect, and help. "Technique" concerns important preconceived actions, such as establishing a frame, maintaining a nonintrusive analytic stance, interpreting the unconscious transference in the here-and-now. I searched for other words and ideas that go more to the heart of what I intend and do. "Creative" emphasizes—as Freud's quote at the beginning of this chapter, indicates the singularity of each analyst's sensibility and voice, how each analyst makes use of his or her "individuality" to foster intimacy and a unique relationship that allows for the sort of deep experiences that help another person. Because this is personal, there is no blueprint for how a therapist does this. *However, there are principles that free the therapist to use his or her creativity and empathy to ground the work emotionally,* which I will describe. There are also ethical horizons. "Engagement" suggests an ethical commitment. The etymology of "engagement" is a "binding pledge or commitment". Our engagement involves an ethically asymmetric responsibility and commitment when we take someone into analysis who then continues under our care.

Elements of creative engagement

Love in the Analytic Framework

First of all, creative engagement has to do with our unique ways of loving within the analytic framework. Love is expressed in our desire to know, understand, and recognize the singularity of a patient in a deep way that fosters intimacy. We express in action our abiding care for the welfare and emotional growth of the patient. This involves communicating in various modes—words, rhythms, gestures, provisions—our understanding of the patient's world of struggles and needs.

I am guided here by Nacht's (1962) seminal article where he affirms that the "final result of analysis", the "reparative gift" the analyst gives, depends on his "inner state of being", "a *real* deep attitude" toward the patient (p. 211, author's ital.). He states emphatically, "No one can cure another if he has not a genuine desire to help him; and no one can have the desire to help unless he *loves,* in the deepest sense of the word (p. 210, author's ital.)". This care and love manifests in our desire to know the patient as fully as we can and communicate that recognition in understandable ways, in the patient's idiom. In this process of communicating, we learn to speak the language of the patient, whether that is through words, gestures, or embodied rhythm. Ultimately, this expression creates a place in us and in the potential space between us, for the patient to be and find the deeper layers of his or herself. *It is an offer of freedom.*

One might be tempted to minimize this as something like, "Love is all you need". In fact, ongoing serious emotional work and self-interrogation are needed by the analyst (for example, how does the patient live in us and what are our real intentions?) in order to develop and maintain this "*real* deep attitude" that gives a quality of real care and authenticity to the interaction. Edwin may come, I hope, to feel and rely on my abiding care, concern, and love. This takes time, as the patient tests in many ways the reality of our intentions. As Nacht states, this is fundamental and necessary for cure.

Presence

Related to love is what I call *embodied presence.* Presence is our spirit of openness and welcoming and emotional availability. Presence is offering a place for another within us, opening a door in us for the patient to come in. We allow for an influx of the patient's emotional states. Presence opens us to live with and within the patient's world, by allowing for influx and interpenetration. The patient can sense our availability.

Presence makes us available to contain emotional states within the dyad, by making emotional links between our emotional experience and the patient's. By taking in the patient and allowing for the range of experiences that arise in us, healing can occur. We make contact with our own early difficult experiences and connect this with the patient's suffering. Our identificatory-empathic responses resonate in the patient, as we work through our own difficult past in the presence of the patient—not necessarily explicitly communicated but communicated by the quality of understanding and recognition.

While a loving *"real* deep attitude" may endure over an extended period, our presence is momentary and in flux and takes emotional work to maintain. We are willing to work toward it because of our attitude of love. What is this work?

As I show in Chapter 4, to make oneself available and present, involves the emotional work *of surrender and mourning.* We let go of constraints in us: our transferences, and our attachments to theory and analytic identity, to ways of feeling stable in order to offer a place for the patient in us. We take on their world. I think Edwin will depend on my presence in the immediacy of the moment, in real time, in order for him to bring in the split-off parts of himself and difficult past experiences. He may then sense that his vulnerability—up to now a liability and dangerous condition—can be made safe and meaningful, and that may give a greater sense of reality to his existence. I must be present for this to happen, but this takes ongoing work.

So, the path to presence is not always easy for me. This active work is sensed by the patient. Edwin will eventually experience the way I am struggling with the emotional material he brings in that at times overwhelms me. I am not unflappable or perfectly contained and containing. In my struggles, Edwin will feel that I have a personal stake in the relationship, that it is not about employing correct technique but emotional work, pain, uncertainty, and personal exposure on my part. I do not aspire to be an omniscient authority but a human being struggling within the relationship as well. One of the most meaningful statements a patient said to me was, "You care more for me than for your theories".

Attuned, improvisational accompaniment

Creative engagement is an offering of attuned accompaniment. We provide forms of accompaniment in an embodied way, giving the patient the experience of our companionship and support for self and relational experimentation and exploration.

Attuned accompaniment holds the patient by providing a "facilitating environment".

As Edwin and I begin, I do not know how to create the specialized conversation with him so that emotions will be shared and potential space opened up. I need to be present to discover this. This often happens in novel ways that I cannot predict, that often arise from my spontaneous improvisation (or the patient's) in searching for new avenues of communication and ways to accompany him—especially when traumatic material breaks through in the sessions.

Creativity

Winnicott (1971) describes creativity as an "alive relation colouring the whole attitude to external reality" (p. 65). Creativity becomes a way of living and relating to the world (and to our patients) that brings out what is genuine, spontaneous, non-habitual, and non-reactive in us. We speak in our own voice from a place of true feeling. It is this sensibility that insists working fully within the constraints of who we are. Spontaneity and play are an important part of personal presence. We engage by drawing on our emotional and imaginative self, on our creative potential to be spontaneous and improvisational, to emotionally move within the relationship in a flexible way. We also draw on our emotional imagination—our vision of the patient's internal world—in order to meet the patient. Thus, to be present analytically means to make use of one's own authentic sense of self in the service of communication. *Presencing happens when we perceive and connect to something real in the patient, that comes from a real place in us.*

Analytic authenticity

Creative engagement also depends on analytic authenticity (see Chapter 2), which is closely related to presence. We have an authentic, original way of being ourselves when inhabiting the position of analyst—what Freud is referring to in the quote above. As each of us finds our own creative ways to engage, each of us has our own particular individual resources to rely on. Whatever ways we participate—ranging from taking in and imaginatively identifying with the patient's emotional world to active, interactive, and interpretive modes of engagement—it is inspired by an alive relation to a creative, spontaneous, and authentic self within us, giving a feeling of realness to our communication.

Developing an authentic analytic voice in training and later on one's own makes for the realness and intimacy and immediacy of the encounter. Our ability to be authentically present and responsive allows us to play and experiment, to come from a real place in us. I will present clinical situations in the course of this book—including with Edwin—when I had to depart from what felt safe for me (which involved departing the safety of orthodox professional approval, ego ideas etc.) in order to provide what I thought was needed. With each patient, the aim was somewhat different and required different modes of being that were still within the repertoire of what I could do.

Making emotional contact with Edwin

In the next two clinical sections, I will illustrate the elements of creative engagement in action with Edwin. First, I'll describe the various ways we communicate and how I understand his communication, and what

I do with it. I hope to show how I go from my emotional experience to an engagement meant to be therapeutic. After this description, I will give a detailed account of a session.

As mentioned, Edwin speaks in the language of the body through pantomime, to which I have a visceral response. Bodily, I take in Edwin's tone of voice, posture and movements, facial expression, cadence, and intensity of speech. All of this tells me something crucial about his feelings and states of mind. I feel intensely and vividly his state of terror and agony. I hold onto this and only say something when I feel I'm not pushing it back into Edwin. A promising sign is that he is ready to make use of me as a container for intolerable states, communicating this bodily. One royal road to the unconscious (in myself and Edwin) is through sensing movement, gesture, and tone, through our "embodied relationship"—a concept I will develop later in Chapter 5.

I imagine that if the session with Edwin were videotaped and analyzed, we would witness a subtle synchronicity or coordination of gestures that he initiated, a rhythmic sharing that reveals attuned responses and counter-responses that build a sense of connection. I move to and with him and he eventually moves with me, in a rhythmic dance. This synchronized dance begins in the first session after I point out my difficulty sensing his emotions that are muffled in his various literary allusions. I can translate the allusions to his emotional states, but they are a step removed from the gut-level communication that follows when I feel his emotions passing through me. This visceral communication is really the basis of an empathic bond that is forming, right from the start. In being present and available, I am making space internally for Edwin, beginning almost immediately.

In the first session, I also seem ready to begin caring for the frightened traumatized younger part of Edwin. Though "coming from afar", a fit between us is established as a result of the entanglement and overlap of each of our unconscious object worlds. Being spontaneous and authentically responsive, I express in various ways my appreciation for his linguistic ability. I enact unknowingly an earlier father-son relationship in his history—and mine. For him, as I subsequently learned, an important part of his early childhood—in his conscious mind, the most important part—

involved precocious intellectual performances for his demanding father to admire and reward him. In parallel motion, I had my own way of trying to impress and gain approval from my father at an early age through performance. So, already an unconscious process arises in me of identification and projection—identifying with the father one wishes to impress to give one a sense of meaning, and also identifying with the father who is impressed. I am in both positions, and, as such, Edwin takes his place in my preexisting object world. The same is true for Edwin, as he immediately relates to me as the father-to-please. The interlocking of transference-countertransference, which forms the text of enactments, is at work. The danger going forward, though, is that our overlapping transferences or the intensity of his visceral communication may lead to collapse, repetition, or mutual defensiveness.

Working through my transferences will allow for something new. And my willingness to permit influx and interpenetration opens a place for Edwin's world to live within me and be contained. A hopeful sign in the first session is that Edwin turns toward a father-therapist who he feels is caring and helpful and accepting, as he simultaneously opens up a tender and vulnerable non-performative younger part of himself. I sense this potential strongly, and that is why I offered to begin an intensive treatment in the first session. Edwin's vulnerability rarely felt or experienced by him, comes forward in response to an openness in me that feels safe and hopeful to him (which he probably could not articulate at this moment).

Over time, the relationship developed and deepened. As we came close to intolerable emotions and memories, he would cancel, became busy at work, travel on business. Nonetheless, our relationship slowly developed, as each iteration of flight and return allowed him greater access to himself—his past experience and current needs. Gradually, I sensed that he trusted the conversation we both engaged in, but that at times I had to firmly maintain that conversation to bring him back to it over and over, after each flight.

A crescendo: Edwin, two years later

Now, I will present in detail a session two years into the analysis. Edwin is nearing something that is traumatic for him to recall and experience. Will I be able to contain the intensity of the emotions and hold Edwin, so that he may recognize parts of himself—truer parts buried by defenses of hyper-performance—and get the care he needs? In this session, I am working guided by the principles of creative engagement outlined above. This example is not so unusual, though the material Edwin brings in is very intense and challenging emotionally, at times hard to tolerate. In making myself available and open, as present as possible, I struggle to contain the intensity and horror of the material involved in living within his world. Sometimes I am not completely successful. But, I believe it is good enough. I am committed to find Edwin and meet him where he is. I am attentive to and actively relate to the younger and vulnerable part of him. *I expect that I will only achieve this through experimentation and creative responses that I do not plan for, that will come up in the immediacy of the situation, and that will be novel for both of us.* I put this overall approach into action by my willingness to improvise and be authentically responsive. I will also try to be embodily attuned and find a way to accompany Edwin that feels supportive and alive. I do not want this to sound so sure and clear. Emotionally, I go through bouts of confusion and uncertainty, struggling to be present by containing difficult emotions.

Before presenting the session, I will provide some necessary historical background. As the only child of two extremely successful parents, Edwin grew up under tremendous pressure to excel and please his parents, especially his father, who was a powerful businessman in the diplomatic corps, but also a terrible alcoholic. He began teaching Edwin English, French, and Italian as a young boy. "To get along and be successful in this world, you need tools of communication", his father insisted. Edwin recalled his fear when his father commanded him to come to listen to broadcasts in languages other than his native one. "Get in here, Edwin" his father roared. Although these were uncomfortable encounters with his father, the radio sessions account for Edwin's fluid command of many languages and his perfect English accent, and he is grateful to his father for this. His father also made Edwin memorize poetry in various languages at a very young age and perform for family and diplomatic colleagues. Having an outstanding facility with many languages early on, Edwin always complied and never thought that much about it. "It's just what I did ... and I was good". The idea of failing or resisting never entered his mind because he seemed so capable of capturing an audience and his parent's admiration—at least for the moment. There was always the next performance. Growing up in the midst of an intellectual and culturally sophisticated family, he recalls no tenderness from his parents—"That would weaken me. I needed a stern hand at home to excel".

An important aspect of the family's background is that they lived through a period of enormous social upheaval and trauma caused by a military coup and a repressive dictatorship. People disappeared and relatives were lost. At the same time, his father loomed large in the home. When drunk, his father frequently verbally abused the mother. When in charge of Edwin, which seemed often, he took him on business trips and while taking on Edwin's education and cultivation of him for a successful career in the world—ideally an ambassadorship.

Edwin suffered depression and anxiety without understanding why. Initially, he thought of his family background as "wonderful", "privileged", "the best a child could hope for—I was so loved". It is striking how he confused attention with love, and how he ignored the political situation in which he grew up. During the course of the first two years of analysis, that picture of his childhood was dismantled as memories of a traumatic nature emerged.

It is in the context of memories of harrowing experiences with his father that this session takes place. Working with traumatic memories, Edwin is gaining a new sense of himself as deeply suffering in childhood and his life-long failed attempts to deal with that suffering. The picture of the revered, god-like father is collapsing in a destabilizing way.

P: Let's carry on ... *(at the same time he gestures as someone cringing and turning away from a frightening accident).*

A: Really. Carry on? Let's go slowly into this because I see you're not comfortable, you seemed scared.

P: Yeah, well things have to be faced! Though I've no idea what will happen or where we are going *(he says softly).*

A: We're not just going to plunge in. *(As I say this gently, he slinks in the chair and looks small.)*

P: I'm in your hands and you know what you're doing. I've seen that, heard that. I'm holding onto that like a piton on a cliff. *(He shrugs and smiles as if to say, "I'm sorry, what can I say?" There is something very tender and young in this gesture and I'm touched and feel protective. I think maybe we can stay like this for a while, calmly being together. I'm a bit scared too, not knowing what will happen next, sensing there are terrible events to encounter. And I surely do not feel at all like the omniscient analyst he thinks I am, the "Dr. M" he mentions frequently.)*

A: I know you're frightened. There are experiences in you that you're afraid to get close to and feel.

P: Actually I came in with something ... something on my mind ... a shard I'm afraid to pick up, but I want to tell you about it. I don't think it's much, but you never know. *(He quotes a Springsteen lyric.)* ... You always find something important there. You're amazing. Very high batting average ... *(He's never been to a baseball game as far as I know—he's a passionate soccer fan—but he wants to talk in my idiom.)* Here goes. For some reason—did I ever tell you that my father was an expert extreme skier? Because of his powerful connections, he had access to parts of the mountain others didn't, very remote and pristine ... I don't know why I'm so afraid—this is really a funny story. I have a film playing in me all the time and I can review the past like an editor, going over the details of every scene. It is clear and vivid, and for some reason this clip came into my mind today in Technicolor. Like certain parts of X *(his hometown)*. I call them up and see the shops, time of day, crowds on the street ... *(laughing)*. Good thing I'm not a director, I'd never finish a movie, lost in the details in the edit room—but there is Tarkovsky. He got away with it. More than away with it. I know I'm not telling you anything new, those long scenes, the lone man walking in ankle-deep water. That scene alone took him a year to finish and nothing happens! Except for the sound of the water, the soft light, the drip drip drip ... you know it of course. It's famous ... By the way, see "City of God"—if you can stand it. Ha Ha.

A: Let's try to stand it. I want us to try to stand it. Let's try to hear and see the image that is in your mind that you brought in and can't forget.

P: At this point there's maybe nothing to stand, really. It's a silly story.

A: Ok, father, skiing ...

P: Ah! *(He curls up in a ball)* What the fuck!

A: Yeah, what the fuck! *(He's telling me something now; now he's talking.)*

P: What is this?...

A: Something inside you, hurting you, scaring you.

P: *(He turns on his side. I almost think he fell asleep or is in some altered hypnotic state. Then he abruptly sits up.)* Ok, this is stupid, nothing. Here it is. My father loved skiing, in extreme situations. He was an excellent skier. Next to his music, he loved skiing the most. He was a beautiful skier. He taught me to ski at a very young age and pushed me to excel on runs often inappropriate for me. I would go along with his friends and there was always a lot of drinking. Funny, I don't have specific memories of that time. But then one incident popped into my head. It's almost too ridiculous to relate. Doctor, how can you hear these banal stories day in and day out from your patients. But then again you always see something in it. The memory is this. I'll play it for you ... watching my father, hanging with the men drinking, he has the idea that now was the time to accelerate my learning curve by going to a very expert part of the mountain. "Edwin, come here, let's go down that run" *(Edwin speaks in his native language first, then he translates. The English translation is neutral but in his native tongue it is powerfully harsh and commanding.)* When my father says this the other men go "Whoa, not that one". I can tell they are anxious and there is a disturbance among them. They are talking fast and soft to each other. Agitated. In my adult mind, and maybe I know this then, that given my father's position and power in the world, they would do whatever he asked. But they were trying to tell him that I should not do this run. My father who is very drunk says, "No, this one. My son can do it. Let him do it!" I don't remember very much. So, I get ready to go down this really very dangerous run myself. Really Doctor Markman, the camera cuts out then except I hear a lot of laughter, mainly from my father. I have a feeling his friends are sympathetic to me. Their laughter is nervous. When I came back to myself, I am laying on the snow surrounded by laughing men. Especially my father laughing. I start laughing too. Then someone points to my arm which is bent in a funny way and that's funny and we're all laughing at that.

They pick me up—this is a funny story isn't it? The rest is even funnier—and we go for dinner at our remote cabin. I don't feel my arm. It doesn't hurt, just looks funny. We gather in a circle outside and the cooks bring on a big meal. The stars, the campfire, the circle of men passing around a bottle of tequila. Father is proudly recounting my bravery to go down such a treacherous run, and my spectacular fall. Then my arm starts to bother me. One man says it's broken and I should have it attended to. Doctor, you really look in pain hearing this.

A: I am. This is a painful, really horrible story.
P: I'm sorry. I don't want to upset you. But don't worry, here comes the funny part!! My father, drunk beyond his usual drunkenness—which is saying a lot—says the cure for fractures is to wrap the limb in aluminum foil. This will expedite the healing process. He asks one of the men to get some and wrap my arm in it. This is something out of Chaplin, don't you think?
A: No, it's terrible and your father is grotesque.
P: Whoa!... Well, you're probably right ..."It's alright ma, I'm only bleeding". That kind of thing … Mama. That's how the story ends. The next day I'm returned home to her. My arm is very swollen and painful and still wrapped up in aluminum foil. I remember the look on her face. It wasn't anger or distress. Just, "Let's get down to business and get this taken care of". All calm action—she's seen worse, I guess. No comfort … She took me to the private hospital for children of the elite. The main reaction I remember, more than my mama's, was the doctor there. I tried to make a joke of it and at first he laughed, "Yeah, drunken fathers". But then he got very mad at my mother for allowing "a

father like that to be in charge of his son". The main thing, the feeling I'm close to, is that it is really funny how inept my father was. Aluminum foil! But now I can't get it out of my head.

A: (*This is a surreal moment. He believes what he is saying should be funny, but every part of him looks terrified.*) It's not really funny. It's only funny if you stay outside of it, outside of yourself. Let's go back to it. I have an idea. Let's look at this story as if you're watching a film of a young boy with his father.

P: (*A long silence. Very unusual.*) I don't, I don't understand. You want me to look at it ... as if I'm not telling it? Like I'm watching it, it's presented to me?

A: Yes. Then we can maybe see what that boy is feeling.

P: I see ... He's very, very scared. But that's not even a word. Scared ... He's all shivering, shaking inside. Poor, poor child. (*He starts to cry.*) He doesn't know what is happening to him. Why is his father doing this to him?... Why doesn't someone help him? What has he done?... I don't like seeing this! I know this is me, but I only feel something if I'm watching it like a movie happening to someone else. I don't want to watch this.

A: I know, and we can stop whenever you want. But I want to help you see and feel what happened to you.

P: (*He gets up and starts wandering around the room.*) I want to leave.

A: Of course you can ... But I'd like you to stay here with me, if you can.

P: Doctor., Oh, that was horrible to see! (*He sits down and cries.*) That poor boy! And no one stopping it! Laughing! Help him, god damn it!!...

A: Yes that young boy is you, and really needs help and protection—deserves help and protection.

P: I *so* don't want it to be me, doctor (*Several minutes of silence go by. Something seems to be gathering in him.*) I can only feel something, fear, outrage, ahh! If it's not me. And especially if that is not my father ... I don't want it to be *my* father ... There is another picture in my head. I'm on a cliff—"Don't go over" I'm telling myself. But you need to know everything ... One time around the same time, same age, I'm in a taxi with my father at night. He is very drunk. He starts arguing with the driver in an abusive way, like "Do you know who you are dealing with! Do you know what I can do to you!" ... You know I'm a bit close to this. It's not a story. In some way I feel more in this. The driver is very calm and actually tells my father to get out of his taxi, calmly and firmly, and because my father is so drunk, he can't really do much about it. As we are getting out the driver looks right at me. He has a sad and caring look on his face. "You'll be ok" he says, and hands me a candy. (*At this point he breaks into sobs.*) I don't know why this is so affecting, his kindness. And he made me feel I have this big burden in my life, and I'm so young! It's not my fault he's like that *(sobs)* ... I can't get over that he went out of his way to do that. I don't think that ever happened and that anyone ever saw what was happening.

A: In his caring gesture, he saw you and you could feel your own sorrow. That you were really suffering.

P: Yes, but why can't I believe, or why is it, was it so rare? One time in high school I got into a fight trying to protect a girl who was being hassled. I was severely beaten up. My face was a mess. I was afraid to go home and face my father. All I remember is feeling humiliated that I was beat up that way, that I couldn't protect myself ... *(He starts crying again, and there was a few minute silence)* ... I know I've told you about the time my mother and grandmother were looking for a relative who disappeared. They would gather in the square. My grandmother told this story. Every day a young boy would come to them and ask about his parents. Then ask for something to eat. He was disheveled and frightened. They would give him something to eat and he would go away. Then he would find them the next day at the square. It became a pattern—until he didn't return. My grandmother thought he had died.

A: Can you tell me what you're feeling?

P: That poor kid. With no one. On his own.

A: *(This is at the very end of the hour and I feel an urgency to say something, to connect this for him.)* Not only that boy, looking for someone to care and sustain him. That boy is you, too. We won't let him disappear.

P: *(Looks stricken. I think his story of the young boy was again outside of him so that he then could feel into his own experience of abandonment and fear.)*

Reprise

This clinical material illustrates the workings of creative engagement. Of course, this is a specific situation at a specific time in a specific analysis, so what I am oriented to in particular is this moment in time for us. Here, my concern is containing the emergence of traumatic memories that had been split off by Edwin's manic performative way of being. To do that, I help him to make contact with a younger, traumatized part, so he will be able to experience these painful memories in ways that turn them from haunting, menacing presences into objective memories. As the session begins, I have no sense of how we will do this. I do know I will try to draw on my own emotional experience in the moment and engage with him in ways that are not pre-formulated but experimental and improvisational.

Initially, I attune to Edwin's rhythms while also being alert to what feelings his manic pace attempts to express and erase. Both defensive and compliant, he struggles with these feelings, thinking that what I want him to do is to be a man and face reality. In retrospect, this is an enactment of the trauma he will describe, where he is identified with his aggressive father. I counter that attitude in my words and ways of communicating. I sense his manic energy and slow him down by the way I talk, giving him a clear sense that I am in no hurry. This is how I attune to him and participate in an embodied way. He doesn't have to "plunge" in for me in his usual inclination to please me. I am hoping and trusting that he does know that when he is ready, I'll accompany him into this terrible world—in fact, I am already accompanying him nonverbally in my rhythmically slow and steady presence.

I have faith we will get there, and, almost simultaneously, he is ready to go forward. As he slows down, we go into the memories. I am in the role of witness and companion. Yes, these things really happened and it's not funny. I slow down his manic counterphobic attempt to plough through by speaking slowly and offering him a reason to slow down. Again, this is embodied participation. I am communicating and accompanying in words and rhythms, very alert to the *adagio* tempo I am expressing, by saying, in a sense, "I can't keep up with your pace, slow down a bit; we can go slow together". I know if I say that directly he will comply and feel he is doing something wrong. So, I communicate in a more musical way, taking the lead for the pace. I think he feels my care by protecting and containing him. I know he's scared. I am trying to bring us into emotional synch before we go forward into his painful world so that he can feel we are together in this. I begin to accompany him at a pace at which he can tolerate his feelings and experience.

As I noted above, only in retrospect do I see the potential transference repetition of a father pushing a willing, counter-phobic, loving son down a treacherous ski run that is way beyond his capacities. However, I love him in a different way, by accompanying him at a pace suited to his emotional age—which is very young at this moment. Though not consciously recognized, my way at the beginning of the session comes from sharing his intense fear. I felt very protective. This loving, parental feeling—what Winnicott calls "maternal identification"—is expressed as much in my embodied way of holding as in my words, and continues throughout the session, informing much of what I do.

Edwin then slows down and a traumatic memory emerges. I try to help him stay with its emotional impact by using metaphors he has developed in the analysis—in particular, viewing film. A spontaneous, unplanned move on my part, I improvise with the possibility that the way to his feelings is through his own idiom of watching film. I know Edwin loves movies and has strong emotional reactions to them. I have found in past sessions that it opens up emotional channels that are usually blocked in his day-to-day life. Perhaps he can view his memories with some distance from the outside as film and then he can slowly move in closer to feel what is going on inside of him. The crucial moment is when, for the first time, he can identify with the frightened child in his memories and recognize the horrible reality of parental neglect and abuse.

An essential element in the "viewing" of his memories is that we are watching it together. For a moment, we are sharing the same images and emotional responses to them and to what happened to him. This companionship and containment were accentuated by the way Edwin and I approached the memory. I am thinking that he will be able to feel into what happened if he himself is a witness alongside of me. We are watching a film about a helpless boy with a drunken, violent father. I am adopting his idiom as the film-watcher with a purpose.

As he identifies with the split-off part of himself, he experiences what it was like to be *that* boy with *that* father—and it is devastating.

Spontaneously, I express my authentic reaction to his father's behavior. These are my true feelings and I'm taking a risk in expressing them so directly and forcefully. It's as if—and I only know this in retrospect—I am a fiercely protective, loving parent. My intense feelings and reactions that come with this shared experience are not "as if", but genuine and authentic in my relationship with him. I am uncertain how he will take such direct emotional involvement. Though he doesn't respond directly, I see that it allows him to go deeper into his feelings about what happened, and subsequent memories that come up are, I believe, a reaction to my reaction.

When the intensity of feeling becomes too much for him, he wants to end the session and leave. I am not insistent that he stay, but I express in an authentic way—coming from a real emotional place in me—that I would like him to stay and that I believe we both can bear it. I don't know this but feel it. At that moment the session turns. By expressing my desire that he stay, he suddenly finds me with him—in the guise of the taxi driver—a sympathetic, caring presence. Up to this point, there was always a part of him wanting to please me, take care of me. More than a detached witness, I am now someone deeply affected by his plight. It is only a small token, a piece of candy, but that gesture of the taxi driver and the concern in his eyes, in *my* eyes, gives him the feeling that someone sees, knows, and is emotionally affected and with him.

Simultaneously, emotionally I am both a caring father and a hurt child. In empathically expressing my protective feelings toward Edwin, I am also feeling something powerful of what it's like to be left alone with this terrifying paternal presence—the very one meant to care for and protect you. I believe that his sense of me comes from the authentic, at times unguarded and passionate, way I am relating to him. Unlike his matter-of-fact and detached mother, I am the enraged ER doctor because I might know something of what it is like to be him.

Then we move into a heartbreaking passage of aloneness and brutality permeated by the violent images of his drunken father, the slope, his broken arm—that is, the starving orphaned child. In a world of violence swirling around him, as much from within his family as from the political crises his family lived through, Edwin speaks of despair and helplessness—the young child without protective parents who is (emotionally) starving. Though I wish to nourish him and give him what he needs despite our limited daily contact, will this be enough? Will he disappear? I honestly do not know at that moment, and it fills me with doubt and fear. Feeling a moment of alarm, I reach out to him at the very end of the session, again spontaneously, by saying, in effect, "I see you and will try to be here at the square to meet you every day. Come back". My last words to him, a kind of plea really, contain the ambiguity of "the boy in the square" ("him"), and of Edwin. It's as if I can't fully allow for that to be Edwin either, that it is too searing at that moment, especially as he is about to leave, parting with this terrible burden, on his own and alone.

Notes

1 This is Pichon-Riviere's (1998) term to describe analytic process, which I will discuss in Chapter 11.

2 A phrase used by Borgogno (2014) to describe initial encounters with our patients.

Chapter 2

The development of analytic authenticity

> If there is one theme in all my work, it's about authenticity and self-expression, it's the idea that some things are in some sense really you, or express what you are, and others aren't.
>
> —Bernard Williams, Interview, *The Guardian*, 2002

> I can define my identity only against the background of things that matter.
>
> —Charles Taylor, *The Ethics of Authenticity*, 1991

> The analyst you become is you and you alone: you have to respect the uniqueness of your personality—that is what you use, not all these interpretations.
>
> —W. R. Bion, *Clinical Seminars*, 1987

Is there a way to talk about the importance of being oneself in doing analytic work? What does "being oneself" actually mean? In what way is it a necessary part of the therapeutic process? Is this idea something already implicitly understood and in no further need of clarification, debate, or study?

In the previous chapter, I introduced the idea of *analytic authenticity*. Complex and controversial, the word "authenticity" rarely comes up in analytic discourse, although the notion inspired early analytic thinkers and still finds its way into the current psychoanalytic conversation under other names. The question for us is: *How do we inhabit within ourselves our very unique way of being an analyst, while also pursuing the analytic project of care for another?*

Here is my definition to start: "Analytic authenticity" means that

DOI: 10.4324/9781003208518-2

each of us has a unique way of being an analyst in the project of attuning to, empathizing with, relating to our patients, which is embodied and made manifest in our practice. I am not talking about authenticity in a general sense, like the search for one's "true self". Rather, it is how our true nature—our unique way of being and our "voice"—is expressed in a caring analytic action, bounded by the needs and emotional development of another.

Developing one's voice and being true to oneself is essential for the work we do. It is the root of our creativity, our wellspring of aliveness and realness. It is the way we participate with the patient in the project of analysis. Our analytic authenticity is not a static state, a place of arrival, a resting place. It is always in process and in development, modified and refined by what we learn about ourselves in action and by what our patients teach us.

The following scene describes a pivotal moment long ago that made a strong impression on me and started me on the path toward developing a sense of my own authentic way of analytic relating. In a seminar conducted by a well-known analyst, a colleague presented an irritatingly passive-aggressive patient who always delayed payment of the bill, among other withholding behaviors. In one session, the patient asked my colleague for a pen to write out a check for services well in arrears. My colleague freely gave him the pen, the check was filled out and signed, and the session continued without further discussion. After hearing this, the eminent analyst calmly asked why he gave the pen to the patient: "Weren't you enacting a subtle sadomasochistic drama? Why couldn't you interpret what was going on?"

We all waited tensely and in dread for our colleague to respond. He replied, "I don't know, but it's just not like me to withhold a pen when he asked for it". A very long pause ensued as we looked on sorrowfully at our friend. I expected the consultant to make an important teaching point about projective identification and enactment, about masochistic surrender. The consultant finally responded, "Yes, it's true, you have to be yourself". There did not seem to be much more to say about this exchange between the patient and analyst and so we went on.

As Taylor (1991) beautifully puts it in *The Ethics of Authenticity*:

> ... each of us has an original way of being human [that] entails that each of us has to discover what it is to be ourselves. But the

discovery can't be made by consulting pre-existing models, by hypothesis. So, it can only be made by articulating it afresh. We discover what we have in us to be by becoming that mode of life, by giving expression in speech and action to what is original in us. (p. 61)

Evolving psychoanalytic theories of authenticity

In his late work and in *The Clinical Diary of Sandor Ferenczi* (Dupont, 1985), Ferenczi began a conversation about authenticity—though he did not explicitly use that word. *The Diary* begins its second paragraph with:

> *Natural and sincere behavior* constitutes the most appropriate and most favorable atmosphere in the analytic situation ... (p.1)

Ferenczi advocates "real sincere sympathy" toward the patient (p. 227). Here and in his last papers, he uses words like "sincerity", "spontaneity", "realness", and "naturalness"—qualities in the analyst that create the right atmosphere for the patient, the right way of welcoming him or her. These qualities emanate from the analyst's humanness and vulnerability and are necessary analytic provisions given to the patient. Ferenczi's sensibility countered "professional hypocrisy"—a coolly detached and uninvolved manner—that typified much of analytic practice at the time. He encouraged the analyst to engage in a real, human, and emotional way. The analyst's natural and sincere expression, Ferenczi believed, is the analyst's way to inspire trust and belief in his or her real intentions. This way of relating also encourages the patient to express his or her reactions to the analyst's real personality and emotional states, especially if problematic. The analyst should not be enigmatic or a "mirror", but open and accessible.[1]

Ferenczi's subtle clinical intuition did not stop with a naïve belief in the simplicity and power of words like "honest", "sincere", and "genuine". It was a place to start in countering certain hypocrisies but did not solve crucial problems. Though he advocated that the analyst abandon a distancing and objective stance, maintaining true "real sincere sympathy" was personally challenging at times. Yes, "professional hypocrisy" can also hide "that we can only with difficulty tolerate certain external and internal features of the patient" (p. 226). A warm and welcoming attitude can hide the same sorts of negative, disturbing feelings. As he noted in 1932/49, patients often sense the analyst's true attitude and feelings, even if the analyst is unaware:

> Whether they recognize the truth by the intonation or color of our voice or by the words we use or in some other way, I cannot tell ... they show a remarkable, almost clairvoyant knowledge about the thoughts and emotions that go on in their analyst's mind. To deceive a patient in this respect seems hardly possible.... (p. 226)

Importantly, Ferenczi broadens the notion of analytic authenticity by taking into account the impact of his de-centered position in the relationship. Our authenticity then becomes an open, unsettled question that depends on what we learn about ourselves from our patient's observations. This openness to the patient becomes an intrinsic part of our authentic way of engaging. Ferenczi recognized the way the analyst's inauthenticity (the analyst's unawareness of his or her true feelings and attitudes) can damage trust and even re-traumatize the patient. Yet, by openly acknowledging his limitations and contingency, he gives a fuller, more realistic and ethical account of analytic authenticity. Ferenczi was playful and experimental and creative, but this was contained by his willingness to openly examine his attitude and feelings and its impact on the patient.

Ferenczi sets the stage for the idea of "relational authenticity".[2] Neri (2008), bringing in more fully Ferenczi's relational perspective, believes that "one has a need and a right to speak with one's own voice in order to express one's own thoughts and feelings" (p. 327). But he distinguishes "being oneself" in this way from authenticity. "Being oneself" for Neri does not take in another. He proposes, following Gallese (2006), the concept of "relational authenticity" to allow for the place of the other. Neri says:

> ... being able to act in an authentic manner when relating to another person is based on an innate capacity for honesty,

immediacy and desire for self-expression. This capacity becomes "relational authenticity" if it is accompanied by the ability to understand and take the other person's sensations, emotions and feelings into account, while expressing oneself. (p. 52)

Here, Neri is describing a complex internal process in the analyst. The challenge is to allow for and manage spontaneity and unique ways of expressing ourselves, channeling our "innate" talent for emotional expression, while simultaneously sensing the way the patient experiences our engagement. For Neri, "being oneself" is put in the service of the patient. It is a delicate balance.

Neri addresses the balance this way:

... giving a degree of free reign to one's feelings ... is not spontaneity *tout court*, but a *"special spontaneity"* that involves tolerating powerful feelings and not evacuating them. The responsibility involved is one of "taking responsibility for one's relationships and becoming aware of the effects of one's words and actions on the other." (p. 336)

Neri defines authenticity in a way that does not simply mean being sincere and direct and saying things that correspond to reality, but also *"saying things that correspond to the reality of relationship"* (p. 335, my ital.). Meanings are made in dialogue and are bounded and framed by the relationship. The implication here is that our actions as analysts are always embedded in an intersubjective matrix, which modifies and relativizes the idea of authenticity.

Teasing out his relational account, Neri considers that authenticity not only "belongs to one or the other of the individuals involved in a relationship, but also [is] a product of their interaction" (p. 337). He goes on: "In the analytic situation, an increase in authenticity is signaled by greater involvement on the part of both analyst and patient: both feel they can reach, and indeed are reaching, something that is essential" (p. 337). Neri expresses the view that authenticity is co-extensive with emotional truth within the relationship.

Neri gives us two complementary accounts of authenticity: a relational one and an intersubjective one. In the relational account, we make use of what is essentially true and original in ourself, while simultaneously sensing the impact on the patient. The intersubjective account describes the way authenticity is co-created and shared in intimate communication, in the "now moments" of interaction, when each participant realizes a fuller and truer sense of who they are. These accounts are both right. Often it is one member in the dyad who expresses him or herself authentically that then alters and tilts the dyad toward an intersubjective experience of authenticity (and emotional truth).

Now I turn to Orange's (2002) contribution, *"There Is No Outside"*, a title that captures her thesis. Her work is complementary to Neri's, though she uses the term "authentic participation" rather than "relational authenticity". Agreeing with Neri that the analyst's expression of authenticity is necessary and compatible with empathy and sensitivity toward the patient, Orange solves the tensions between attunement to self and to another by doing away with the self-other binary altogether. She stresses that there is a false dichotomy between self-concerns and concerns-for-another. Instead, Orange uses the term "authentic participation" to unify the self and other in relationship: "Authentic participation in an intersubjective system is being within that system in a way that is faithful to one's sense of the system" (p. 687).

This elaborates Neri's argument for relational authenticity. One cannot be authentic on one's own. Authenticity only becomes meaningful and is defined by participation in a relationship, a relationship with professed values and intentions. The unique analytic dyad modifies the "system" due to the uniqueness of the field it creates. Emotions and states of mind are shared, not residing in one or the other in the interaction. As Orange states, "There is no outside". She expresses this view best here:

Empathy ... and attunement ... require not abandonment of my own ongoing organization of experience, no loss of personal authenticity or genuineness. Authenticity does not require an outside, a denial that one's perspective is inevitably embedded in a conversation or form of life. A parent who puts aside, or brackets, his or her own perspective or needs for the sake of an infant is not inauthentic but may be profoundly faithful to his or her own values. (p. 699)

There are two crucial ways Orange broadens the idea of authenticity. First, by establishing that authenticity is an ethical commitment to a project that is an essential part of who we are—like her example of maternal preoccupation. Our values are intrinsic to our subjectivity and subsequent actions. Faithfulness to the project is being authentically who we are—they are not opposed or in conflict. Our project involves the care and empathic understanding of our patients. Second, *how* we do this is highly personal and creative. For Orange, that project assumes a relational foundation of the analyst's "inevitable and continuous participation", to quote Aron (1996). Though we are committed to allowing for and developing our authentic personal style and voice, Orange emphasizes that that personal style is contingent. We know that ours is not the only or even the best way to be an analyst. It is (only) *our* way. Nonetheless, the way we express our authenticity is in our personal way of engaging.

I now turn to Winnicott, whose concept of the True Self adds something new to the concept of authenticity. Devoting much of his attention to the self and subjectivity, Winnicott (1971) writes that creative expression comes from the True Self: "Creativity belongs to being alive … It is a way of being that "colours the whole attitude toward reality" (p. 64). In one of his last contributions (1986), he writes:

To be a creative a person must exist and have a feeling of existing, not in conscious awareness, but as a basic place to operate from…. Creativity is then the doing that arises out of being. (pp. 39–40)

I want to unpack these poetically condensed ideas that link aliveness, creativity, a sense of being-existing, and the self. The feeling of existing is to be in touch with a vitally alive part in us, of being in this body-mind in this world. This feeling of existing comes from a "basic place" that is the True Self. Our actions in the world that come from the True Self-Basic Place are intrinsically creative: spontaneous, non-reactive, original—authentically, singularly, who we are. Winnicott (1963) says of the True Self:

> I suggest that in health there is a core to the personality that corresponds to the True Self. I suggest that this core never communicates with the world of perceived objects, and that the individual person knows that it must never be communicated with or influenced by external reality (p. 187).

What Winnicott adds to the notion of relational authenticity is this private and pristine picture of authenticity that exists before engagement with others.

My involvement in the session with Edwin in Chapter 1 illustrates this dual sense of authenticity. A true, spontaneous, and alive part of me emerges in the way I comment, react, and direct his attention. I sense that I am attuned and empathic, but there's no certainty in this. I also sense that at each moment we are taking a risk into unknown territory. For me, the feeling of risk comes from my recognition of the unprecedented nature of my own action. Yes, "there is no outside", but what is inside feels uniquely, at times, fearfully mine. At that moment of spontaneous action, I am, like Neri writes, keenly aware of what effect I am having. Yet my actions were not wholly geared to the patient. They are framed by the moment but not determined by it.

We draw on both sides of authenticity in being an analyst: relational authenticity and the expression of engagement from the "basic place" in us—where "some things are in some sense really you" as an analyst.

Analytic authenticity and supervision

I want to begin this section by describing a part of my personal journey toward authenticity—my way of being myself, of personally participating in analytic relationships. Early in training, I had two very different supervisors. One supervisor formulated the material I presented into elegant and pithy transference interpretations. The idea was that I would take on her words as a model of how to interpret and each week refine my work in the direction of her detailed and nuanced sense of a good interpretation. She was kind and generous. This approach of learning to be an analyst felt invaluable to me at the time. I liked words and the understanding of what is hidden, and the intellectual appeal was great. I think I progressed well enough in this direction. I became more able to track unconscious phantasy in the moment-to-moment-interaction. Coming out of medical school with an emphasis on knowledge and surety, I was looking for the same sense of the one right way to do analysis. I believed there was such a thing and someone so clear, confident, and smart surely must have found it. I was acting more and more in concert with the role she embodied as an analyst. Her ear was finely tuned to the present moment in ways that still strongly influence me now in how I attend.

My own personal way of being and expressing myself was not relevant to her theory of therapeutic action—though I could imagine how much she affected her patients by her careful listening that was part of her personal way of being. These things though were not up for discussion and were not how I would learn from her to be an analyst.

I was at the beginning of my work with patients and the only other model I had for how to do this was my analyst in what was called a "didactic analysis". Her model was one of a relatively active and attuned analyst whose comments focused on where I was emotionally at each moment. She was sensitive and her comments were frequent and never far from my experience, often consisting of simple, single sentences. She didn't seem ambitious or overly invested in what she said to me. Given my early history, this was a very good fit. She gave me a feeling of space, calm, patience, and real un-self-interested interest. I sensed her as an alive and vital person who came through as much in the silences as in the way she spoke and responded. In a way, she was nothing like my first supervisor, whose authority and mastery, and active mentorship were quite impressive. Yet, both had a strong and beneficial affect on me through their way of being.

I was in a quandary about how to be an analyst. At the time of my training, that was not a question to discuss. I knew it would be ridiculous to imitate my analyst. First of all, how do you copy someone's embodied presence, restraint, and attention—their very way of being? Of all the things the happened in my analysis, including my analyst's perceptive comments about me, it was her way of being the mattered most, that affected me most. I did imitate her words though. For a long time, I ended my own sessions with the same words she ended mine: "Let's go on next time". That seemed so intrinsically *her* in the relationship with me—open, firm, yet gentle. I did internalize a kind of quiet presence and attention to the emotional moment that grew in me. That is, I took in her way of being that deeply affected me. But I am very much not like her. I talk more and am more reactive and emotionally expressive, utter sentences far from Hemingway's succinct phrasing that often wanders around before getting to the point of what I want to say, before finally reaching my point. I can get distracted by interesting digressions that unconsciously emerge and I lose my way at times. I inject my subjectivity into the mix much more, which is my way of being in relationships.

Then, I met my second supervisor. He worked with me by simultaneously translating the patient's associations into unconscious thought and desire. He never offered suggestions about how to make use of his insights despite my frequent queries of, "So what would you say?" His inscrutability made me anxious, yet he offered me the freedom to work it out myself, to play with and experiment with what he gave me. I came back each week with new material and my attempts to make some use of his understandings. He had a certain capacity for deep listening that was well beyond me then, or now, so there was no temptation to act or be like him—except again, as with my analyst, I internalized the quality of attention, spaciousness, and freedom he gave me. He never commented on my interventions, never judged the way I engaged with the patient but continued his decoding of the patient's state of mind and unconscious reactions to me. The transference was never discussed as a "topic". What he taught me had to do with listening deeply—"the patient never changes the subject", he would say—"the rest, you work out yourself".

I felt very drawn to my first supervisor, yet, with my second supervisor I noticed more change in my way of being with patients. In supervision with him, I started to inhabit more of myself in the work. At the time, I could not formulate the difference between the two supervisors and the tension arising from my attachments and gratitude. As my work developed over time, involving contact with various supervisors and consultants, I realized that my second supervisor was a rare breed. As I thought more about him and my analyst in the middle of my career, the metaphor that came to me was that every analyst needs to recognize and develop his or her own voice. One's voice is a signature of an embodied self: something in the voice is enduring while at the same time expressing a great range of feeling and states of mind in timbre, tone, cadence, intensity. I came to value and try to develop my personal way of being and relating, avoiding whatever I encountered in theory or learning situations that muted the vitality of expression and personal feeling. I was drawn to theorists like Ferenczi, Winnicott, and Bion, who opened up horizons of freedom and experimentation to develop my own voice further.

Here is another story that makes this point. Like the incident in a training case conference that I described at the beginning of this chapter, this situation also had a salutary impact on me early on in my journey. I was sitting next to a revered, prolific senior analyst at a party. We were discussing how one develops an analytic practice. I was expecting him to encourage me to continue to teach and start writing. Instead, he told this story. When he had just completed his training and had already contributed some fine papers to the literature, he sat waiting in his office for referrals to come. None did. This was distressing and confusing. Then at an analytic institute dinner dance, he cut up the floor with his graceful steps and obvious pleasure in moving with the rhythm, in beautiful, effortless harmony with his partner. Shortly after this dance, he started to fill his practice with patients. He laughed in telling me this, like, "Go figure. Aren't we all *meshuganah* in this field?" What really *did* cause this shift in referrals? This analyst had a very alive presence—one could feel that. The dance demonstrated to his colleagues this personal liveliness that perhaps was hidden in professional meetings and the decorum of analytic conversation, presentations, and writing. Now they could see on display his authentic way of being, his vitality and *joie du vivre* that must permeate his work with his patients in ways that inspired the trust of his colleagues. He could freely and gracefully dance with others.

I also learned a lot from students that deepened the value I place on authenticity. These experiences changed my way of supervising as well. One candidate I supervised immediately comes to mind in this regard.

He often would bring in a stack of papers that supposedly had his process notes, but he never referred to them. Instead, he spoke extemporaneously, digressively, and, at times, incomprehensively—at least to me. This worried me. His narrative, nonetheless, surprisingly, gave me a real feel for what was going on in the work and the relationship, communicated though in his non-linear, visceral, and idiosyncratic way. Obviously, his was not a fine-grained, nuanced report offered, but the way the analytic experience lived in him. He did not do this consciously or deliberately. At that time in my career, I felt that I needed the actual process notes to better supervise. I asked him a few times about bringing in some process notes. But he just could not bring himself to take notes or write them after. He had to do it his way. Though I could not fully follow the things he said to his patients or his formulations logically, I did get a palpable sense of the relationship and his conscious and not so conscious feelings about the patient.

This supervisee's patients were clearly helped by him. I realized over time that he had a very creative, non-discursive, and emotional way of reaching them. My understanding of him shifted as I learned his way of being himself with his patients. I opened up to his unique voice that he fiercely guarded, resisting pressures from training and analytic orthodoxy, including initially from me. He would not be pinned down by convention or written process that did not really capture what was happening for him—the flux and flow of embodied analytic experience. What was obvious in him was a deep sensitivity to a wide range of emotional states, a musical ear, and an original voice. He recognized his patients in ways that clearly transformed them while communicating in his unusual, idiosyncratic way. His language must have reached them. He is an original and he taught me the broader range of freedom to interact as an analyst, and also, as a supervisor.

Another supervisee had a quiet, sensitive, and shy way of being. I misinterpreted her sensitivity as timidity, encouraging her to engage the patient more assertively within the relationship. Despite my efforts, she had the strength to remain faithful to her own sensibility in the work. She did learn about phantasy, enactment, countertransference, and so on. But the way she put these ideas into practice did not alter her steady, serious, and capacious presence. As with my other supervisee, her patients emotionally developed within themselves and in the analytic relationship, in obvious, vivid ways. As I worked with her over the years, it came as no surprise that she often had a full practice and patients rarely left due to an impasse.

Crucially, I also learned a lot from my patients. It may go without saying that many of our patients detect the instability of our authentic voice. As we work together and they get a sense of my "basic place" of relating and communicating, they can tell and often tell me when the signal is garbled. The off-notes in my voice can have deeply disturbing effects on some patients. *My way of being is part of the frame, and so it follows that, when I am off, it is disruptive, painful, and disorienting in a fundamental way—a subtle but not less impactful disruption of the frame.* To emphasize here, I am not talking about my analytic stance—evenly hovering attention, receptivity, and more generic elements of my engagement. I am speaking about attributes of my being, my nature that, in doing analysis, can go off-line at times. It seems to be something they count on, and at times, my patients can sense this before I can.

Evolving analytic authenticity with James

The following clinical examples show how my thinking about authenticity developed in my adult work and how I came to recognize it more clearly.

The first example is James, who was at the beginning of his candidacy when we started working and I was at the beginning of my career as a training analyst. Over our fairly long time together, my way of being came more fully to the fore. Initially, beginning my career as a training analyst, I wanted to (often could not) fit into the culture of my institute, striving to embody its values in a "didactic analysis". My own vulnerability to accommodate manifested in caution and constraint, making me a pretty reserved and quiet analyst with James at first.

I think James shared these values and expectations of how an analyst should act and behave, being socialized in the culture of analysis we shared. He rarely asked questions of me and censored his curiosity. He completely—at least consciously—accepted my way of being with him, associating "freely" and without the apparent need of my interventions. This was not a good fit because it made for a somewhat flat relationship. Interestingly, I think, and he confirmed this, there was something about my attention and genuine interest in him that was communicated, which meant a lot to him and helped him in spite of my reserve.

This more constrained way of working with adults was completely at odds with my adolescent work at the time and the way I was evolving in other therapies. As this was early in my career, I did not theorize what was happening. I think this change in me came organically, gradually, and not deliberately. It was palpable though. Only later could the lessons be articulated as I am doing now.

After some considerable time together, as James and I approached the possibility of termination, he remarked, "You've really changed as an analyst. At first, I found it pretty confusing even though I liked it. It felt liberating for me. But I did wonder—is this OK? Is this analysis? And what then were we doing before? What is it that made you change this way?" James is a cautious person—or at least accommodating—until we approached possible termination.

As James and I looked back on the time spent together and what it meant to him, he talked about a change in me that occurred after a year into the work. He described this change as my being much more interactive, responsive, challenging, and personal. I asked questions more. I reacted more emotionally to his associations and offered more specific emotional responses. I used metaphor and humor more freely, with my own subjective, idiosyncratic figures of speech. There was a more-ness in my being with him. James remarked that I became a more alive presence, and he had a stronger sense of who I was as a person and an analyst. This made him feel more connected to me as a less idealized, more ordinary person. He said, "If you can be vague at times, think out loud, be off point, ask me for clarifications, admit confusions, then so can I … with you and in my own work". James was letting me know about the impact on him of my growing sense of being myself. Because we worked together for a long time, we could retrospectively see how my changes gradually affected him.

James eventually wanted to know what had happened to me to cause these changes. I told him some of what I am writing now: My search for my own voice and some of the influences that helped me along the way. "But there must have been some important life experiences, too?" he asked. I answered that of course there were. I gestured to certain important losses along the way that emotionally pushed me on to become my own person, in my family of origin, and in the analytic family of institutions and teachers and personal analysts. Only as I write this now do I see James's own parallel development in his readiness to leave me and the analysis to become his own person and analyst.

Analytic authenticity and its lack: working with Ellie

A very different way of recognizing my authenticity and its lack came up in my work with Ellie. As with James, we worked for quite a while together, spanning from early in my career to a time when I could in real-time make more use of what was happening. Ellie made me quite aware, painfully so at times, when I hid behind the authority of my role during heightened moments of discomfort. These were times of inauthenticity on my part that I fell into unconsciously. A brilliant scientist with a healthy dose of skepticism and empirical analysis, Ellie often wanted to know the "why" of the analytic setup and my behavior. She interrogated almost every element of the procedure— asking how this or that way is supposed to help her. In her view, many elements and ways of "conducting" an analysis did not.

Ellie would have little to none of this without a good explanation. You can imagine trying to give an explanation to a person well-schooled in the scientific philosophy of Karl Popper. So why should she trust my account of what matters? For example, "Why don't you answer my questions? Why don't you tell me more about yourself? Why are you reserved and wait for me to speak first?" Or, "This is not your natural voice. This is not how you would talk to a friend— why such care?" She continued with, "What if you started first and revealed yourself—that would help me be more open. What if we could just have a regular conversation about who knows what? That would feel much better. Why do I have to stay on the topic of me and my supposed problems … it all just makes me clam up?"

I am very grateful to Ellie who confronted me early in my career with the brutal honesty of a teenager combined with a mind like Bertrand Russell. I was no match for her on either account. Ellie brought me closer to my way of working with adolescents along with a rigorous interrogation of my basic assumptions in the work. What allowed me to be so affected by her was my wish to help her and to put aside ideas I was attached to or protected me or gave me confidence. She was quite unhappy and lonely. Though I could see how Ellie needed great control of me and other relationships, going in a traditional direction missed the point of what fundamentally needed to happen in our work.

This was painfully brought to light whenever I lapsed into a false way of being in relating to her. For example, during moments of difficulty between us, I might sound more assured than I truly felt because I wanted to convince her that I still maintained a dispassionate and calm analytic state. This would happen almost automatically at times, coming from old ways of dealing with interpersonal distress and identifying with an ideal way analysts should be and behave. With teenagers, you just immediately lose them at this point. With Ellie, I could immediately see the disastrous effect this had on her. She would get disorganized and panicky, which could last until our next meeting when only my being more authentic would restore her. For Ellie, inauthenticity was an encounter with deadness and despair. It was as if, when she encountered falseness in me that *I* took to be real, she was thrown into the Night of the Living Dead—zombie land.

Early on I had to go over this sequence with Ellie many times: a confrontation with an inauthentic though presented-as-authentic analyst, leading to potentially long periods of dissociation, which was resolved only by hearing again the alive voice of an authentic analyst. Even if my authentic voice was palpably confused, irritated, and apologetic, as long as it was inhabited in me as *true*, she (and I) came back to the world of the living.

As I engaged from a more real and authentic place, my work with Ellie became less traumatizing to her. This basic place with Ellie involved me letting go of the protections of the role of the analyst in order to experience vulnerability and the emotional truth in the moment. When I could do this, I was more alive and spontaneous in a way that cannot be faked. At times I surprised myself with what I said—and surprised her too. Rather than upending and distressing, these times yielded vivid responses from her—some not always positive toward me, but vital and enlivening for both of us. Like a canary in the coal mine, Ellie had an unerring response to authenticity and falseness.

When I was more authentic, something precious and expansive happened.

Ellie was also one of my patients who taught me that my authentic, reliable way of being is an important part of the frame. Giving her control of our exchanges—for example, starting the session with my thoughts about her, or revealing parts of my history or emotional responses to her—eventually gave her access to a dependent part of herself that was protected by a challenging and skeptical exterior. If she could trust me to be real and authentic, if she could see the way I struggled with this and at times failed, that I was willing to make corrections and adaptations to her, she then could allow for more openness and vulnerability in herself as well. But I had to go first in order to earn that trust through trial and error while tolerating the discomfort of being called out when false.

As I digested these and similar experiences with other patients, I started to recognize and allow for more authenticity as an analyst. In my development, I continue to read, but even learning new things does not alter something basic in who I am as an analyst. Today, when I discuss work with colleagues, I pay close attention to the way they work, their particular forms of relating, noticing resonances and differences. Without consciously doing so, I personalize their modes of being that feel right to me—that fit me. This feels importantly different from how I related early on to teachers and supervisors.

The very personal side of authenticity

My authentic way of participating has a certain slant. It is "my way" (minus Sinatra's assured tone) that comes from an alive "basic place" in me. I am hesitant because I neither want to reify something that feels in motion nor to valorize these ways of being either. The list below describes tendencies, generalities contributing to analytic authenticity. As I said in Chapter 1, I believe I am different within each dyad, with each patient. And, I try to be very mindful of the impact and difficulty each of these may cause the particular patient. Nonetheless, these aspects of myself are enduring. These ways of being could be theorized as some form of technique, I imagine, but they are not techniques. They are who I am as an analyst—my "basic place":

I often play first and think/plan later (in the context of the person I know).

I take leaps and chances.

I'm sensitive by nature to giving space while narrowing in on the patient's emotional states.

I don't stray too far away from immediate emotional states. I don't naturally and easily have continual "reveries". I am rarely struck by lightning by my own associations.

I'm sensitive and responsive by nature to the non-verbal part of communication.

I go with the patient, including various actions and interactions, before understanding what it means. I surrender to enactment and often enjoy it.

I like discovery. I like finding out and learning—sometimes too much.

I'm very curious—sometimes too much.

I reach out until I learn it is intrusive and impinging.

I speak in metaphors a lot—sometimes too much.

I try to hold and enlarge the present moment with attention—language—embodied attunement.

Conversely, I like being didactic and speaking to the big picture, including reconstructing the past—sometimes too much.

I tend to see areas of emotional growth and the patient's potential more than repetition—defense—perversion. I definitely miss things.

I share my interests and pleasures. My enthusiasm is not hidden. I tend to be expressive.

I speak to the patient conversationally, casually, simply. My sentences can go on and on at times.

I make fun of myself at times. So do my patients.

I give myself the liberty to improvise, make mistakes, and be creative in order to be with and meet the patient.

This list does not include my aspirations, such as wanting to contain difficult states of mind or to be present with a person in agony or grief. These are my true intentions, but my way of doing this is somehow contained in those things I listed above. For example, when I am with a person who is deeply suffering from grief and loneliness, I find my way of sharing these states and eventually have something to say. My way involves a tendency to resonate in the non-verbal register while simply being with the emotion, perhaps through play, shared interests, deep resonating silence, or storytelling.

Analytic authenticity, training, and beyond

When I presented these ideas to psychoanalytic clinicians with a range of experience, many wished that they had encountered the notion of authenticity earlier in their training and careers. Bion's (1987) famous quote in the *Clinical Seminars* is that once you finish your training, that is when you can become an analyst. But why wait until then? Why not inculcate the aspiration to use one's unique and original creative vitality from the beginning of your training? Why not consider ways for that development to occur? What would this look like? I understand that this is a difficult task early in training when it's only natural to find a structure to hold onto for support when there isn't an internal model and one's voice is still undeveloped. Nonetheless, to have authenticity as a goal—and finding settings where you can find your voice—helps you evolve toward this aim.

To foster authenticity, a learning experience would encourage, from the beginning, the development of the two parts of authenticity: our original, unique way of being human (our True Self) in our work, and our relational commitment to the values of practicing psychoanalysis, in the personal and contingent way we do it, appreciating both tradition and innovation. This approach would encourage the freedom to make mistakes that come with experimentation, improvisation, and play in order to find our singular voice in this process. This type of training would discourage imitation and mimetic use of another analyst's words and naturally lead to a search for personal forms of expression and attunement. I understand how tempting it is to borrow the language and understanding of others when we are uncertain or new to this difficult job. But if we start from a place where we cultivate our own way of communicating within the analytic setting, we have the opportunity to learn from experience, *our* experience. This may also involve "trying on" approaches while searching for what feels right.

Finally, developing confidence and faith in what is true in us and trusting in our own particular forms of vitality is not achieved in isolation. It is important that in training and beyond the clinician's spontaneous gestures are met with recognition and support by teachers, consultants, and colleagues. The sense of being real and finding our "basic place" from which to work is liberating and vitalizing. Once on this path, authenticity will continue to develop throughout one's career.

Notes

1 Ferenczi's revolutionary ideas came from his openness to hear his patients' negative reactions to the "standard technique" of the time, which was also his technique as passed on by Freud in the analytic culture and in his personal analysis with Freud. Ferenczi's willingness to learn from his patients changed the course of his work and the generations of analysts he influenced.

2 Later, in Chapter 7, I will discuss authenticity as it arises out of the mutual nature of analytic work.

Chapter 3

Embodied presence: the analyst's home base

The more I am present to myself, the more others exist for me.
—Gabriel Marcel, *Homo Viator*, 1945

The power to grasp is above all a power to lend ourselves, that is to say, to let ourselves be grasped.
—Gabriel Marcel, *Presence and Immortality*, 1959

The first "sense" of availability lies in the meaning it has for the life of our bodies. The openness of the personal body is an initial availability. A kind of bodily awareness goes ahead of our reflected consciousness, so that with the advent of every act, every intent of consciousness, we find that our life is always already a life in the world.
—Joe McCown, *Availability: Gabriel Marcel and the Phenomenology of Human Openness*, 1978

Introduction to presence and analytic openness

In Chapter 2, I described a primary element of creative engagement: developing an analytic way of working that is truly one's own—analytic authenticity. In this chapter, I explore the place where we emotionally work *from*—the emotional home base from which we engage that manifests our embodied presence. Like a hub in the wheel of our intended therapeutic actions, presence grounds all that emanates, at each moment. When we communicate our availability, openness, and hospitality in an embodied way—the internal space we make for another—the patient senses this and it is intrinsically therapeutic.

DOI: 10.4324/9781003208518-3

When one of my patients once said to me: "You're not with me!" it raised the crucial question: What does it mean to *be with* her? Or not?

The moment we engage with our patients by word and action, we immediately communicate our basic mindset and attitude. Are we open, accessible, receptive? Or are we preoccupied with things in our own world, intent on going down our own path, perhaps harboring and struggling with difficult feelings toward them? These messages are given by our personal body that "go ahead of our reflected consciousness", often out of our awareness. But any intervention we make reveals our interests, moods, and attitudes. The patient may sense the non-verbal meaning of our intended interventions and is affected by it. An intervention that comes from an embodied emotional place in the analyst can be more powerful than the verbal content—positively and negatively.

To affirm our receptivity, we can develop self-awareness that affirms presence in us: a calm sense of openness to the patient. When we are present and available for the patient, a space expands in us to receive them. In this state, we don't fall sway to emotions that block the patient's communication that is signaled by inner tension, agitation, or distraction.

Gabriel Marcel and human openness

I have been deeply influenced in my thinking about presence by Gabriel Marcel, a French existentialist, phenomenologist, and ethics philosopher working in the same period as Sartre, de Beauvoir, and Merleau-Ponty. His writing on human openness clarifies my approach as an analyst—the desirable emotional and ethical position I strive to inhabit with my patients.

Marcel considered presence the embodied manifestation of "availability"—an internal state of openness to another, a welcoming and readiness to respond, a yielding to what is encountered that makes space for the other. His term, *disponibility*, from which "availability" is translated, literally means "putting oneself at another's disposal".

Marcel (1933) writes,

> A presence is a reality; it is a kind of influx; it depends upon us to
> be permeable to this influx.... Creative fidelity consists in
> maintaining ourselves actively in a permeable state. (p. 40)

Presence is an offering to another—a "reality"—that is a concrete,
palpably felt entity (atmosphere or mood) communicated from one
person to another. Marcel writes that presence "reveals itself immediately" (p.42) in tone, gesture, movement, and word choice.
Participatory, not passive, presence is a way of being-with, an open-
relating-with that is more than what one says, but rather who one is,
how one is, and what one does. *Presence is our emotional state of
availability tangible in the interaction.*

Availability—related to receptivity, openness, and permeability—
requires emotional work. And what Marcel calls "creative fidelity" to
permeability is necessary because permeability must be actively,
creatively, and faithfully "maintained", as it is fragile and in flux.
Anxiety and other internal obstacles that crop up threaten our presence. Marcel links "fidelity" to "creative" to stress the improvisational and flexible state necessary for presence, as a live response to
another in real time and the changing climate within the relationship.

Receptivity is a rich emotional experience. McCown (1978), in
describing Marcel's idea of receptivity, writes,

> The human meaning of receptivity, then, is to introduce the other
> into a qualified (and privileged) zone of our experience or life, a
> region which is uniquely our own, which we have readied or
> prepared by investing something of ourselves in it ... it is not passive
> ... like the power of taking upon ourselves or into ourselves ... or
> better yet, the power of opening ourselves ... (p. 19, italics mine)

Further on McCown says,

> Availability may be thought of according to the image of an open
> door. Availability makes ready and makes room for other-
> ness. (p. 20)

These ideas suggest the internal work of making ready and making
room for another—that simultaneously alters the receiver. For an

analyst, this means a clearing out by working through our own transferences to the patent, attachments to our preferred theories, and to authority figures and institutions. All this clutters up the room. (In Chapter 4, I discuss the emotional work of removing clutter as surrender and mourning.)

There is more to availability. An intriguing aspect of Marcel's work centers on the idea of "self-presencing"—what his quote at the top of this chapter gestures toward. Presence for oneself, "at home in oneself", possessing oneself, means being in touch with and having access to an authentic place in ourselves that is simultaneously open to another. This place actualizes in communication. In fact, we need the other in order to be self-actualized. Marcel believes, quoting McCown again: "We constitute ourselves as an interiority, as we recognize the reality of the other" (p.43). Marcel (1940) puts the same idea this way:

I can only communicate with myself when I communicate with the other, when the other becomes thou for me. And this comes about thanks to a *movement of interior relaxation* by which I put an end to a sort of contraction through which I shrivel and at the same time distort myself. (p. 50, my italics)

This is a profound expression of self-communication and openness. It adds an ethical dimension from Buber's *I and Thou* (1923/2000) as well. The existence of the patient places demands on us to put an end to our "contraction". This work involves relaxation … but relaxation from what? I think Marcel means a letting go of the tense holding onto aspects of ourselves meant to prevent influx and vulnerability, meant to establish our own boundaries in an I–it rather than an I–Thou relation. This tight grasping to enlarge and protect ourselves actually removes us—"shrivels" and distorts us—from what is actually essential in us that allows us to be open to the patient. It is the opposite of self-presencing. Marcel is saying that, when we are away from ourselves, we are indifferent to others and unable to be present. So, to offer presence to another, we have to be present for ourselves, dwelling in an authentic place of receptivity toward ourselves as well. But, how do we do this?

Recognizing presence in ourselves

There is a *sensate* correlate to inner openness and availability. We are alerted by bodily states and perceptions. In my experience, presence has particular bodymind[1] qualities: a richer perceptual world, a bodily fluidity and relaxation, a clearer awareness of oneself in space, a sense of time slowing down, a settled-in feeling, a keen attention, and attentiveness. This is often foreshadowed by letting go and surrendering (discussed further in Chapter 4). This is the "openness of our personal body".

This internal, somatic dimension of presence is homeport in the tidal seas of analytic interaction, a place from which to attend and act and, under duress, a place to return. Presence is not a perfect Zen-like state. It is more like acceptance, a porousness, and surrender to what is happening that allows us to be with and accompany the patient, especially during the lived experience of challenging episodes in the analysis.

I am describing a desired state in the analyst that we struggle to maintain, even though we feel the importance of striving for it (creative fidelity). Presence results from the analyst, in an ongoing manner, actively facing lapses, dissociation, defensive self-protection, complementary counter-transferences, and difficulties in self-containment. Ideally, we are in an evolving and never-ending movement toward presence, as we work through obstacles—signaled palpably, bodily by "constriction" and "shriveling" that block openness. Clinical examples follow that illustrate my way of doing the emotional work to find—at least in the moment—a state of presence.

Therapeutic aspects of presence

The analyst's presence is intrinsically therapeutic, as McCown (1978) writes:

> We know whether someone is present or not because, when the other is present, he renews us in some way and makes us more fully ourselves than we would have been alone. (p. 41)

In encountering presence, our patients may feel spacious, secure, and accepted. These feelings are a necessary condition for them to trust us enough to bring in dissociated and traumatic aspects of their personality, and ultimately for analytic process and cure. Likewise, it follows that our welcoming and accepting mindset enhances self-awareness and self-possession in our patients.

Presence as an emotional attitude or stance challenges traditional aspects of technique that advocate neutrality, abstinence, and interpretation alone as the vehicles for change. I am sure that analysts from differing theoretical perspectives bring this quality into their analytic relationship, though only recently has it been identified as a part of the technique, but, it has been relegated to additional or adjunctive factors in therapeutic action. I am proposing that these additional factors are in fact necessary and foundational, and without this grounding of real analytic presence, interpretation—the traditionally accepted *sine quo non* of analytic technique—can be hollow. The teachers who meant the most to me, as I described in the Introduction, had presence, no matter what their theoretical perspective.

Nacht's (1962) paper, "The Curative Factors in Psycho-Analysis", contains language strikingly similar to Marcel's, making one wonder whether these ethical ideas were current in French circles at the time.[2] Writing from a clinical point of view, he is concerned with therapeutic action. He mentions Ferenczi and, perhaps one of the few times since Ferenczi, there is an emphasis on the analyst's way of being that comprises the core of cure. He writes,

> It is what the analyst *is* rather than what he *says* that matters … the basic relationship of the patient to the analyst springs from what his unconscious *perceives* of the unconscious of the doctor, perhaps even more than the interpretations that are given him. (p. 207)

Nacht goes on to say that integration and emotional growth "is only possible … in an atmosphere of peace and security; the patient will only find this in a really tranquil relationship with the analyst" (p. 208). There are clear echoes of Ferenczi here.

Nacht uses the word "presence" to describe his way of being: "*behind* the analyst's silence the patient should sense a watchful presence which *really exists* and is felt as helpful" (p. 208). The silent behavior of the analyst was a basic stance at the time, yet Nacht rightly emphasizes that whatever the behavior of the analyst—silence or speech—the patient can *sense* the attitude behind it. Nacht's idea of presence is:

> ... [An] openheartedness ... enabling him [analyst] to be spontaneously and intuitively what he should be given at any moment in the *actual* analytical situation ... [the analytic situation being] a living relationship between one person and another. (author's italics. p. 208)

Veszy-Wagner (1964) writes that Nacht views presence similar to Marcel, as a "constant accessibility"; an "unconditional (kindly) reception"; an "unlimited patience"; and an "ability to give". Veszy-Wagner continues:

> The patient should find "a good object" in the therapist and *the effective* management of the transference depends less on the technical abilities of the therapist than on his deeply felt and genuine attitude toward the patient. (p. 79)

For Nacht (1962), the curative unconscious attitude toward the patient is one of compassion, acceptance, and, indeed, love—the love of care, concern, the "language of tenderness" to use Ferenczi's expression. Nacht's description of "presence" is similar to my own, although I am referring to something more variable, precarious, and nuanced than a constant loving and nurturant attitude. I agree with Nacht's view that presence is a requirement for proper analysis and the substrate on which the analysis rests, and acknowledges that his analytic failures came from failures of presence. I would also add that presence may become a major *agent for change* in its own right, especially around failures of presence and its repair.

Ferenczi (1915) called the "dialogue of unconsciouses" between patient and analyst the fundamental medium of communication. Nacht (1962) puts that this way:

> It is precisely these exchanges between one unconscious and another which form the strongest bond in the analytical

relationship. The essence of this relationship is non-verbal, can be felt as reassuring, provided the object is felt as "good". (p. 210)

Presence is at the heart of transformational change. Seligman (2018), in describing attention *as* presence, believes that the "central role of attention [is] a core analytic virtue" (p. 258)—and uses descriptions of presence-attention, such as "vital, creative and energetic" (p. 259). Given the powerful therapeutic effect of presence, it is important to understand what pulls us away from this state.

Emotional obstacles to presence

There are obstacles to presence, when our intentions and ways of being and acting foreclose, misdirect, or are misattuned. (I more fully discuss our emotional work to establish presence in Chapters 4 and 5.) These obstacles may come from many places in us. From one angle, the way the patient represents an internal object might obscure our empathic connection to the patient, *as a subject*. Racker (1953, 1957) calls this "complementary countertransference"[3]—really our own disruptive transference to our patient. From another angle, in struggling to manage difficult emotional states, either communicated or elicited by the patient, or particular challenges in the work that threaten the stability of our sense of self and purpose, we can be taken out of contact with the patient and taken into internal states meant to protect us or to provide narcissistic provisions, and even falling into dis-sociated states. Finally, from yet another angle—possibly a curative one—we can be taken over by the patient's emotions and states, losing our analytic place, becoming ill with the patient for some time, as described by Borgogno (2014) and Bollas (1983). The analyst is then brought into the patient's world viscerally, possibly involving intense unwanted and disturbing emotions, altered states of mind, dissocia-tion, and confusion. How do we find our way back to presence? What use do we make of these emotions that help the patient? Paradoxically, by not resisting these states, by surrendering, relaxing, and living within them (i.e., containing them), we restore presence in ourselves and for the patient. The restoration of presence in us, as I have been describing is a therapeutic action in itself. Again, this work will be described in more depth in the next chapter.

Clinical illustration: Julie, a connoisseur of presence

Many if not most of the clinical examples in this book involve in some way establishing presence between myself and the patient. The following example with Julie provides a view of the dynamics of presence within me and also between Julie and me.

Julie started her analysis as a serious and eager person who wanted to "delve deeply into my problems". Right from start, I often heard her say, "You're not really here"; "I can't feel you with me. I'm all distracted now—you've distracted me"; "What's wrong with you today?"; "The way you said that sounds wooden"; "Are you here today with me?" Her sense of my absence, however subtle, immediately grounded her to a halt and stopped her associations and reflections about herself. The frequency and intensity of these and similar comments came somewhat as a surprise and disturbed me, since our initial meetings gave me the feeling of good contact and a beginning understanding. This feeling—at least on my side—continued. Something very different was happening. I was struck by how disrupted Julie was by what seemed to me the most subtle shifts in my attention and receptivity, and how agitated I became by her observations.

Julie was one of those patients who teaches us how to be a better analyst. She did this by bearing down on what is most difficult to maintain in most of us and brought home Marcel's (1940) idea of a commitment to permeability and influx. She taught me a lot about presence because she was a connoisseur. When I first started working with her, I felt that I constantly disrupted her. Almost anything I said disturbed her flow of associations. Yet my silence — especially in an understandably cautious way—was equally difficult for her. The way I was silent felt off and disturbing to her. I gradually came to understand that Julie had an almost uncanny way of gauging my state of mind when I was not present—to myself and to her—detecting the most subtle agitations and preoccupations in me.

At first and for some time, I felt oppressed and controlled. It was like those situations when tech support remotely commandeers one's computer screen. I felt irritated when I irritated her. I was angry because my task felt impossible: I was caught between being too careful or too carelessly spontaneous—both were states that lacked presence. In this state of my resistance, I only seemed to make matters worse. I was tempted to comment on her need to have my complete and exclusive attention, but by saying that I would certainly have conveyed my annoyance by blaming her. I had to sit tight and see what would happen next, in her and in me.

I had yet to encounter a patient before Julie who seemed to so immediately grasp my availability—at times before I had my own sense of it. Her observations made me aware that at certain times I habitually found a comfort zone with her that slightly yet palpably took me away. I also noticed that I justified these meanderings in my mind as my associations meant to pick up on her unconscious—my own "free floating attention" and "reverie". As I paid more attention to this experience, which was difficult and which I resisted, I could detect an absence, an elsewhere-ness, signaled by a slightly dis-embodied state. I would lose track of my body sensations and the perceptual world around me. I was often not fully present in the present. The emotional work of yielding to her observations and noticing what was there and not there in me shifted me toward presence. This occurred over a long period as I came to disrupt her less and less, and as I actually enjoyed giving myself over to her as attentively as I could. All of this was primarily communicated in my tone and movements, in the way I said things, in peaceful quiet at times, and in managing times of agitation when I did not remove myself but stayed in the experience with her.

I can sum up what presence meant to Julie: She felt *I was glad to be with her*. I was not impatient or distracted, attending to more im-portant and interesting matters. In my experience, the meanings of presence vary from patient to patient, but there is this core com-munication of pleasure to be with and attend to the person.

To Julie, I was a discreet person. She did not want me to disappear, to be unobtrusive, to be a "subjective object". Instead, she wanted to feel a palpable sense of my openness and availability, and she had a highly attuned detector aimed exactly at that point. Julie would comment that feeling my presence was a powerful experience for her. She would say, "You're in that soulful place"; "Now I can feel you with me"; "You're really here, what a relief!... I feel I'm settling in now". At these times, her associations flowed in unpredictable and lively ways.

My being "really here" with Julie had definite somatosensory and emotional qualities. One emotion of my presence was relaxed contentment. I was paying attention and attending with my whole body to the movement of air and shifting scents in the room; the dancing pattern of shadows on the wall; the full dimensions and colors in Julie's voice. My gestures felt easy and my imagination roamed. In this relaxed state, what I wanted to say to her arose naturally and spontaneously. It's not that I said everything that came into my head, but the words, whether spoken or kept to myself, had a fresh embodied lightness. At times she described her reaction to this state as entering a deep warm place. It nourished her.

Presence is transient and contingent and unstable. We are always at risk of lapsing into other states. The work is to continuously monitor ourselves for self-presence, often alerted by the quality of perception of our bodily sensations and the world around us.

Some of the most powerful moments occurred when Julie sensed something off or different in me and risked mentioning it. There was a familiar pattern to this. "I get the sense you're not here, you're troubled or preoccupied ... is that true?" At times I was aware of her observations, and I said as much. I also said I'd seriously look into what she said. Almost always I could find something that took me away from being present with myself and her, knowing this from the somatosensory experiences I have come to recognized as presence. For example, I'd feel restless. I would not really notice anything definite in my sensory world, like I was living in a fog or a black and white movie. This could be really subtle, but there, nonetheless. Julie was deeply affected when I could validate her observations. My willingness to consider what she saw and not put it back on her and to get to the bottom of it had a tremendous impact on her.

In spite of these repeated positive and emotionally meaningful exchanges, I still often struggled to be as present as Julie needed me to be, which was 100%. Part of this had to do with how much is involved in the active process of presence, and how much work goes into relaxation and surrender and letting go of automatic self-protective processes in me. For example, when we first started, earlier in my career, I rather liked the protection of being in the analytic role, putting the patient on the couch, being the one seeing and commenting, of having the patient be the one in need. There is a kind of invulnerability in that position that is appealing and can become ritualized and then not thought about—even valorized in certain theories. I resisted how much I was in view and how much my state of mind had an impact, both positively and negatively. The boundary between me and the patient became more and more permeable, allowing states of mind to be immediately accessed between us.

One development in my search for presence early in my work with Julie was the realization and acceptance that obviously I could never be perfect. In accepting this fact, I become more open and permeable to her. In quite admirable ways Julie was after the truth—truth she could bear even if it was disappointing but rang true. What she could not tolerate was anything allusive or defensive.

Although I offered Julie helpful insights at times, and a reliable, steady, warm way of being with her, what she constantly came back to and credited to her change and emotional growth was my presence. "When I sense you are truly here with me, involved with me no matter where I am or what I feel, it is as if my life, my existence has value to me. It's meaningful and I'm hopeful about the new experiences to be had". Her life concretely bore out these statements.

Gradually, the felt sense of being with her would stay with her from session to session and over the weekend. During separations, she would say we had engaging conversations in her head, that I walked beside her in her life. This sense of my presence outside the session moved her in new directions. Julie was a reserved, socially cautious person. For the first time in her memory, she began to seek out relationships, enjoy being with people, and make concrete changes in her life circumstances.

As she became more expansive, she also became more anxious. Would I be there next time, in the same way, to meet her and attend to her? She had trouble sleeping and went through periods of withdrawal to prevent being disappointed and let down by me. As we interpreted these anxieties and defenses, particularly that her excitement and erotic feelings felt dangerous in herself, she calmed down and could contain her feelings and then engage more deeply in the work. As we worked through this turmoil, she talked of having a love for me inside of her, but that love was *hers,* she had it, and it made life feel vital and meaningful. This love was something solid in her, her way of feeling real, that pushed her further into the world of new experiences.

Over many months, her sense of self strengthened. She began to focus on the last moment in each session, on the way I said "goodbye"—a farewell that seemed "impersonal, almost inhuman". She felt I had dismissed her from my presence and my mind. So now, during the separations, a heightened feeling of distress returned, all hinging on the last word I uttered—or, rather, the way I uttered it.

I understood that this had to do in part with the possibility of her leaving analysis at some real point. These thoughts were coming up more and more in her associations: the money she would save and what she could do with it; the freedom more time would offer, and so on. Her musings meant that ending was a reality for her at some point, and that question was, "Would she be able to take me with her; would I offer myself to her as she left in the same ways I've been doing in the sessions?"

We both knew something of this, and the interpretations felt a bit like low-hanging fruit. It would be relieving for me to encapsulate the experience of endings that way, focusing on her anxieties of not having me inside her when she left. But then I would be removing myself from the reality of what was going on in me during those parting moments. Was *I* really present all the way to the end?

This opened up for me the realization that how I generally end sessions was in fact perfunctory. But there was something very specific with Julie. I associated to a story I heard about when Freud lit up a cigar after making a compelling interpretation of a patient's dream. My perfunctory ending had a sort of self-satisfaction in it, especially when the session was particularly meaningful. On a deeper level, this was my way of turning toward the experience we just had and holding onto it, and not allowing in myself the feelings of sadness that come with endings and departures. Perhaps this had to do with my problems with endings, and if I could not be present to them, it would be difficult for Julie to be. I recognized *my* ambivalent feelings about her terminating. I felt very good about the work she had thus far accomplished, and it was a real pleasure and deeply rewarding to be a part of her emotional growth. I was attached to her and felt good about myself in the work with her. I would feel real loss when she left and got on with her life without me. This was now a reality between us that I had to face.

This helped me get back to myself more fully in those last moments of the session. Now when I spoke it was not disembodied but with a real emotional presence that contained a recognition of endings, filled with sadness and hope and love. She sensed this and it relieved her. But in her characteristic way, she started to play with the endings and orchestrate them to her liking—literally who would say what and when—certainly making it clear who was leaving whom. My continued efforts to be present actually led to a successful outcome: she would leave me and go off into her own life. The more present I was, even in that last moment of goodbye, the more possible it would be for her to leave, thus creating an absence within me that she sensed, and that helped her leave me.

Conclusion

Not everyone we see has Julie's sensitivity to disruption, her vigilance, and unerring ear, the courage to confront and refuse to accommodate, or her way of making good use of the provision of presence. She presented many challenges to me by rousing me out of habitual ways of listening and attending. It is a cliché but nonetheless true to note that we learn the most from the patients who are personally very challenging.

The work with Julie expanded my sensitivity to maintaining presence and facing lapses with all my patients—especially those who do not have the courage and voice Julie had to bring subtle absences to my attention. I believe presence to be the most basic and necessary way we are with patients. And yet, it is quite fragile, subject to our internal conflicts and mood shifts. Even so, we can commit to being "creatively faithful" to it.

Notes

1 "Bodymind" is Dewey's term for the non-duality of human experience.
2 Nacht was one of the founders of the French Psychoanalytic Society.
3 Racker's (1953, 1957) groundbreaking work on countertransference divided the concept into two clinically useful experiences. "Complementary countertransference" refers to the analyst relating to the patient as an internal object, in effect the analyst's transference to the patient. "Concordant countertransference" means the analyst relates to and identifies with the patient as a subject in an empathic connection.

Chapter 4

The analyst's emotional work of surrender and mourning

> The value of ideas lies in the experiences to which they lead.
> —John Dewey, *Art as Experience*, 1934

In the last chapter, we encountered these words from Gabriel Marcel (1940) in describing how we gain presence and availability: "... thanks to a *movement of interior relaxation* by which I put an end to a sort of contraction ..." (p. 50. my emphasis). This movement of interior relaxation from contraction, a movement from one emotional state to another, is really surrendering and letting go. It is giving up those attachments that keep us stable, secure, defined, and removed, contracting and distorting us. These attachments create a particular texture and tension in our relationship with patients that sharply contrast with surrendering and opening up to be present. We come to embody the therapeutic action of presence through surrender ("internal relaxation") and mourning.

Mourning is the struggle to give up and let go of attachments that protect yet constrict us—attachments that do not allow for openness to the patient's inner world, being with and living within their experience. Our emotions are transformed in this work, from contraction to openness. This transformation happens with all patients and many times during an analysis.

In this chapter, I give a framework for understanding the nature of our emotional experience and how psychoanalytic theories try to make sense of this experience. This will provide a context for my central idea that the analyst's essential emotional work is to gain

DOI: 10.4324/9781003208518-4

presence and availability through surrendering and mourning. At the end of this chapter, I give a detailed clinical example.

Here is an ordinary moment in a session. As Dr. N spoke calmly about the weekend with his family, I noticed a physical tightening in my body and a slight feeling of nausea. There was pressure in my head, and a feeling of dread came over me, making me wish that I could be relaxing somewhere else. I started shifting in my chair to relieve these uncomfortable sensations, chiding myself for my physical-emotional distractions, urging myself to pay closer attention to my patient and his ongoing narrative. I commented on something in his story that caught my attention, feeling relief in seeming to join him in his world. I wasn't sure though whether this relief connected me more to him or took me away from a deeper, though less formed connection present in my emotional-physical response.

This complex experience contained physical sensations, feelings, emotionally colored thoughts, movement, and speech. The episode was not pleasant yet it comprised an integrated way of being—even if distressing. This is common for psychoanalytic therapists: while listening or reacting or interacting, we are immersed in an emotional state, some states more present and intense than others, but emotional states that are always there. They can be in our face, so to speak, physically taking us over, or quiet, requiring more attention and self-awareness, but still influencing our perceptions and actions. This is where we start in our encounter with patients (and ourselves), living in an emotional milieu from which thoughts, fantasies, desires, and plans emerge. We naturally pay attention to emotional states in our patients, which signal important feelings, states of aliveness or dissociation, a sense of relational contact. But what about our emotional states? How do we understand them?

Clinical theories can offer guidance in understanding and dealing with our emotions. These help us orient to what we feel, answering questions like: Where do these feelings come from? What meaning do they have? How do I use my emotional responses in the session? What do my feelings say about the patient's inner world and the nature of the relationship?

Our explicit and implicit theories also do something with, and to, our experience. How theory helps us understand the relevance of our emotions has crucial consequences. Are our emotions the result of the patient's pressures or are they communications? Or, can our emotions at times be considered entirely independent of what the patient is doing? Do our emotions enter into the relationship and affect the process? Some theories protect the analyst from exposure, from being seen by the patient. This security gives the analyst a sense of space and freedom to think about the patient but at the expense of knowing our impact on the patient and their impact on us. Other theories bring us more immediately and fully into the interaction.

Before considering the various psychoanalytic interpretations of our emotional states, we first need to take up a more fundamental question: What are emotions?

The analyst's lived emotions

The vast topic of emotion cannot be fully explored here. I will narrow down our discussion to the clinical significance of our emotional experience as analysts. Because emotions are bodily-mental experiences, I will start with a description of the analyst's embodied subjectivity—the basic human quality we bring to the relationship.

Damasio (2010) makes an important contribution to understanding our emotional states. Separating emotion and feeling, he says that emotions are physical correlates of "what is happening", which, when conscious and put into words, become "feelings". Feelings emerge first as images. Damasio describes the trajectory in which "sensory patterns signaling pain, pleasure, and emotions become images, [then] ... feelings" (p. 55). Bion (1961) also describes the way raw sensory-emotional states are transformed into "proto-mental" qualities in the form of pictograms. Images and bodily expression then become attached to words in early development through the recognition and naming by primary caretakers, or later, by therapists

In addition to Damasio's ideas, important empirical and philosophical contributions tell us that subjectivity is embodied.[1] Our perceptions, feelings, thoughts, and phantasies emerge from bodily states. These bodily states form a constant background varying in shape and intensity, coloring the world we inhabit. We are in the world, in ourselves, and with others as embodied minds, accompanied by an evolving, ever-present emotional soundtrack. This soundtrack, full of variations in texture, color, light, and cadence, moves in time in response to internal-external interactions. Emotions give us a first-person perspective that this experience is *mine*. And, a crucial dimension of our feelings is also what they simultaneously are telling us about the emotional state of another. This is the *foundation of intersubjectivity*: embodied minds sense the embodied mental states of others and are affected by it. This allows us to share emotional experiences, which can be conscious or out of our awareness. Ferenczi's (1916) notion of the "dialogue of unconsciouses" points to the same idea: a two-way street of emotional information passed back and forth between analyst and patient. We are permeable to the emotions of others, at times even before they are aware of their own feelings. That is why we can know another's emotional state while it is outside of their awareness. There is therapeutic value in naming the patient's emotions, giving them a handle on their experience by making emotions conscious as feelings. The same is true of the analyst's position vis-à-vis the patient: the patient may sense our emotions before we know our feelings as well, and name them as well.

In summary, feelings, and their underlying counterpart in emotions, are our basic orientation to ourselves and others. This orientation colors our way of being in the world and signals what is going on in and around us. Thus, feelings give us a sense of ourselves—actually give us a crucial quality of subjectivity, the me-ness, the first-person perspective of our experience, as well a channel to another.

Given the centrality of emotions in bringing us into the world of others and understanding *who* we are and *how* we are in relationship to others, and they with us, what is the place of our emotional life in analytic work?

Psychoanalytic perspectives on the analyst's emotions

In reviewing theories that interpret our emotional states, the question becomes how do these theories bring us in relation to our emotional self and to our patients—not the truth-value of the theories—but how do they organize, orient, and give shape to our experience? Here, I will take up and track the analyst's emotional life, focusing on central clinical concepts dealing with the analyst's emotion in the interaction. While not an exhaustive review, it is a personal account of the theories that have most influenced me in formulating my view of analytic emotional experience.

Countertransference

The concept of countertransference first described by Freud brought in our subjectivity as part of the analytic experience. Two aspects of our emotional position worried Freud. He stated that countertransference is "a result of the patient's influence on [the physician's] unconscious feelings" (1910, p. 144), which he felt makes us vulnerable to acting out with the patient. His other worry was that our emotions may distort our objectivity and color our observations. Freud wanted us to tune our mind to the patient's unconscious like a telephone receiver, picking up unconscious transmitted messages. Static from our emotions would garble that message.

In a letter to Jung, Freud (1909) wrote of the "need to dominate counter-transference, which is after all a permanent problem for us" (p. 231). Though Freud may have been curious and open regarding his own emotional states as evidenced in some of his letters, he publicly expressed a rather adversarial attitude toward the analyst's feelings for and with the patient. Freud, himself, actually allowed for "real relationships" with his patients,[2] but subsequent writers eventually developed "standard technique" that codified "objectivity", "anonymity" and "abstinence".

We see a contradiction in Freud between the personal and idiosyncratic ways he worked and expressed himself with patients, and his theoretical emphasis on managing ("dominating") one's feelings to maintain objectivity. Freud did not let himself theorize his personal clinical expressiveness. This tension was resolved in the direction of abstinence and wariness toward our emotions.

Projective identification and containment

Gradually, different views came into the conversation that considered our emotions as an aid rather than obstacle to understanding the patient's inner world.[3] As a route to empathic understanding, what we feel and our receptive stance may reveal important things about the unconscious object relationship and state of mind of the patient. This thinking is an advance because it is more welcoming toward our emotions, although they are still considered dangerous if expressed or enacted.

However, if we understand that we are participating regardless of our intentions, how is this theorized? A more interactive view of countertransference comes from the Neo- Kleinian and Bionian tradition in the evolving concept of projective identification. This concept gets at the "how" and "why" of mutual influence. In the neo-Kleinian view, the analyst is under pressure to comply with the patient's unconscious relationship in order to maintain the patient's "psychic equilibrium", keeping the dependent part of the self, split off and out of contact. The pressure to enact is defensive for analyst and patient, and often hard for the analyst to perceive and resist, and instead is lived out in the session. According to Joseph (1975), if the analyst can resist the pressures of projective identification, he or she gains access to the part of the patient's protected self in need of care. For Joseph, enactments are seen as defensive but common. Importantly, Joseph shifts attention toward the ever-present action component of emotion, a more realistic view of the vulnerability in both parties to enact. This expansion of the concept of countertransference to projective identification, from phantasy to action still puts the source, the originator of enactments, in the patient, who pressures the analyst to live out a defensive, unconscious object relationship. The value of this model is that the analyst's emotions and actions are a crucial object of reflection and knowledge. The blind spot in this theory is that the analyst's transference, independent of the patient, is not adequately theorized.

Feldman (1997) brings in a subtle intersubjective perspective when he underscored the analyst's independent contribution in projective identification. He views projective identification as a two-way street, asserting that the analyst also pressures the patient to maintain a stable sense of self and identity to maintain dyadic equilibrium. Importantly, Feldman brings mutual influence into the model of the relationship.

Bion's work prior to 1967 continues this tradition of the patient-oriented flow of emotion, with an important twist. The source of the analyst's emotional experience derives from aspects of the patient's world communicated non-verbally through projective identification that is meant to be understood as communication, contained, and transformed from raw emotion into thought through "alpha function". Un-metabolized unbearable states in the patient are communicated to/deposited in the stronger mind of the analyst. Our disrupted states in relation to our patients are then considered, not as obstacles or pressures to enact, but important bits of the patients' raw experience to be held onto, *lived with and through*. This is a welcoming attitude towards disturbing experience—however painful it is for the analyst. Emotions are endured, unmetabolized experience borne—not to avoid enactment but to transform the patient's embodied modes of communication.

There is another variant to projective identification worth mentioning. Some patients reverse roles with the analyst so that their unconscious experience, their position in difficult or traumatic relationships, is passed to the analyst to live out. What differs from the containing experiences Bion describes is that what is given for the analyst to absorb is an emotional state in relation to another, not unmentalized bits of the patient's mind.

All the theories discussed so far give shape to the analyst's various emotional states. After Freud, as the idea of countertransference broadened, theories tended to view the patient as originator of the emotional vector, and the analyst as receiver-reactor-metabolizer.

A new paradigm and my personal approach to emotional experience

I want to turn now to my perspective on our emotions and how I approach them. A paradigm shift occurred in the 1980s when analysts began to consider the inevitability of their emotion-in-action and the view of inevitable shared emotional states. This shift came from several directions: the publication of *The Clinical Diary of Sandor Ferenczi* (Dupont, 1988); in Latin America Pichon-Riviere's theory of the *vinculo* [the link] and the dynamic analytic field theory of the Barangers (1983); and the work of the Relational Group in the United States. These contributions enlarged our understanding of the influence of the analyst's emotions on the therapeutic process in important ways, implying that a new kind of emotional work is required of the analyst. Intersubjectivity is the grounding principle for all these contributions. In this vision, we enter into and live within the patient's inner world through our shared emotional states and responses—both conscious and unconscious. The patient also lives within the world of *our* transferences. There is a free flow of emotion that results in an interlocking sequence of psychic and physical actions. Both patient and analyst bring unconscious object relations into play in creating enactments. McLaughlin's (1991) earlier work on enactments advanced the progress of this intersubjective dynamic model. Grossmark's (2012) later more radical view depicts enactments as the interpretable text of the analysis, previously conceived of as the patient's free associations.

Analytic process is conceived of as a free-flowing often unconscious sharing of emotional states that make up enactments and then understanding. The crucial part of the process is the analyst maintaining an open circuit of communication at all levels of representation and expression. But blocks can occur in the progression. Ferenczi (1933/49, 1988), followed by Balint (1950), believed obstacles to progress are not due to the patient's resistance but the analyst's unconscious transferences that block this circuit of emotional communication. Our conscious and unconscious emotional life can be expressed in the mix in ways that burden the patient or stymie communication. The more we recognize the *inevitability* of this, the less likely it will become an entrenched obstacle to progress that leads to impasse. Ferenczi found that in many cases his unconscious transferences to patients limited his receptivity, at times conveying negative reactions toward his patient. He found that the only way forward was to better understand himself by listening carefully to the patient's observations, assuming that their perceptions were not only transferential but contained a germ of truth, always, about a problematic aspect of his character. Racker (1968) famously stated that "the first distortion of truth in the 'myth of analytic situation' is that analysis is an interaction between a sick person and a healthy one" (p. 132).

This view requires us to make our emotional life our responsibility to recognize and work with as our own and, not necessarily, at least a first, used to "understand" the patient. Our first move is to foster open communication and shared emotional states. Our emotions not infrequently cause constriction or blind spots in us. We can become preoccupied with our own feelings and lose the patient, as I described in Chapter 3. Within an intersubjective matrix, in the flow of experiences, it is sometimes difficult to know whose feelings are whose. This is a phenomenological truth. But, here, I am describing a pragmatic approach to our emotional experience that gets at its more problematic dimension: as a corrective to earlier perspectives that point to the patient as the source of our emotional experience. When the patient is considered the source, there is a danger in denying our own feelings and contribution. We need to sort ourselves out first, beginning with the emotional work necessary to be open and responsive to the patient in order to be present. This work puts us in a more receptive attitude to our emotional life and the patient's as well.

The emotional work of surrender and mourning

After much lead-up, I come to the heart of this chapter. I have described how various theories frame our attitude toward our emotional reactions. What follows now is my personal perspective on working with our emotions.

Hageman (2002) writes

> ... it is through the experience of surrender that we break out of the confines of our false selves and allow ourselves to be found, known, penetrated, and recognized. (p. 32)

Surrender is the necessary first emotional step. We give up the hard and clear boundaries that separate us from the patient, we give up our sense of control and surety, and we give up our firm sense of identity as analysts and the more rigid, habitual ways we know ourselves. Mourning is the actual emotional work of letting go of such attachments that block surrendering.

Mourning describes the difficult emotional struggle of letting go of attachments to ways of being and feeling that (defensively) support the way we experience ourselves and our patients. Unconsciously, we need things from the patient and the work that are based on our early relationship history and defenses, and our unconscious motivations to heal others. We seek in our work reassurance of our goodness, capacity to repair, narcissistic needs for love, and early omnipotent feelings of power and control. We might also seek masochistic relations out of guilt. When trauma is a part of our background, we can be prone to denial, omniscience, and dissociation to preserve an intact sense of self. These often unconscious or split-off parts in us resist awareness. If observed and enacted in the relationship, we may feel shame and humiliation. All this is to say that the analyst's position is a contingent one. The recognition of this, the experience of this involves loss—a recognized loss that initiates mourning.

Yet, this recognition of loss has an important upside. By surrendering and mourning, the analyst then becomes open to what is going on in the patient and the relationship. This expanded self-awareness can only occur *within the relationship,* given the limits of self-analysis and self-reflection, and even consultation (which is of course helpful if we are open to investigating our transferences with the consultant). *We ultimately though come to know ourselves in interaction with another, in real time.*

How is mourning done in the analytic relationship? Marcel (1933) discusses obstacles to presence in an uncannily psychoanalytic way: "To be incapable of presence is to be in some manner not only occupied but encumbered with one's own self" (p. 24)—in other words, the analyst's transference and narcissistic defenses. Marcel uses terms such as "obduracy," "fixation", "constriction". As analysts we are familiar with ways we can feel blocked, yet often the specific "fixations" or "countertransference reactions" are not in our awareness. We *can* be aware that we are relating to the patient more as an object for our own use—however altruistically. We can also be aware of our constriction, limited imagination, lack of emotional freedom—*signals* of a transference problem in us.

The next section will describe how the patient helps us become aware of obstacles to openness.

How do we work through emotional states that block empathy and availability? We can come to know what embodied presence feels like by first detecting a momentary feeling-state tonal shift toward availability—like a shift in a key of music — an "interior surrender". What is emotionally held tightly is loosened. This shift can be felt as physical relaxation, richer sensory experience, and a widening of consciousness. This shift is inevitably accompanied by a loosening of many attachments—to one's theories (about how the work should go, what analysis is, and what an analyst does) and to one's own boundaries.

This loosening is a quiet or more noisy psychic upheaval. Our habits and our need for control, "understanding", and psychic equilibrium are disrupted. Paradoxically, this disruption is a good sign because it allows us to better receive and attune to our patients. This upheaval brings with it two painful states—loneliness and alterity—which I will discuss in Chapter 8.

The patient helps us to surrender and mourn

Along with signals of contraction how is our self-awareness expanded in order to recognize our transferences (complementary counter-transferences)? At any moment in the session, we have limited self-awareness of the ways we are being and relating in a relationship with the patient. We are decentered. We are more apt to see in others than ourselves our subtle often implicit emotions and attitudes expressed non-verbally. So, self-awareness in relational action can helpfully, and most often, come from being seen by the patient. The fact of mutuality, or rather, our willing recognition of the fact of mutuality, expands our self-awareness. (In Chapter 7, I argue that self-discovery begins in dialogue.) A full sense of ourselves consists in seeing ourselves as an "I" and a "me", and the movement back and forth between the two. "I" is our subjective sense of ourselves, and "we" the way we imaginatively see ourselves as others see us, as an object to others. Often the way we get to "me" and back to "I" is to observe and take in the other's reaction to us. This is a crucial process of expanding self-awareness that occurs from the patient's observations and reactions. The "me" often resists being seen—the pleasure and safety of anonymity and neutrality that may even be built into our technical frame. To be exposed in our work feels dystonic and uncomfortable. But it is so necessary. It comes with mutuality.

Forms of surrender and mourning

We therapeutically engage patients through *holding, containing, and "being-with"*, and *living through transformational moments.* These experiences depend on the specific ways we surrender and mourn.

Holding

Winnicott's (1960) idea of "*holding*" derives from his observation of infants in development. An infant requires a kind of provision that is physical and environmental that allows for the development of a True Self through "going on being". In analysis, as the analyst adapts to the needs of the patient-child, this action is sensate and "atmospheric" in the interaction. Related to holding is Balint's (1969) concept of the "unobtrusive analyst" who provides a protective medium for emotional development in which our subjectivity is limited. This means that the patient is not forced to relate to us. Instead, we adapt to the patient in ways the patient does not consciously encounter.[4]

What is called upon emotionally in holding is for the analyst to tolerate being a subjective object, one whose subjectivity recedes into the background. It is challenging for us to not be recognized as a subject, and to defer our own needs for connection and more symbolic ways of relating. Many students have questioned whether it is really "analytic" to "do nothing" except manage the environment in a way that minimizes intrusion. Actually, as Slochower (1996, 2013) describes, the analyst must manage a great deal of tension to minimize intrusion, knowing that the stakes are high, while at the same time accepting inevitable failure.

In surrender and mourning, with a more regressed patient, we then let go of our needs and the sort of security a more "mature" patient gives us: symbolic communication, a more defined analytic role, the gratification of giving "understanding", and the familiarity of more predictable interactions. That is, holding involves deprivation for us.

However important the provision of holding is for the patient, the analyst will either 1) reach the limit of what she or he can provide in a certain moment, or 2) inadvertently disrupt the patient. In both situations, we will fail the patient. Also, we cannot fully make up for the deprivations in our patient's childhood. A "basic fault" remains. There is a limit to how much we can repair or restore in the patient. As we accept the limitation in us and the impact on the patient of their early environment, so may the patient recognize this and mourn as well.

Containing and "being-with"

Bion (1963) developed the concept of containment in which the analyst takes on non-mentalized experience and most difficult aspects of the patient's internal world. Different from holding, "containing" means having the patient live within us. What does this demand emotionally from us? In the pragmatic sense, "containing" actually means "self-containing", in which we *hold onto the patient's and our own resulting emotional state*—not giving this back to the patient— and *being-with and living with and within* this emotional world.

This form of intense receptivity can open up us to confused, dissociated, and non-symbolized emotional states. We can be taken over and carried away by the state of the patient and our response to it, losing all awareness of what is going on. The analyst does not simply share painful bodily states of distress, dissociation, or psychic deadness, but is possessed by these states. When this happens, we may not at first have the awareness to recognize and put into words for ourselves what is going on. Borgogno (2014) writes about how the analyst may become "sick" with the patient:

> Psychoanalytic knowledge is not intellectual but *visceral*, saying that if analysts are truly to understand their patients they must take on their suffering in such a way as to *become the patient*. (p. 301, author's ital.)

Similarly, Bollas (1983) encourages the analyst to surrender to the patient's world,

> Provided the analyst can tolerate the necessary loss of personal identity within the clinical situation, I think he is more able to achieve the necessary *process identification* which allows him to receive and process the patient's transferences. (p. 5, author's ital.)

Losing oneself in this way does have value. If we can tolerate and work through these difficult embodied states by becoming aware of them, returning to our sense of our own body-in-relationship, and regaining receptivity to the patient, we can then know the patient at a deep experiential level.

Paradoxically, we come back to ourselves by settling in, being released from a *resisting* that contributes its own tension and detachment. When we feel overwhelmed by confusion or loss of boundaries, even our loss of identity as analysts when infused with the patient's world, we can surrender as Bollas suggests, and mourn. We have to accept and tolerate the very uncomfortable emotions we share with the patient and the loss of our privileged status—at least for a time. (In Chapter 8, I describe how we also have to live with the discomfort of uncertainty.) And, as withholding, it is inevitable we will fail and not be able to contain all that we take in. We may become "heady" and intellectual, or project our own distress onto the patient (the susceptibility to complementary countertransference is great), or feel persecuted, and so on.

It is also challenging to find ourselves in a difficult emotional position in relation to the patient during periods of role reversal. We resist feeling masochistic or sadistic, uncaring and hostile, inadequate and confused. This is a particular form of being-with and containing in *content*, but the emotional work is the same: surrendering to the position we are in and letting go of more comfortable ways of being and viewing ourselves.

How we tolerate uncertainty and confusion is a personal matter. Our reactions to disruption bring out our own particular defensive solutions. We all have historical, relatively stable ways of maintaining equilibrium—for example, under the strain of containing another, we may tilt toward a collapse into our patient, or we may maintain a highly differentiated, impermeable state, either of which compromises containment and blocks communication.

Transformative moments

There is a class of emotions we face when the relationship frame or accepted ways of being together breaks down. We enter into heightened, turbulent, and intense passages of shared living. It becomes especially personal.[5] These moments can arise from failures on our part, from entry into new areas of experience in which we express more than we knew or intended, from the patient having a surprising impact on us that is witnessed, or from the patient's emotional growth that disrupts the status quo. Our vulnerability in the relationship is heightened, often unexpectedly. "Now moments" are times when there is a potential for something new in the relationship and a new shared way of being in the relationship. There is a new sense of who we are and who the patient is. But in order for these moments to fruitfully play out, we have to let go of habitual ways of relating and feeling stable. We have to let go of what is known and predictable. In a state of surrender and mourning, we accept the alterity of another in relationships and the limit to what can be known about them. When this is borne, when we can accept and also help the patient contain the turbulence of what is non-repetitive and new, the dyad is changed by these moments, and each grows emotionally.

Clinical example of Dr. N

Earlier, I briefly mentioned my patient, Dr. N. Now I will describe in detail an emotional therapeutic process with him that required me to surrender and mourn. There was a period in which my transference to Dr. N resisted the emotional position I was in with him, so I became a stonewalling and rejecting object. As I worked through my reactions to him, I was able to embody and accept a world full of dread and hopelessness that we shared—though for Dr. N this world was at first split off and denied. Eventually, this world-sharing brought Dr. N in contact with a young and terrified child in himself he could express directly to me: the vulnerable part that I could then attend to in a different way.

Dr. N is a married man in his early 30s who came for treatment because he felt burdened by life and found no pleasure in it. He seemed to be liked by colleagues, patients, and friends, as well as by his wife and child, but he had little interest in deepening these relationships. He relayed images of his life in a vague, two-dimensional way. I could never grasp what his life was really like, but the tone was usually grim and barren. An oppressive sense of futility pervaded the atmosphere. I was infused by his mood. A sense of physical oppression and heaviness inhabited my body and I instinctively moved in ways to relieve or at least contain it, but with little success. I would try to comment on things he said but that was not the point. The point was this deadening world we shared and that I resisted. What seemed most prominent to me was the inescapability of this terrible, claustrophobic mood. I felt a collapse in my ability to think about what was going on—at least while in his presence. I found it intolerable and wanted to emotionally flee.

With Dr. N, I did not start with a view that he is doing something to me—aggressively invading me or intending to collapse my thinking. Nor did I start with the idea that the mood between us was created by him alone. My first attempt was to see if I could tolerate what was going on and understand two elements: 1) What is getting in the way of my being with this experience? 2) How am I contributing to it? I consider my emotional responses *mine* to live with and tolerate. I want to understand how the patient lives in me—what sort of transference figure is he to me, and how does my emotional response to him help shape our interaction? These questions can get answered by what the patient has to tell me.

Here is how it evolved. Dr. N and I settled into something negative and static and repetitive. The claustrophobic discomfort was intense. Within the dread and deadness that we shared, I tried to understand what was going on. But in reaction to my attempts to open up the meaning of his narratives, he felt that I did not understand him. Whenever I tried to show him what motivated his view of each of us was—to escape a sense of anxiety with me, to rid himself of anything positive, etc.—it intensified his insistence that I did not understand him and that I was detached from him. My comments were in fact irrelevant to what was going on at a deeper level but *enacted* the central dynamic. My interpretations actually communicated the way I was trapped in a dreadful place and how I tried to escape from it—in part by putting the responsibility on him. What I mean is that my comments were intended to affect him and change our experience of the work, himself, and me, and not contain or bear it. This was all meta-communicated to him.

The following vignette is an example of that exchange. The content of my interpretations is not necessarily wrong, but my unconscious intention to alter something between us for my own needs ultimately render my comments fundamentally, emotionally wrong.

P: I feel the way I always do when I come, a kind of dread. I know nothing will happen and that you can't help me … well, it's not how I always feel, I know. A few hours ago I was thinking about talking about a different kind of feeling in my body since I've been swimming, and I'm learning how to do it better. More of a glide. *(His voice is gaining energy.)* So I'm not dragging so much in the water. Now I'm dragging.

A: You were coming in feeling lighter and stronger and something interfered that now gives you a feeling futility. *(I am caught up in the destructive aspect still, rather than seeing if he can widen his feeling of "gliding".)*

P: But it is futile, isn't it? I mean nothing ever changes in me.

A: You were just noticing that something was changing in you and you wanted to tell me. There's probably more to say about that. *(I'm feeling quite alert and engaged at this point, which I'm sure I communicated.)*

P: That doesn't really mean anything. I go up and down and usually end up down, especially with you. It doesn't matter what steps I take forward. It's always taken away and this here is the main thing. The better feeling is a blip.

A: Right now you want to take the vitality out of you, especially in my presence, so that we will both feel defeated. *(I'm sure there is an accusatory tone here.)*

P: *(long pause)* ... Come on. You're over there in that comfy chair and nothing can really touch you. I'm the one suffering! Maybe you're even enjoying this a bit *(a slight laugh)*. No really, I think you think I can feel better and that you want to feel you've been helpful. But let's cut the la la la stuff.

The more I attempted to get us out of this dynamic, the deeper in it I felt. I noticed how we were on a constant emotional seesaw: If I seem alive and invested, he goes flatline. This all happens in the nonverbal register of our conversation, and the sense is that there truly is no way out of this.

In time, his persistent responses to what I offered—that I did not understand him—helped me. I became much more aware of how claustrophobic and irritated I felt, frustrated by what appeared to be his resistance to accepting my comments, and his dedication to hopelessness. In a way that felt bad, I realized that a good part of what I was trying to do was save *myself* from something uncomfortable that I felt he was doing to me. That is, he was a persecuting object to me in a complementary transference. There was a menace lurking that I located within him that executed all vitality.

So, as I listened to his reactions, I became aware of my anxiety with him and hostility toward him, which allowed a surrendering and mourning to begin. There were antecedents in my own history of being trapped in a hopeless relationship, in which all of my efforts proved useless. I could not get through to him by repeating efforts from my past, with all the same feelings of frustration and dread. In gaining some emotional awareness of this, something relaxed in me. Yet, it also brought up feelings of helplessness and hopelessness that I had trouble bearing when young. I gradually became open and present to my experience with Dr. N and was gradually able to tolerate these difficult feelings.

There are specific elements of this surrender-mourning process. With Dr. N, I had to give up a sense of my own reparative powers in our relationship as expressed in my (traditional) role as (healing) analyst. I also had to accept the very negative feelings I had toward Dr. N, which also tarnished the picture of myself as an accepting, benevolent person. And I had to accept being shut out by Dr. N from moments of life and the goodness he might feel when apart from me.

As I became more relaxed and quieter, Dr, N took a dramatic action that heightened my feelings of oppression. He began to research me on the Internet and report to me his findings. Now I felt the menace concretely in the room. This was a world of spying and shaming and intrusion. Because I had done some of the emotional work of surrender and mourning, I was more prepared for this. In this concrete persecution of me, I could now feel into the internal world in which he suffered and that we shared. There was a "we" now. In this world we shared, I could begin to take in and accept his feeling of persecution.

As a result of these reflections, I began to sense the threat I posed to him and the sadomasochistic structure that enfolded the two of us. I think what was most important in this emotional transition was the feeling that I did not need to save him, that *my interpretations did not need to—perhaps could not—do anything*. Also important was the feeling that we were in something together. I had to allow myself to live in this persecuting world without feeling compelled to alter it. As a result, I did not offer something "useful". I accepted and tolerated the experience we both shared. This emotional movement in me traces the arc from surrender and mourning to presence.

What set off this arc for me was that I became curious about the quality, the emotional texture of feeling persecuted. In this shift, I opened up to Dr. N., feeling a greater sense of freedom, imagination, and with time slowing down. I did not need to flee. The sessions no longer trickled by. Unbidden metaphors and reveries came to mind. Some were spatial, such as a sense of claustrophobia. And I think perhaps most *a propos*, I found myself thinking about Stalin's reign of terror that I had been reading about—particularly the story about a gathering where Stalin made a toast at a meeting. The small group of elites kept clapping after the toast. The clapping went on and on, as everyone was afraid to be the first one to stop clapping. Finally, one of the higher officials said, "OK, let's get down to work". At which point the clapping stopped and party business began. This official was murdered shortly after this incident. You simply could not survive having your own mind—at least not in public.

And, so, in a session, thinking about this while feeling a kind of terror and persecution, the Internet spying on me, and all, I came to appreciate in a way more immediate than before what was being actualized: a part of the patient, Stalinesque, was absolutely terrifying and sadistic. Putting these sorts of experiences into imagery or words involves both acceptance of its reality and a sort of separation—there is this entity alive and in the room. When I commented on what he was doing with the Internet and so on, I spoke of the atmosphere in the room we both shared and had to deal with. I did not make an interpretation in which he was the agent of the aggression—for example, "You're trying to intimidate me, confuse me, etc.", while pointing to his excitement and triumph.

Instead, I started by describing the sort of metaphors that came to me. The subject of the metaphors was not attributed to either of us. I mentioned my thoughts about Stalin and his tactics, and the eerie story of the meeting. I said, "We are the officials around the room with Stalin, afraid to stop clapping". Dr. N's first response was to laugh excitedly, but it also aroused his curiosity:

P: Hah, so you like to read about the USSR! I thought you might be Russian … I don't know what to say. What am I supposed to do with that? … It actually scares me that you said that. Isn't that a bit exaggerated?

A: Is it?

P: ... I don't know ... *(His manic pace is slowing, and he seems disturbed. At this moment I sensed a shift in the emotional atmosphere between us. We were both at a loss as to what to say. There was a very long uncharacteristic silence. I think we were both absorbing what it is like to live in that climate.)* ... I know I would constantly complain to you that I can't get anything done, that nothing ever happens or goes anywhere. I never felt very much when I talked to you like that. Except for annoyance with you and with me. For some reason that I don't understand, I feel very sad. And scared. *(He starts to cry.)* I really wonder whether you or anyone can help me. No, I *really* wonder, I really feel that. This is real what's happening to me.

At this moment I felt connected to him in a different way. I was moved that he was conveying a true fear we both felt. It *was* possible I could not help him—that this terror and deadness was extremely powerful was realistic, not fantastical. He expressed this, not as a complaint, but as an accurate emotional picture of our work together. This was a transformational moment we shared, an emotional truth that was novel, alive, and barely contained by language.

What emerged within our conversation, what he could then describe, was a vicious, devaluing internal presence that drained the life out of any impulse or desire to the point that the alive part of him felt useless and dying. He experienced this destructive object as very powerful and exciting, but also terrifying. For example, he described a certain kind of excitement in watching the two of us "flail" and make no progress. There was an internal sense of victory and triumph over anything alive, tender, or hopeful. "Maybe I'm Molotov to Stalin", he said. The more he could describe this aspect of his experience, the more distance he gained. He said, "There are three of us here, and one always watches, demeans, ridicules, mocks ... and threatens".

A usual pattern to his verbal expressions emerged. First, he would comment in a slightly manic way, as if he now really understood and could put his situation into words. But immediately after, the reality of his words, what it means to be Molotov, or subjected to a reign of terror, would sink in and affect him, and he would appear afraid. At those moments, he made sincere gestures toward me to gain my interest and help—I was on his side and he was not alone. I felt often, as he spoke, a sense of time slowing down, images coming to mind, and a feeling of acceptance.

One final point: The idea of a pathological organization or an intrusive internal object as dynamically alive in Dr. N is not wrong. Nor would an interpretation of that internal organization be wrong. The main question is how to emotionally approach this in a way that makes contact with the vulnerable, terrorized part of the patient. This can powerfully happen when the emotions are shared and a shared language arises from the immediacy of the experience—one we offer when present.

Conclusion

The analyst works to be present and open to the patient's emotional communication. The heart of this work is to surrender ("internal relaxation") and mourn (give up forms of self-protection). Whether we are in the mode of holding, containing, being-with, or interpreting, when we can surrender and then mourn, we allow ourselves to accept and tolerate our emotional state and our contingent position in the relationship, however confusing and destabilizing. It is from this emotional place that we move toward the patient with presence and availability. It is from this state of mind and being that transformation is possible. This view clearly goes against the picture of the analyst as contained, in control, and objective, a view that forecloses the most human and alive moments between ourselves and our patients, moments that are made possible when we are able to surrender to our difficult emotional experience, and mourn.

Notes

1 See Chapter 5, "Embodied Attunement and Participation", for a review of this topic.
2 See Lipton (1997, 1999).
3 See Heimann (1950) for an early discussion of countertransference as part of therapeutic technique.
4 Holding is one form of accompaniment that I describe in Chapter 6.
5 I will discuss this topic further in Chapters 9 and 10.

Chapter 5

Embodied attunement and participation

> The information carried by interpersonal rhythms does not move directly from one person to another. Thus information cannot easily be conceptualized as messages since the information is always simultaneously shared and always about the state of the relationship.
>
> Paul Byers, 1976

Experiencing the analytic relationship as embodied brings with it significant clinical consequences and possibilities for our attention, participation, and therapeutic action.

My appreciation of the embodied relationship and its clinical potential first came from clinical experience—my struggles and limited success with certain patients. With these patients, I was having difficulty picking up what was going on and connecting to them. I was facing the limits of reaching them through interpretation. In searching for other ways of connecting, I extended my attention to the embodied dimension of my experience, which widened my focus of engagement. I did not completely abandon the way I listened to and at times interpreted unconscious fantasy as expressed in words or enactments. But my embodied receptivity added another crucial dimension of listening and engaging—the powerful communicative language of the body. I attend to the embodied dimension in a way that allows me to receive messages about the state of the relationship and the state of the patient. I call this *embodied attunement*—a specific mode of analytic attention. One direction of my attention is toward the embodied register within the dyad—sensing shared rhythms, tone of voice, and movement, or dis-syncopation and

DOI: 10.4324/9781003208518-5

misattunement that signal the state of the relationship. An ear dedicated to the "music and dance" at the embodied level also gives me a sense of the degree of emotional sharing—an essential ingredient in therapeutic action—that is intersubjective,[1] as interactive rhythms are codetermined. At the same time, I turn my attention inward, toward my own bodily reactions and proto-emotional states.

Embodied analytic participation is a deliberate action is an interpretation in another mode. Even when my speech reaches the patient, I attend, deliberately, to its resonance, tempo, and other musical factors. I can enhance emotional states by emphasizing the patient's mode of expression, often by engaging in similar nonverbal qualities. For example, this can happen in an antiphony of call and response in the rhythm of the patient-analyst interaction. I can also bring out more quiet states in the patient by an enlivening engagement, as when I increase the intensity of my vocal cadence or tone. I may offer an accompanying counterpoint, in a dialogue of "overlapping play" (Winnicott 1968). Finally, I can disrupt the rhythms so that new forms of interaction occur, bringing the patient into a more embodied, emotionally connected state. Just as the analyst listens to the patient's words and eventually decides to comment, so we can decide to intervene in the language of embodiment.

What guides me in these interventions? The patient's embodied state and the pulse of the relationship direct my actions. The patient senses my embodied receptivity in my *presence* and *availability* as I described in Chapter 3. When patient and analyst are in the mode of emotional sharing and creating, in something that is sensed, the analyst's participation can be one of partnership, companionship, play, and accompaniment (see the next chapter).

However, some patients, beset by dissociation, psychic deadness, or high levels of anxiety arising in the face of intimacy and dependency, cannot enter into this sort of relating. These people require the analyst's "live company" (Alvarez, 1992) to find a new, more enlivened pulse. With the analyst in a more differentiated position, the patient can feel disrupted. That is understandable. The analyst is disrupting the ways the patient feels safe, even at the cost of psychic deadness. If the analyst can tolerate disturbing the patient, a more fruitful way of being and relating can eventually found. The analyst inevitably struggles with his or her own experiences of dissociation and deadness to move to a more alive, differentiated place.

Finally, in an attempt to bring the patient into a more embodied state, the analyst can focus directly on the patient's bodily awareness or on the sensory object world shared by patient and analyst. This can be particularly effective when direct relational contact occasions high anxiety or is experienced as a demand for compliance and submission.

Forms of embodied participation are unique to each dyad and vary over time. I hope to show through the following example how my understanding of the embodied dimension developed, the process I go through in becoming aware of what is going on, the sorts of participation available, and its effect on the patient and process. Often I must undergo a process of working through my own resistance in order to become more open and available. This vignette takes a slice out of the complex and rich interaction between patient and analyst, swirling with unconscious communication and influence.

Clinical illustration: two encounters with Carl

My experience with Carl charts the course of my analytic listening and attention, ranging from a tendency to focus on words and speech that reveal the unconscious transference for interpretation to a broadened awareness of and receptivity to embodied communication that yields new ways of participating. An interval of four years separated the two encounters. During that interval, a change occurred in the way I worked.

Carl is a gifted artist with a beautiful, metaphorical way of speaking. The analytic work proceeded conventionally through associations, dreams, and interpretations. His rich language elicited interpretations from me that focused on his anxieties in asserting himself in relationships—including ours—and a surprising inhibition in his capacity for creative living, given his work. Surprisingly, though his artistic endeavors met with serious success, he seemed to lack a creative response to life. At the time, I had the impression he was working through serious inhibitions of a neurotic nature, as his associations wended their way through his history and current interpersonal relationships in what appeared to be freer and freer ways. Links were not hard to make between his difficult childhood (an alcoholic and at times violent mother and a father who disappeared unexpectedly) and his current difficulties.

What might have caught my attention in a more significant way is that while narrating he did not seem anxious; he was *talking about* his anxiety and suffering in a way that had less of an emotional effect on me than I would have expected. The historical and transference material used for understanding his inhibitions did not deepen his experience with me, his emotional understanding of what had happened to him, or my emotional responses to him. I was only later able to appreciate this flat atmosphere.

Carl's dream imagery had a solitary quality that emphasized, as did his art, motionless landscape and a subdued, quiet mood. He also tended to be quite still on the couch. At times I felt bored and physically drained, overtaken by a bodily heaviness that seemed at odds with the vividness of his verbal associations. I did not focus on my physical responses at the time.

In one session, Carl told me, quite out of the blue, that he was stopping the analysis at the end of the month. He said he appreciated the work we had done, which he credited with allowing him to begin a promising romantic relationship, but after a year was ready to stop. He seemed content in a rather distant way. I did not sense that he felt any ambivalence or loss.

I was caught completely off guard by his decision. I had no inkling of why he wanted to stop. We surely had more to do, and we seemed to be working well together. His decision felt hollow and disturbed me quite a bit. I was put off and troubled by his cavalier, detached attitude. I felt treated like someone of little worth and that our relationship had no real value. Obviously, I had missed something crucial. Carl was emphatic and untroubled. So, we ended.

Carl's abrupt departure left me feeling abandoned, confused, and angry. I could not make sense of what happened. What had I missed? What had I not understood? It was striking that my intense feelings became defined, took shape, only when I was left alone with them and deprived of the person with whom I would want to share and try to understand this experience. He became an enigma I might never understand.

Surprisingly, Carl returned a few years later because he had broken up with a girlfriend he liked and was confused about his decision—he had expected to marry her. Though feeling low and out of sorts, we returned to the same rhythm of our previous work, as if no time had elapsed: lengthy, vivid stories and memories that I enjoyed, as I made what felt like correct interpretations, and that he elaborated in apparently meaningful ways. When I brought my work with Carl into consultation, it seemed clear that an enactment was occurring, but the consultant and I could not determine its nature. Perhaps it was a "bastion". Further, although I was interested in understanding what had happened that led to his leaving the analysis years earlier, Carl and I made no inroads into comprehending his state of mind when he made the decision to leave.

It was at this time that I began to widen my attention in my work, and for the first time took in our connection by tuning to my bodily responses and at times listening less closely to his words. As I mentioned earlier, this change was prompted by limitations in my work with certain patients. So, now with Carl, I felt less attached to "understanding" what felt like a traumatic rupture—at least to me—in the first go-round. And I listened now in a less directed way to the words he spoke.

I noticed something different going on: a subtle, persistent, tight stillness between us that we both contributed to, a narrow range of rhythm and movement, a fixed cadence that was at odds with his "lively" narrative. Our sparse gestures seemed constrained. I could not tell who was responsible for this constriction, which until now had been hidden in plain view. I would have liked to blame Carl for it, for making me feel so stifled and constrained, which would have relieved and satisfied me, giving me a pleasurable feeling of retaliation for the troubling emotions he had roused in me when he left. But I could not really endorse that view. We were in something, creating something, together.

Working this way allowed me to notice other things. The most vital moments occurred when Carl entered the office. He would steal a glance my way and then abruptly turn to the couch so he could start talking as soon as possible. He needed to escape a dangerous situation, and his escape lay in speaking and telling stories. He seemed afraid of a living contact—with himself and with me.

Milner (1960) writes about "sinking down into total internal body awareness".[2] As I sank down in embodied awareness, I noticed I felt heavy and listless and the office colorless: as if a state of dying, a major decathexis was going on. I now saw that we actually were sharing a drab life together, on the edge of death, frozen in time and movement, carried in the body and in my perceptions. In marked contrast to the colorful material Carl produced, this world that was noticed only in passing during the first phase of the analysis, now it took on great significance.

A part of my daily practice is to take a "second look" at an analytic relationship, a kind of meditation outside the session (Baranger et al., 1983). The embodied attention I am now describing includes not only reflection and reverie but also a focus on my somatic experience with a patient,[3] which I then can heighten and clarify, putting into relief certain sensations and perceptions.

These somatic insights evoked vivid imagery. The sense of physical death and dying was intense as if we were preserved in a lifeless chamber with a slowly diminishing oxygen supply. Movement would use up our supply too quickly—so stay still! I became aware that we shared this state, that my sense of my own decreasing vitality and live engagement matched this deeper experience in Carl. My physical sensations and emotions, as Damasio (2010) and Bion (1961b) have both described, were transformed into imagery and metaphor. This transformation allowed me to think about what was going on and how to go forward.

I made a clinical decision at this point. Though I wanted to enliven the relationship and the two of us individually, it was important that this come from the possibility of new, nonrepetitive experience and not from my own urgency and difficulty containing these painful feelings. I had to live in this world in a conscious and settled way before intervening. I considered putting this state of the relationship into words. Would that help Carl bear and know more about his experience, knowing that I recognized his state, even if he did not have access to it? Perhaps I could say something about the deadness and the anxieties underneath, or even something about my state of mind when with him.

When I tried verbal contact, though, by describing the atmosphere between us and the feeling of constriction, often using metaphors, words did not touch him. He made use of my comments the way he used previous comments, creating his own metaphors of the situation, talking *about* what was going on. And, if I pointed that out, we would be in for an infinite regression: he would protect himself, detaching with words the more I used words to reach him. We would be "talking about talking about". There was a subtle form of dissociation going on in him that was actually mediated by his speaking—a form of self-hypnosis. I now understood that this needed to be interrupted, so that an experiencing self could be present in Carl to experience what was going on in him and between us.

I started to engage and communicate in the language of the body. I became more alive and "real", freer with emotional expression that differentiated me from his/our usual state. This differentiation was made possible only by my tolerating the "emotional field"[4] we shared. I became more active in my movements and gestures, and quickened the cadence of my speech. I leaned forward in my chair to intensify the volume of my speech as I moved physically closer to him. I certainly wanted to feel more enlivened myself, but I felt no urgency. I clearly felt the desire to do something, to allow for and offer a different way of being together. In this way, I moved out of a more receptive and dissociated mode into an enlivening, active one. This move could be authentic only if I had truly "sojourned in the land of the dead" with him and knew something first hand about that world. I was not rising above it but was emotionally knowing the world he was in, and that we had been in.

My expressiveness made Carl anxious. He was disturbed and disrupted in his flow of imagery and memories. He complained—which was something new—that I would not let him follow his thoughts and that I was being intrusive. He said, rather weakly, that he wanted to set another termination date. I was firm in insisting that I understood his need to flee from an alive connection with me and that something scared him deeply. Through this difficult exchange, between his discomfort and my firmness, a real clash occurred, and Carl came into increased emotional contact with himself and me. My change in rhythm did not suit him. I had "knocked him off his game", he complained. "Aren't analysts supposed to allow people to do what they want?", he argued. Though some of his attacks hurt—he could be biting and sarcastic—and I had an urge to withdraw at times, I saw this offense as his best new defense, importantly an alive defense, as he emerged from a deadened symbiotic world with me.

Although we clashed, Carl felt I was emotionally present with him in a different, more separate way. How did I know this? I sensed it in several ways. Carl maintained longer visual contact with me in his entering and leaving the sessions. Sometimes I added words to his gaze, such as, "Here we are", with a slight nod. His language became less metaphoric and more concrete. He referred to specific things about himself and me and the surround—the time of day, the light in the office, other patients coming and going. There was more emotional heft to his words and tone. I spoke to his fear of me in a way that did not inspire more fear but conveyed my caring: "I know this is very hard and you really don't like it. But we need to get under the smooth way you talk with me, and I with you, to see how you really feel, to know how you feel".

Carl offered no direct responses to my comments, but I noticed much more movement on the couch. On the wall next to the couch hangs a weaving with tied strings at the bottom. He started to play with the dangling strings, rubbing them between his fingers, tying and untying, and swinging them around in a plainly self-soothing way, like a child caressing a blanket. A transitional object. Carl was freer to use his body, to seek comfort in it, and explore the world around him.

Carl asked about the weaving, its origins and dyes, and where I purchased it, as he continued to play with the strings. He noticed the weaving's colors and how they related to the color of the couch and rug in a "harmonious" way. Was the weaving my body, or perhaps more likely a transitional space arising out of our interaction? I wondered, but I did not interrupt him. I joined his experience and way of being. We talked about texture and color and shape, and the emotional experience he was having. He described qualities of "warmth", "harmony", and "vivid" color that he enjoyed in the surroundings and that he could freely explore.

We were now sharing a different world, one of aliveness and curiosity, though not without dissonance. We were living in the world together, doing something important in play where emotions are expressed in perceiving the things around us. Our doing something together, our playing, was not instrumental—it did not set out to change anything. It was a created world within the play. In other words, if I encouraged understanding at this point, I would have deprived Carl of the chance to make use of me and the environment as potential space, an intermediary area where he would not have to adapt to the realities of "doing analytic work" and "understanding". This period lasted for a few months. His gaze lingered longer and longer on me, my clothes and expression, and on the atmosphere in the office.

Eventually, Carl brought up what had happened when he first saw me:

> I was afraid to be more alive and open with you. I was pissed off you pushed me... though, if we continued as in the past, I would not be here, feel myself here with you, feel in myself, and get nothing out of this. That's what happened last time. Staring session after session at a blank canvas. Then trying to make marks that look good to please you. But it reflected nothing real in me. I had nothing real for you or for me then... just a blank canvas between us. What I was really afraid of is that there's nothing *in me,* that I'm a fake. It was desolate. I don't feel that now.

This time around, I had changed, attending to the embodied feel of the connection as a place from which to start, pay attention to, live through, and eventually participate in. This position affected how I spoke to him. Gradually, Carl's words took on greater depth and resonance. He spoke with feeling about his experience in the first phase of analysis and the quiet despair he felt. He wondered if I knew the state he was in—could I have reached him then?—since it was only in retrospect that he had words for his past disembodied ex-perience. Only *now,* when not in a dissociated state, could he know the kind of experience he had with me *then.* Before, he did not ex-perience it, so he could not communicate it. This is very important. When Carl or other patients are in a kind of automaton, detached mode, they are not experiencing. Words, images, and ideas are not repressed but detached from an experiencing self. When Carl felt himself in the room with me, it was only then that "words came" that represented his internal state. In speaking this way, there was hope for something new to happen between us and in him.[5]

A transformation occurred between Carl and me in this second time around. An ongoing deadened self-experience in Carl was heightened when the possibility of intimacy with another presented itself. This deadened, likely traumatized, part of him did find expression in his art, which, while rendered beautifully, evoked feelings of stillness, and lifelessness in the viewer. And, as I described, it did find expression in the nonverbal embodied relationship with me: lifelessness, suffocation, any movement leading to death. A therapeutic process could occur when that deadened part of him became engaged in a lively way. "The living core of the individual personality", to use Winnicott's language, could not be accessed through language. The "living core" was established through engaging the psyche-soma. Then play began to take shape, coming from a living part of him: the play of the strings of the weaving, the form and colors of the office that represented his alive emotional relationship to me. It was only once his "living core" was available that words and symbols came to life, expressing that living core: the sense of blankness and emptiness, the need to adapt to me, and so on.

Carl's metaphor of a blank canvas communicated emotions originally felt in the body that, until that moment, were not symbolized and not repressed but were now felt as real.[6] What made this possible was a concrete bodily experience of connection—in our case a difficult and disruptive one—that fostered Carl's greater self-awareness and self-possession, which ushered him into a more embodied self-experience. What then ensued was a capacity for play and symbolic thought. This connection to me and within himself arose from a deliberate action on my part to engage him through embodied participation. What signals to me that compliance was not the primary motive in the new phase of analysis was the obvious vitality and authenticity in Carl's way of being. One cannot be certain, of course, but one goes with one's best sense of what is happening.

A brief review of the embodiment literature

In searching for modes of embodied engagement with patients, I have been inspired and supported by a body of literature that posits the mind as embodied and shared from the earliest interactions, from which cognitive and emotional growth evolve and a sense of self develops. Several disciplines have converged on the view that the mind and the development of self are inseparable from the body (Damasio, 1994; Schore, 1994, 2011). This literature also establishes the importance of bodily communication and its connection to the clinical situation.

These influences did not result from a systematic search; rather, as I think happens with many analysts, I found useful theories organically when I was open to take them in. I found resonance and language to account for what I intuitively and empirically was encountering in my clinical experience. We find the "right" theory—pragmatically right—when we need it.

Thinking that inspired and resonated with me I found in Betty Joseph's emphasis on *mutual action* within the analytic dyad as the material for interpretation (1983) and in the enactment literature (Renik, 1990; McLaughlin, 1987), which stresses the inevitability of interaction when words fail to communicate the dynamics of the relationship. Also, insights by Ferenczi (1931) and Winnicott (1968) concerning the importance of play in adult treatments freed me to engage noninterpretively with patients when needed. Another influence was Balint's emphasis on the limits of language in communicating with patients in the area of the basic fault (1968), and the need for the analyst to provide a supporting atmosphere or medium, like water, which gave me theoretical support to follow what feels right with certain patients.

Bion's work (1957, 1959, 1961a, 1961b, 1967) was most crucial in expanding my awareness of analytic communication beyond speech. His view that communication in the clinical encounter occurs primarily in emotional transmission through projective identification—through transferred bodily feelings—widened my attention to the nonverbal, bodily dimension of clinical experience. What was most crucial is his later work, which emphasizes "being" before "knowing", experience before concepts in his description of shared emotional experience (at-one-ment, "O").[7] My current work builds on these experiences and influences and is further shaped by an intersubjective view of the encounter that naturally follows from them.

As I searched for a "language" that evokes and gives shape to this nonverbal dimension, I found that music, particularly jazz, suits this purpose (Markman, 2006, 2011, 2017, 2020). The metaphor of music helped me conceptualize what I was doing intuitively. At that time, I encountered the work of (Trevarthen, 2008; Trevarthen and Malloch, 2002; Malloch and Trevarthen, 2009) and his concept of "communicative musicality", the idea that human interaction *is* musical by nature and that an aspect of what we do analytically is *intrinsically* musical—rhythmic, sonorous, and gestural. He describes how a shared emotional world of companionship and recognition arises from mother-infant play of rhythm-pulse, tone, and gesture. The intersubjective world of the infant bathes in emotional meanings carried musicality, and the self as agent emerges from this interaction.

Being attuned to and participating in this register with patients fosters a shared emotional world, one in which the patient finds a greater sense of vitality and self-establishment. The language of the body manifests emotional narratives that eventually—as with Carl—may find verbal expression. Along with other nonverbal qualities, the relational connection is carried by its pulse and rhythm—the "music and dance" of the relationship (Harrison, 2014). This dance may involve a waltz of complementary exchanges or the tango of conflict and dissonance.

For example, working within the sensibility of the embodied analytic relationship can reveal the way many patients struggle at a fundamental level of existence to feel alive, to know and experience the present moment, as well as the past, to inhabit an experiencing self. Disruptions and trauma in early development weaken a person's link between the emotional body and self-awareness—a disruption in "going on being", as Winnicott (1960) calls it, an interference in the development of an alive and creative locus of the self. The analyst's sense of the patient's painfully disrupted and at times dissociated state is primarily and often forcefully conveyed through the language of the body. In this register, I pick up something about a patient's self-states: my somatosensory reactions turn out to be a gauge of the patient's disembodied experience. The analyst can play an important role in enabling the patient to return to or initiate a continuity of being and experiencing. Without the analyst's alive presence—conveyed through bodily expression, movement, and vocal qualities of tone and cadence—the cutoff, often traumatized, part of the patient may not be reached and revived.

A sense of self begins in infancy through interaction with primary objects via co-created rhythmic coordination of movement, facial expression, gaze and body movement, sound, and song, giving the child an experience of recognition in a shared emotional world. In this way, the mind begins as shared and dialogical through early interaction with others in a reciprocal mode of recognition between the primary object and child. This is the "bottom slice" of relating that continues throughout life (Harrison, 2014).

During development, bodily experience gives a person a constant emotional background and sense of what is going on (Damasio, 1999), within us and in relationships, and is the basis of feeling recognized, appreciated, and engaged. Our bodily sensations, perceptions, and emotions are an experiential mode of knowing self and other.

Sletvold (2014), a Norwegian analyst, who might be described as a relational neo-Reichian, views "the mind... as basically an ongoing process of registering, feeling, and sensing... what is happening and changing in our bodies as we continually interact with our environment" (p. 1). He adds that "the human body interacting with the environment grounds what we call mind" (p. 4).[8] Early development proceeds with interaction with the human world: "the mind is shaped by the feeling and sensing of our own and other people's moving bodies" (p. 7). Sletvold pictures the body as our "basic perceptual system" (p. 7) aimed internally in registering reactions, sensations, and emotions, and aimed externally in gauging the nature of the relationship.

Mark Johnson (2018), a philosopher of aesthetics and mind, argues that what gives meaning to experience are qualities, not concepts, conferred by feeling: "All our conceptual systems and forms of symbolic interaction are rooted in body-based meaning" (p. 2). Thomas Alexander (1987), a philosopher in the pragmatic tradition of John Dewey, offers a view of humans as aesthetic, meaning-making creatures who draw on their deepest sensory, motor, and affective processes to make sense of and orient themselves in their world. He describes a "visceral engagement with meaning" in which "we enact meaning through bodily movement, feeling, and imaginations" (p. 128).

Infant research and developmental neuroscience have provided empirical evidence for these ideas. Intersubjective bodily experience is foundational for the development of self, the recognition of others, and the substrate for symbolic thinking and growth of the mind. This exciting area of research, which looks at mother-infant interaction in micro-moments—particularly shared rhythms in movement and vocal expression—has led to a major shift in analytic theorizing, showing that the capacity for thinking and embodied consciousness develops from interactions with an engaged primary object in early development. This work also posits a nonverbal "core self" emerging in the first year of life (Stern, 2000; Schore, 1994, 2011) from early interaction.

In turning to the application of infant psychology to clinical work, Fonagy and Target (2007) have comprehensively reviewed this developmental research and laid out its clinical implications. They explore how symbolic thought—metaphoric language, fantasies, narratives, and anticipations—"emerges out of a multilayered sensory emotional and *enacted experience* with the primary object" (p. 411). These ideas clearly connect to analytic practice: "the rootedness of mental structures in early sensory and affective experience is perhaps most evident in the psychoanalytic encounter and is arguably the heart of psychoanalytic work" (p. 425).

This suggests that the "multilayered sensory emotional and enacted experience", the bodily dimension, is the *primary text,* created by interaction between patient and analyst. "Since the mind never, properly speaking, separates from the body, the very nature of thought will be influenced by characteristics of the primary object relation" (p. 432). Interestingly, then, Fonagy and Target suggest that all of our metaphors of intimacy—"close, holding, containing, attuned"—derive from the "physical sensation evoked by the action language of metaphor"; thus, "affects (bodily experience) organize the mind" (p. 431).

Continuing in this vein, Beebe et al. (2005) believe that linguistic forms of intersubjectivity continue to depend on pre- or nonlinguistic forms. This suggests that all psychoanalytic treatments are dependent on pre- and nonlinguistic forms of communicative competence and intersubjectivity, not just those with more disturbed patients (p. 63).

The work of Fonagy and Target, Beebe, and Trevarthen, offer an enhanced appreciation of this embodied expressive mode. "When language fails", Beebe et al. (2005) write, "the psychoanalytic dyad can still have access to prelinguistic and implicit forms of communicative competence" (p. 63).

Several founding analytic theorists considered the mind-body experience[9] in development, but the application of these theories to practice is recently more appreciated and developed.[10] Though Wilhelm Reich (1949) explored direct unconscious communication through posture and facial expression, his ideas did not enter the mainstream of clinical analysis. Several current analysts have taken up embodied experience in analysis based on the theoretical contributions mentioned above. This is important work, giving a phenomenological-theoretical account of the nature of the analytic relationship, while showing its relevance in work with dissociated, traumatized patients (Lombardi, 2008, 2011). Importantly, embodiment has recently been brought into the theory of the dynamic field. For example, Sletvold (2014) uses the term "embodied intersubjectivity" to formulate the nature of the analytic dynamic field—an embodied view of the field developed by the Barangers (Baranger et al. 1983).

Knoblauch (2000, 2005, 2011), from a relational perspective, writes about his experience of the embodied aspect of the relationship with a special sensitivity, given his background as a musician. Knoblauch implicitly understands embodied attunement, as his detailed clinical examples show. Through musical metaphors he explores the way bodily messages are passed back and forth or shared simultaneously, influencing each subject, and, like Reich, the way the body communicates unconscious content.

Goldberg (2012, 2018) goes further in describing a somatosensory orientation and mode of attention, a "framing posture" toward bodily experience in ways that are similar to what I am developing here. He writes of entering "the session primarily in a state of psycho-physical attentiveness and anticipation, rather than a readiness to understand or make connections among associations" (2018, p. 18).

Goldberg experiments with analytic action and the frame to bring the patient back into his or her body, in the analyst's presence. What marks a difference in emphasis between Goldberg's view and mine is my focus on the embodied intersubjective nature of the analytic process. His view, directed more toward the patient and giving little sense of two bodies together, does not aim to be intersubjective or interactive, where the rhythms of patient and analyst interlock, merge, or create dissonance. What stands out is the novelty and clarity of Goldberg's stance—his mode of attention to the sensorium, his openness to the unknown, and his willingness to experiment—that fosters an embodied orientation and attention in the clinical process.

The body of work I have reviewed has important clinical relevance. When one attunes to embodied experience, events become understood as emergent qualities of experience that are not necessarily structured by unconscious fantasies or enacted object relations. From the convincing contributions of several theorists, what stands out is novelty, in a more improvisational approach that responds to the newness and the potentiality of the moment. As the analytic relationship happens in time, temporality embraces patient and analyst in action and movement. Both participate in this flowing stream. Our bodies move in time, creating tension and intensity by the arc of tone, movement, and gesture that generates a shared emotional narrative without words, having no prescribed meaning or outcome, allowing for spontaneity and improvisation. When things go well there is a "playing together in a relationship". In Winnicott's words, "Psychotherapy has to do with two people playing together" (1968, p. 591).

Often freedom and "two people playing together" do not occur. Instead, we find ourselves out of synch and unattuned to each other. The patient is afraid or ashamed to engage in this way and self-protects using various forms of withdrawal or disruption. Or the patient senses something in the analyst that prevents trust and spontaneity. This is a jagged dance, out of rhythm and time. As embodied knowing is democratic, the patient senses our states as much as we theirs. Certain patients have even greater awareness than we do of this communicative dimension of the body, coming to it perhaps out of a survival mechanism to quickly and accurately read the other's intent in an early environment of danger. We have to assume that our patients' awareness is active and responsive, and that may account either for truth and freedom to play, or wariness and skittishness based on their sense of the analyst's state of mind. We can be in or out of synch, as I noted above, and this matters a lot.

Therapeutic actions of embodied attunement

Patients seek a sharing of what Trevarthen (2009) calls "time in the mind". Through play and relational experimentation, they seek companionship in a felt, shared world, and support and accompaniment in their emotional growth for self-presencing and self-elaboration—things that happen in the embodied dimension, as shown in Carl's play with the wall weaving. This connection is especially important for patients whose early environment lacked this kind of support, due to deprivation or impingement. But I would argue that all patients need this sort of engagement as a foundational part of the analytic relationship.

So, what are the spheres of therapeutic action providing embodied attunement and participation? First, the analyst offers the patient an experience of a shared world, an "I am with you" in rhythm and time. Such "unison" experiences can be transformational. Knoblauch (2000) writes that he and his patient "were both recognizing and being understood by each other... [when our] bodies moved from out of time, to in time" (p. 13)—not only metaphorically but concretely. That is the basis of "unison", a shared world. All patients, regardless of symptoms, history, and personality organization, are looking for an experience of care, acceptance, support, and accompaniment, bringing them into a world of others. As I have emphasized, a shared world is not necessarily smooth and easy. Often, it involves suffering of many sorts. When the analyst is attuned to bodily communication, the force of this shared suffering can be intense and sometimes hard for the analyst to bear.

Second, through experiences of misattunement and its correction, the patient develops trust in the sincerity, honesty, and flexibility of the analyst, as well as in her ability to affect the analyst positively. This is where the analyst is put to the test, where patients can develop confidence in their perceptions and ways of knowing—confidence to "rock the boat" without sinking it. This sequence can have a profound impact on the patient's developing self and sense of separateness. It also provides an opportunity to experience dissociated parts of self-experience in the analyst's failures and ensuing recognition and support.

A range of embodied action

In this section, I will discuss situations familiar to most analysts that call for embodied interventions, including adaptations in the setting. These interventions may be a regular part of clinical practice, though perhaps not usually thought of in terms of embodied action.

First, changes in the analytic setting almost always occur in the realm of the embodied relationship and hold important meanings and potential for communication (Bleger, 1967; Goldberg, 2018). Some aspects of the setting are necessary to create a safe, reliable space for the patient's explorations and imaginings, such as a regular time, consistency, and ethical boundaries. But other aspects can be flexible, as when the patient needs to experience and express herself in a more action-embodied or playful way. The setting is a living part of the encounter that the analyst can make use of it to reach the patient in an embodied way. Carl used the wall hanging in this manner. Some patients bring in family photographs, their artwork, or a pet. Like many analysts, I take interest in these actions, as a child therapist would engage in the play around any of the child's productions.

Many aspects of what we do as part of the setting, such as greetings and the physical setup (lighting, physical distance between analyst and patient, and so on) can also be used expressively by the patient. Some patients move their chair closer, turn away, sit in a chair as far away from me as possible, adjust the blinds for more or less light, wrap themselves in a blanket, read a story out loud. These are all embodied actions that patients initiate and that ask for the analyst's playful, perhaps noninterpretive, response.

Clinical illustration: Anne

Anne suffered her emotions physically, as pain coursed through her entire body. To deal with this pain, she would ask to listen to certain pieces of music with me. She did not want to talk about herself, declining to describe her pain and what it might mean. Instead, she wanted to do something with me. As we listened together, her response was striking. Upon hearing the first few notes, she would relax while looking intently at me. She might then close her eyes when she sensed my relaxed presence—I was with her. We would share rhythms and emotions created by the music. Over time the music changed, from soothing sounds to more enlivened, even dissonant ones. The determining aspect of the experience, regardless of the music played, rested on my willingness to share with her the physical-emotional states evoked by the music. Anne then found in her body, in response to the music, various modes of being that had been cut off due to the emotional and physical pain she suffered as a child, and now as an adult. Her body relaxed and her gestures became more fluid. For her body to become a source of pleasure rather than pain—for this transformation to occur—the embodied experience of sharing this state with me was necessary.

Clinical illustration: Sarah

While on the couch, Sarah would frantically search to find me, seeking what I wanted and expected. She was often unable to compose or express her own thoughts and feelings. I came to feel that the only way I could offer myself in a more concrete, alive, and less constrained and enigmatic way was to ask her to sit up and face me. That change was freeing for both of us. At first, there was an immediate, very intense feeling of two people together that I had not felt when she was on the couch. Facing each other, I realized we had been sharing a kind of dissociation—words floating between us without ballast. Now a feeling of mutual exploration prevailed: what we looked like, our facial expressions, the immediate impact that our words and gestures had on the other. I felt drawn to her face and gestures in a curious, more intense way: a whole new modality of experience opened up. She expressed the same feeling: for example, the delight, even wonder, at seeing me smile or move around. Rather than frantically searching for direction—a desperation that must have resonated in her primary object relationships—she had me and my presence in the natural way one has another in intimate relationships. I could sense how relaxed and even delighted she felt exploring this person who before had been only a voice, whose embodied presence she only glimpsed. This gave her more of a sense of herself in relation to me, a real object in her world, as a separate person. Providing a medium in which I was more in view and physically present—literally and figuratively—offered Sarah what she needed in a foundational way in order to gain a greater sense of herself, and freedom to explore a relationship with another.

Clinical illustration: Edward

Another example of this challenging emotional work came up with Edward, who could be silent for long periods of time, sometimes the entire session or several sessions. In the silence, he communicated distress, deadness, and dissociation. He could not tell me in words what was going on. My inquires and hypotheses were met mostly with silence. I sensed his dissociated deadness because I felt physically disoriented and lightheaded myself, and my office became blurry and lacking in color. I struggled to mentally stay in the room, feeling like the office was tilting and that I might slide out the window. These sensations were painfully distressing, as I clamored to return to "sanity" and to feel physically back in balance.

In the silences, I was living within Edward's world. Our states were symbiotic, working against psychic separateness, awareness, and self-establishment. We were both floating off in space, like the astronaut unmoored from the mother ship drifting into an empty universe in *2001: A Space Odyssey*. I had no sense of my own separate experience from which to understand Edward, and I could not have used the analogy of the film while in this shared state.

Gradually, once I recognized the merged state we were in, I knew I needed to alter the situation, though not in an anxious way. Edward was "speaking" in a somatic channel in a mode that was direct, immediate, and for a time overwhelming. Rather than resist, which further removed me from the experience, I accepted the discomfort, surrendered to it, and experienced it. Paradoxically, experiencing such dissociative symptoms allowed me to return to an embodied state. Noting my experience to myself—"I'm floating, dizzy, lightheaded"—I would put into words to myself the perceptual state of my office, the intensity of shadows, and lack of tonal variation. These "notations" were meant not to change the sensations but to bring them to consciousness, to experience them and contain them, to observe them with greater awareness and clarity. In so doing and not resisting I could calm down and be present.

Once calm, I began to speak to him. I pointed to our shared embodied experience and world, mindful of the cadence and tone of my voice, now slow and relaxed. My intervention was directed at shared attention, through words and the musicality of expression—a slow waltz perhaps. For example, "Look at that" or "Did you hear/see/ notice that?" I wanted to see if we could share a world together, if he could feel himself in a world with me, without direct comment about the state of our relationship or the anxieties he might be feeling and reacting to. Often, not always of course, he could begin to find himself back with me, following my simple phrases with his own that described concrete aspects of the world we shared. The content established an embodied shared rhythm of two differentiated subjects. Over the course of the sessions, I felt an expansion and richness in his tone and intensity that conveyed a more alive, self-possessed self.

Here is an example of a conversation between the two of us that disrupted the dissociation:

A: (*After a ten-minute silence in which I experienced the usual physical disorientation: Time slows down and it feels much longer than ten minutes. I gradually find my way back to the physical aspects of a shared world through the "noting" I described above.*) It's really stormy out there today. Did you get wet coming here?

P: Not so bad... yeah... I like days like this. I guess because it feels good to be inside, you know. A bit cozy, I guess.

A: In here now?

P: Hmm, I guess so... I like all the wood in your office. It's warm.

A: I'm glad you do.

P: Did you think a lot about it? I mean, did you mean to make it this way. With the wood, and the books?

A: Yeah, I was hoping it would be warm and welcoming.

P: It is... (*He gets anxious and I'm again starting to feel woozy.*)

A: Well, are there other things you notice here?

P: (*After a long pause, in which I do not know what is happening, but I feel like I am moving back into the office.*) This seems crazy. I'm uncomfortable to mention it. But I like your voice. I'm listening to your voice. I think it's calming me down. I was real anxious coming here.

A: And your voice sounds more resonant.

P: How did you choose that picture? (*He faces a large abstract painting, mainly curves, in oranges and brown.*)

A: I like the color and movement.

P: The paint is thick, textured-like. That's cool.

A: Yeah, you like that? What does that do for you?

P: It makes me feel like it's something to touch. I'd like to check it out.

A: You can touch it if you like.

P: No, I'm settled here. It's nice lying down and looking around and imagining touching.

I wanted to start off my comments slowly and calmly, to initiate the conversation and find something in the world we could share while bringing in our own individual perceptions. This was a deliberate action on my part, with a specific aim. My first question intended to convey two things about our shared world and his embodied experience in that world. First, something like, "I think we are in the same world together (the storm, the office), and, if so, how is it affecting you?" that conveyed, "I'm thinking of him, imagining him outside, wondering how he is doing". This is not insignificant—this communication of a curious, concerned analyst interested in imagining his experience when not with me (and with me, as well). It shows that I have him in mind even when we are not together, that I consider him a subject in his own right, having his own world that I am not in at that moment.

When I could initiate something like this, Edward was often responsive. Here, with each exchange, Edward enlarged the perceptual field consonant with his increasingly embodied state. He was not just going along with me but was authentically bringing something of himself, adding his own perceptions in unexpected ways. This gave me the sense I could continue, take the next step, and build on what he offered and then see where he would take it. Though I did not bring his attention to our exchanges and relationship, it's clear that he got more personal and intimate, from the world outside the office, to qualities in the office, to the sound of my voice. I also sensed an expansion in the perceptual realm: hearing, seeing, touching, feeling, and temperature (warmth). As this was going on, I too was experiencing greater perceptual intensity of the world around me, noticing new aspects of the picture and tonal qualities of the wood, and noticing *his* voice, while my body was feeling more energetic and focused. The rhythm of our exchange picked up and, with this greater intimacy, Edward was also regulating its rhythm and intensity, such as turning away from my voice to the painting. I would describe this exchange as embodied intersubjectivity, creating a "third" that captures the dance between us, originating in shared rhythms and a perceptual world that feels connected, playful, and serious.

The concrete world we were speaking about has metaphoric meaning: the office as a warm, safe haven from the storm, its physicality representing my emotional qualities and body. I felt content to leave our shared exchange in the action of the concrete, as when a child in play therapy is *doing, creating*. I prefer to wait for Edward to speak to me in a consciously symbolic way when he needs and wants to.

This condensed vignette might give the impression that transformations are immediate, linear. Rather, change takes place over a long period of time. My working through difficult states lasted for a period in which I did not know what to say or do. Gradually I found myself. Once I had gone through the emotional work of containing difficult states of dissociation, I could direct our attention to a shared embodied world. Edward would then respond and find himself in the world with me. He eventually used elements of that world to signify his internal world and the world of our relationship—the warmth, color, shape, and texture of the picture, and so on. These shared therapeutic moments, often initiated by me, were repeated many times before a new and secure level of Edward's self-embodiment was established.

Conclusion

The infant can employ a transitional object when the internal object is alive and real and good enough (not too persecutory). But this internal object depends for its qualities on the existence and aliveness and behavior of the external object. (Winnicott, 1953, p. 9)

Here, Winnicott points to embodied analytic participation and therapeutic action. Describing crucial domains of analytic engagement—existence, aliveness, and behavior—he suggests that the development of a creative and vital sense of self depends on an alive and good internal object, and that that internal object depends on the real actions of an external object, in this case the analyst. *Existence* refers to the way the patient feels a real, concrete, attentive presence in the analyst. Then, the patient is not alone and is recognized. Then, the analyst's actual *aliveness* conveyed in ways of being—through the analyst's warmth and vitality in tone, cadence, gesture—invites the patient into a cathected, enlivened world of engagement and real experience. Finally, *behavior* means deliberate involvement, intentional participation. There is a reality to the analyst's presence conveyed through the medium of embodiment—those original, first forms of nonlinguistic communication. Winnicott's embodied modes— existence, aliveness, and behavior—offer the patient a shared world of emergent possibilities that go against the pull of repetition, stasis, and habit, and instead toward creativity, spontaneity, and potential space, strengthening not only the self but good internal objects.

The rhythmically embodied shared world I am describing is both simultaneous and moving in time. The dyad is in a unique moment, at each moment. Embodied attunement determines a spectrum of possible ways of participating *in time*—depending on the uniqueness of the dyad and what is happening at each moment.

Notes

1 Beatrice Beebe's definition of intersubjective as "what is between two minds" encompasses the full complexity of how two minds interrelate, align, or disrupt and regain alignment (Beebe et al., p. 73).

2 Milner's full quote: "Inner ground of being as a real psycho-physical background to all one's conscious thoughts can be directly experienced by a wide focus directed inwards... attention deliberately attends to sinking itself down into the total body awareness, not seeking at all correct interpretations, in fact not looking for ideas at all although interpretations may arise from this state spontaneously" (p. 196).

3 I have incorporated in my consultation work this practice of helping clinicians attend to the somatic dimension of their experience with patients. Insights that were not readily available gained our attention with this shift—or rather, widening—of attention.

4 Bion (1961a) studied the "emotional field" in groups, which was the first description of a "dynamic field".

5 I think that the movement of analytic process, the deepening resonance of associations and meaning, comes from the patient's (and analyst's) corresponding

deepening shared presence that afterwards, like an *après-coup*, leads to embodied speech and representation.

6 For a similar metaphoric description of the transformation of unrepresented states, see Levine (2012).

7 Ogden (2019) makes a clear, contrasting grouping of theories and therapeutic aims, around "being" (ontology) and "knowing" (epistemology).

8 Sletvold draws on Merleau-Ponty's (1945) view that "the body exists first and foremost as immediate experience"; Merleau-Ponty's basic argument, writes Sletvold, is "that we come to know ourselves and our world... from a 'pre-objective realm' constituted by our bodies" (2014, p. 5).

9 See, Freud's "The ego is first and foremost a body ego" (1923); Isaacs's (1948) theory of phantasy arising from bodily drives and functions; and Bion's (1961b) beta elements (sensory substrates for emotion) transformed symbolically via alpha function.

10 See Goldberg (2012), Lombardi (2008, 2010, 2013), Knoblauch (2000, 2005), Boston Change Process Study Group (1998), and Elise (2017). From different theoretical perspectives these writers draw attention to the body (and bodies) in the consulting room, and how to communicate and participate at that level.

Chapter 6

The analyst as improvisational accompanist[1]

Analytic work should be as spontaneous as possible.

Pichon-Rivière, 2017

In this chapter, I will extend and refine my view of the embodied analytic relationship by describing the crucial role of the analyst as an improvisational accompanist.

While listening to a jazz quartet—the drummer laying down a pulse for the group to share and the soloist to improvise—one feels the beauty of the drummer's supportive role: the responsive flexibility of his accompanying work to create a collective pulse for shared emotional experience. Small jazz ensemble performance provides a musical metaphor for an important aspect of analytic engagement. Accompaniment is an integral role in this musical fabric, analogous to the *analyst as improvisational accompanist*. As the jazz rhythm section lays down vitalizing accompaniment for the soloist to "say something", I strive to accompany my patient, providing a temporal framework, a pulse that affirms emotionally shared states, recognition, differentiation, and creative expression. Pulse is not simply "beat", but a three-dimensional affective form involving intensity, tone, rhythm, and movement. In accompanying, I work to find the right pulse, the right accompaniment for the patient. The patient *senses* when I am with them, when the accompaniment is right, and knows this in the feel of the interaction—not necessarily by what I say. Nebbiosi (2008) writes, "The experience of sharing a rhythmic-affective form with another is a significant confirmation of the meaning of the

DOI: 10.4324/9781003208518-6

relationship" (p. 217). Accompaniment expresses my "presence": by saying in a palpable way, "I am with you". Where the analogy with jazz is incomplete is that the analyst-accompanist has the responsibility in an asymmetric relationship to find and provide what is needed and take responsibility when his or her accompaniment fails.

The two components of successful analytic accompaniment are recognition and improvisational participation. Recognition requires embodied awareness—in myself and the relationship—of what is going on and what is needed, imparting what feels like the right form of accompaniment. It is improvisational because the "right form" is salient at a particular moment and may shift.

We can see in jazz that the role of accompanist requires dedicated attention to the shared rhythmic dimension of the interaction. I want to make the same claim for a *mode of psychoanalytic attention* of embodied self-awareness and sensitivity—*embodied attunement*—to the pulse of the interaction. Directed action of accompaniment follows from this, depending on the nature of the patient's needs and emotional state. By refining our accompaniment to meet clinical situations and challenges, we enlarge the range of creative analytic engagement.

Music as metaphor

Music is a compelling metaphor for what happens between patient and analyst at the rhythmic nonverbal register.[2] When Langer (1953) writes that "music is our myth of the inner life" (p. 245), we can also say that ensemble playing is our myth of the inner life of a shared emotional relationship, an emotionally meaningful world without words. As Langer (1942) beautifully puts it, "... *music articulates forms which language cannot set form to*" (p. 233, italics in original). Musical metaphors expand analytic attention to grasp *forms* of interaction, nonverbal ways of relating—not dynamic content—many consider the bedrock of what happens in relationships. The form of expression and interaction get at the way we feel into our own experience and those of others.[3]

Trevarthen's studies of the infant-parent interaction give us a look at music's communicative power and interactional importance. Trevarthen and Malloch's (2002) term "communicative musicality" describes a shared non-verbal, rhythmic, and embodied aspect of relating—storytelling without words—through pulse, tone, and gesture beginning early in life, between infant and caretaker. Through rhythmic sharing, a synchronizing in the medium of musicality, felt emotional states are passed back and forth, recognized, and elaborated.

Knoblauch (2000), in *The Musical Edge of Therapeutic Dialogue,* uses a jazz metaphor to explore, among many aspects of listening, accompaniment as an improvisational part of clinical technique. His focus on the idea of the analyst following *and* leading, and the importance of surprise, is very prescient and relevant. I have incorporated many of his ideas explicitly and implicitly in this paper.

I am extending Knoblauch's work, first by allocating accompaniment a primary mode of clinical engagement, while exploring the emotional work and enhanced bodily awareness accompaniment requires. Second, I am offering a provisional repertoire of accompanying forms based on jazz accompaniment. Further, I will develop important aspects of asymmetry and responsibility, the specific mode of attention called "embodied attunement". Knoblauch opened up the metaphor of accompaniment that I think merits deeper investigation into its qualities and clinical implications.

Forms and therapeutic action of improvisational accompaniment

Jazz offers vivid models of forms of accompaniment, represented by iconic drummers that range from Elvin Jones's steady textured beat, to Tony Williams and Eric Harland's spacious, responsive interplay, to Paul Motian's unobtrusive loose weave, to Sunny Murray's disruptive independent contrapuntal rhythm. Likewise, the analyst can be like a steady drummer, providing a strong pulse and attuned presence in tone, rhythm, intensity, and words, pushing things along, or holding things up. Or the analyst can offer a more diffuse, less hard-edged rhythmic accompaniment, what Balint (1968) calls the "unobtrusive analyst". Or the analyst can open space for interactive play, even using a more disruptive rhythmic accompaniment meant to enliven and provoke. These forms are determined by the particular momentary needs of the patient, as sensed by the analyst at the embodied level of communication. How the analyst senses which form of rhythmic engagement will be taken up in a section below.

Just as the point of jazz accompaniment is to share, contain, and enhance emotional experience, ultimately to promote the soloist's greater improvisational freedom, there is a similar aim of accompaniment in analysis. Accompaniment offers the patient-soloist a shared world of emotional experience, active engagement, recognition, and witnessing—whatever personal rhythms and emotions are given to the analyst-accompanist. The patient is offered the radical, often unprecedented, experience of acceptance, welcoming, being-with-ness, and attunement, but in ways the patient knows cannot be easy. This gives the patient a way out of isolation, non-relating, and hopelessness—a way out of a being entrapped in protective defenses. I would argue that whether a person comes from a traumatic background or not, the experience of sharing rhythmic-affective forms is significant in "confirming of the meaning of the relationship"—an important element in emotional growth. The patient feels recognized by the analyst's verbal and non-verbal attunement in a way that strengthens his or her sense of self and the capacity for self-presencing. Many patients need this sort of accompaniment before elaborating their own voice and solo.

Based on experiences of solid support and recognition, accompaniment then can fuel the patient's improvisations, allowing him or her to move away from the analyst and create a clear differentiated voice. As the patient separates, he or she ventures out into new or difficult territory, with the analyst's presence following. Over time, the person develops greater confidence in self-expression, taking chances while still relying on supportive accompaniment.

Part of the work of accompaniment, and a crucial aspect of therapeutic action, involves failures of accompaniment. We could be in the wrong key or time signature, and as happens in jazz ensembles, an intensified listening and greater mutual understanding than previously experienced ensue. Through heightened episodes that result from disruption of accompaniment, and our subsequent re-attunement as we struggle to regain attunement in an open, non-enigmatic way, the patient gains trust in us and her object world, her perceptions, and her ability to act and impact her object. She gains a greater sense of what is real. These moments of re-alignment and mutual understanding are intensely meaningful. The therapeutic effect is contingent upon our recognition of failure and its effect on the patient, and the responsibility we take for these mis-attuned episodes.

The work of accompaniment

The shared emotional experience is not always—or even often—pleasant and easy. The *work of accompaniment* involves our increasing capacity to bear uncertainty, confusion, and suffering, allowing us to be with the patient in various forms of accompaniment. Our instrument for finding the right form of accompaniment is *embodied attunement*, meaning our kinesthetic sensing of ourselves and our patients, knowing their rhythm, affect, and experience as communicated through the body. It *shifts the direction of our attention*, from primarily on the patient's words and associations, or our "reveries", to the immediacy of bodily and perceptual experience in ourselves and in the dyad. This way of attending has a concrete "now-ness" and "here-ness". The consistency of time and space that frames the analytic experience allows for increased attention to our sensorial-perceptual experience. The sense of my body in space, in relation to the patient, my sense of movement, the sound and colors and atmosphere, all move in response to the interaction, where emotions are first recognized through the body, then put into words as feelings.

Clinical illustration: John and getting it right

John was an unusually sensitive and perceptive patient. He was exquisitely reactive to intrusion and abandonment and needed just the right rhythm from me in order to stay with his own mind and experience. In contrast to many patients who make silent accommodations to our frame and way of working, John "knew" what he needed from me to get on. It could not be otherwise. What he needed was a felt sense of my struggles to get the accompaniment right, while surviving my multiple failures.

If I could stay with him and endure his stinging accusations of my lapses, he would go on with what he wanted to explore. I understood from this that he did not want any intrusions that he discerned—

often accurately—came from my own needs. This exposure was uncomfortable. He picked up on real aspects of my personality that I was not especially proud of and that did indeed interfere. When I hung in there and tried to relax physically into the immediacy of what was going on between us, I could find the right rhythm and he would go on and be with himself. I needed to be present, not too laid back: he could not tolerate silence on one hand or liveliness on the other. After many attempts, I "found" the right rhythm and tone, guided by his constant feedback. I discovered this by trial and error and through a heightened awareness of my bodily state that often involved physical manifestations of shame and stress. When I surrendered to these feelings and could accept them, I was able to respond in spontaneous ways in the give and take in the moment. My aim was to find a relaxed groove in myself that I could then offer him.

With each patient, unless there is an immediately intuitive sense of how to be, which is rare for me to have, there is work in finding the right accompaniment. The challenge is that "rightness" can shift frequently. The work initially involves accepting failure and being in the dark, tolerating difficult bodily states and feelings. Because failures come from necessary experimentation, we are constantly at risk of missing the mark. But being too cautious is in itself a kind of weak accompaniment that makes it difficult for many patients. With John, I found a form of accompaniment that was a soft and steady rhythm, closely following his lead, using bodily clues to his state of mind and need for quiet or more active support. I was almost always active, rarely silent, giving him a sense that I enjoyed listening and being there with him. This took time. I needed to tolerate his intense scrutiny and exposure and the negative feelings it evoked in me to find a relaxed set point.

John made the state of my body and mind a prerequisite for being in his own mind. He sensed immediately my bodily state and thus my state of being with him. When I relaxed in my chair, tilting it fully back, he would comment, "I like that you're at ease with me. It makes me feel you want to be here". My tone of voice, its depth and timbre, registered immediately as well. If I spoke out of pressure, coming from my need for contact or meaning, he would unfailingly decry my "thin voice" or "fast tempo". If I asked a question that related more to my need to know than what he was developing, he would tell me to stop interrupting him: "Is it OK for me to go on with what's on *my* mind?" I thought of him as a real connoisseur of the quality of accompaniment, and he taught me how to handle failures of accompaniment that allowed for his continued emotional growth.

I am not presenting John in the usual form of a verbal dialogue. This is intentional and necessary. What happened between us, the real juice of the interaction, was in the emotional rhythmic exchanges and my internal work to recognize and contain my emotional states so as to be with him in a relaxed way, so that "the dance and music of the relationship" was like an easy, slow Blues ballad. Many questions might arise from this account regarding enactments, counter-transference pressures, and projective identification.[4] Yet, I believe there is value in waiting until I have provided a basic and necessary presence as accompanist. Accompaniment that involves the analyst's containing-metabolizing function as an emotional form of engagement has therapeutic value, I believe. My main job though was to get back to John and his world, to get back to accompanying him, and not continue to work through my world of memories, or "make sense" of what happened between us. If I could detect that John was disturbed in a way that led to a kind of manic flight, not wanting to confront me with my absence, then I might slow down the interaction to see what more emotionally lies there, and to take responsibility for my absence.

My solid and reliable accompaniment, when I could accomplish this, eventually allowed John to take my attention and care more and more for granted. This was freeing: he could feel himself, his needs, and desires in my presence. He eventually "knew" when my embodied state communicated relaxed openness and nonacquisitiveness when I was not preoccupied with my needs or disturbed by his freedom and spontaneity. He summed it up quite beautifully: "If you're calm and relaxed, I feel you want to be here for me, with me, and I can go on". Perhaps even more telling, he said at one emotional moment. "I think you care more about me than your own theories".

Forms of accompaniment

The following clinical examples show a range of accompaniment, from an active, constant pulse to more spacious accompaniment, and from active-interactive engagement to disruption. I am not suggesting that certain forms are constant with each patient, or even within a session. There is often modulation as the situation calls for. The musical examples are referenced at the end of the paper and might provide an enjoyable and illustrative accompaniment to your reading.

Clinical illustration: Phillip, with steady support of accompaniment

A certain form of accompaniment gives the patient a steady rhythmic support. On John Coltrane's *Impressions*, the drummer Elvin Jones is palpably and energetically there in a way that is both strong *and* relaxed. Elvin Jones's pulse says, *"There is no getting off this train"*, as he pulls the group along while giving the soloist a solid and reliable floor of support. "I am here with you; I won't let you go", he speaks, "no matter where you go". Coltrane depends on Jones to carry him and push the beat, allowing Coltrane to extend his narrative in fresh, surprising, and passionate ways.

With Phillip, our analytic pair starts in rhythmic disarray and remains jagged for a time. Recognizing this, I try to generate a strong pulse to engage and support him. Once the pulse is established, he can begin to stretch out. The pulse between Philip and me was fragile and would drop off when he felt I was not with him. The disruptions for Philip often involved his suspiciousness, expecting my criticism, boredom, or disinterest. If I could supply a calm and steady rhythm, a steady ease of tempo—communicating acceptance and interest in the musicality of my response—he would be very receptive and join me. This experience often required a passthrough disruption.

In this session, as Philip greets me with a smile, he abruptly shifts his gaze in doubt. The tempo has stopped. There is a sensation of dropping or falling. "You're less friendly today, you're not on my side", said Philip by facial expression, a slight movement in his hands, and overall stiffness in his posture—as if taking a step backward. A moment of promise collapses into punctuated rhythm, tension, and heavy silence, as he then slowly makes his way to the couch, carefully lowering himself down, bracing himself. This says to me, "What am I in for?"

I am immediately disappointed and a let-down: "Oh no, we're in this world again". Despite being here many times before, I feel a slight panic. I have to fight the urge to change his reaction or somehow "understand" by using what I already know. Should I point out his suspicion and anticipated rejection, aiming to get at the unconscious phantasy guiding him (and also perhaps to deny the accuracy of his perception)? When I am tense and feel on the spot, I have a tendency to get "thoughtful" and a bit heady, to figure something out and put it quickly into words. When I resist this urge, we can continue the conversation without words by making myself open to John through observation of *my* bodily state. Just this shift in my attention to my bodily state shifts my presence with him. I must take into account the *way I am* and find a way to accept what is going on by making space for it. What had I communicated that he responded to? Perhaps it was I who disrupted the rhythm?

I recall some physical tension in me upon greeting him: a physical reserve and a quieter "Hi". Yes, I was guarded. I was the one suspicious and slightly closed off in our initial contact, so not responding to the invitation of his smile. This was the disrupted non-accompanying state I offered that led him to withdraw in a self-protective silent retreat. As I filter through these feelings and associated sensations, my body relaxes a bit and feels more supple and open, as does my mind. I am aware that my breathing is deepening, slowing down. Simultaneously, I sense that he seems more relaxed as well: there is a lighter feeling to the silence and a sense of possibility. These moments are hard to put into words. I sensed we were sharing a physical space in subtle rhythm of movement that was now warm and encouraging, that the quality of our silence shifted to a peaceful register. Something important was communicated without words at the level of bodily resonance and I felt the two of us settling in. This is the beginning of my accompaniment, a grounding rhythm he can sense, share, and build on. In the somatic register, I am saying, "OK, go on, tell me, I'm listening". In this shared peaceful state I noticed that the light in the office is softer and the sounds from outside less intrusive. "I am glad to be here, I like doing this" comes to mind. I sink more deeply into my chair.

I then started a steady accompaniment, offering in a relaxed way, "That was a tense start, but we've found a good way through it to be together now". "Yeah, I felt you really don't like me ... I know I'm difficult at times and I'm very wary. You get that for sure and it must make you tense". "Well", I responded, "maybe, but I bring my own tensions into the picture too". He gives a laugh, "I don't know why but that's relieving. You were tense at the beginning, then? I'm never sure what I see". "Yes, and it messed you up, stopped us in our tracks". "It stopped me for sure, I didn't feel like talking to you". (I was concerned he could be going along with me, being compliant, rather than using my steady leading accompaniment to get deeper into his own experience. So, I remained actively present and less directive.) "That's rough", I say (meaning, "I'm here, let's go on".). "It's hard when we don't connect. I am so affected when I pick up something negative in you. I always feel I've done something wrong". (This is emotionally poignant, taking responsibility for what goes wrong in relationships, and this goes way back.) "Now you see I have a part in it. You didn't cause it". "I'm grateful you say that", he says.

I am providing a steady rhythmic accompaniment, taking the tone, length of expression, and intensity, and matching his, not in a mannered way, but loose. The content is important, of course, but at another level he senses that I am with him and will receive him, adding a bit for him to tell me more. Adding something of my experience in an emotionally present way gives Philip a stronger sense of himself and his experience. This interaction feels warm and important, and I sense we both feel that. He feels my comfort and openness, in marked contrast to our meeting at the beginning of the session. I believe the patient recognized a shift in me without my putting it into words, that *I* was no longer on guard. Then I could initiate a rhythm of welcoming and openness. The pulse was there, strongly. But I have to initiate it. The accompaniment that initially was absent, confused, and conflicted; with internal work and my accompaniment, the patient could go on.

The patient's thoughts began to roam more freely, soloing. For some patients, it can take a long time to tolerate the sense of separateness that soloing requires. Philip's jagged staccato rhythm of self-interruption was met by my steady stream of supportive responses; this allowed him to go a bit further. Philip made use of a constant strong rhythm that did not vary. Any break in my pulse felt to him like tentativeness, withdrawal, or a negative reaction. I had to learn this patiently through experience.

Clinical illustration: Betty, with unobtrusive accompaniment

This rhythmic accompaniment is not immediate and pulsing, more a sound "medium" of support, finding the patient where she is, not urging her on or directing her, but carefully and lightly following. The pulse is fluid and expansive in a quiet way, drawing less attention to the drummer as a differentiated voice. Musically, this can be heard in Paul Motian's work on *River's Run*. The drummer's support here is palpably there, but less conspicuous. He creates a fine yet firm tissue that surrounds the soloist. His touch is light, non-repetitive, not driving the beat but suggesting it, creating spaces with silence or minimal fills. You can almost take his voice for granted—almost, yet the pulse is there, making his presence a vital atmosphere of support.

Here is how that same form of accompaniment worked with Betty, a successful doctor who came to therapy to discuss problems with her "fussy child". From the initial session, she could not get physically comfortable. The couch, which she first tried, lacked proper support—it was "was weak and uneven". She lay on the "too hard" floor, tried all the chairs in my office, paced, sat on pillows. Nowhere felt right. She chose one chair as the lesser of evils. Understandably, she often talked about somatic discomforts of one sort or another that moved throughout her entire body and affected her mind. There was a kind of insistently repetitive rhythm, unvarying in intensity and form. For example, the beginning of sessions often sounded like this:

P: I can't think … I'm not doing well at work … I'm not doing well at all … I'm stuck … my back hurts and I'm tired … I can't get comfortable here. Maybe I'll walk around. (*She stands up and paces for a moment. Then sits down.*) The bureaucracy at work is killing me, causing me so much work … Incompetent … I never should have left X. (*This is said in jagged broken rhythm matched by her movements, which are broken and abrupt.*)

At first, I interrupted her rhythm by suggesting the symbolic meaning of her bodily experience. My long comments concerned the concrete aspects of the uncomfortable office as representations of her emotional experience with me, and in herself. I often thought about and, at times, interpreted the sort of transference-countertransference we were in. For example, the inadequate mother unable to soothe her

baby. In response, she would insist on the *real* difficulty of this chair
or that couch, or this situation or that somatic pain. As we went
through these exchanges, a deadening shared rhythm began to have a
life of its own, the back and forth of two agitated and frustrated
bodies matching each other. My feeling of failure to bring her bodily
experience into a symbolic realm frustrated me and made me tense.
My voice sounded sharp and clipped as I began to have feelings of
suffocation and pressure. Over time I recognized that I was dominating her with stabbing comments, giving *her* little room to get
comfortable, relax, and breathe.

I was not *accompanying* her in the world in which she actually
lived, but rather *matched* her state. There is an important distinction
between matching (especially negative matching and merger) and
accompaniment by a separate and attuned presence. Matching is the
absence of accompaniment. Instead, my accompaniment needed to
welcome her and provide space for her, to share this uncomfortable
repetitive experience in a containing way rather than simply vibrate
at her rhythmic frequency—to pick up the rhythm where she moved
and suffered, and tune into it from a calm place in me. Though I
approximated her rhythms, the vitality form was different in me,
calmer and relaxed. I found a way of being together that accepted
wherever she happened to be without intruding my desires or ideas
about how things should go. All the while I related to her physical
states *as* physical states, not symbols or metaphors. I could then
empathize with where she lived. I accompanied her as someone in
pain, perhaps pain that will never end. I would ask simple questions,
taking interest in whatever held her attention, allowing her to
expand her somatic story. Her pains had an impact on me. For
example, in this session:

P: God I'm sick today ... my neck ... everything is falling apart
A: I see that. Your body's really tense.
P: It's especially tense in my shoulders and neck ... too much time
     at the computer ... like this (She shows me.)
A: That looks like it hurts, that way.
P: Yeah. (I immediately notice her shoulders relaxing and there is a
     long silent pause.) I'll try to be aware of that.

Although her painful somatic narrative continued, it was given in a more related, relaxed, and emotional way, with more detail and nuance. I could tell she wanted me to hear it all and she sensed I wanted to hear it all. I think she felt a shift in me: I was with her, wanting to be with her, and communicated this in the spreading arc of my tone, cadence, and relaxed presence. The first change I noted was that she seemed more comfortable in the chair and moved around less. She was not scouting her next move. Her body relaxed and she gestured more freely.

At one point, she told me she loved to dance as a child and wondered if she should try a dance class now. She requested more time with me without needing (or was able?) to explain why. And, things very slowly changed in her life, such as trying new relationships and activities. I would describe this kind of treatment as support at the most fundamental level of being—though pain in her core, she could share that with me; it was the beginning of going-on-being with her pain. Betty found more comfort in herself that opened up possibilities not there before. I would analogize my work here to the way Paul Motion creates a broad and flexible rhythmic container of warm space that does not push the pulse or announce a more differentiated presence on my part—soothing and patient.

Clinical illustration: Barry, with interactive, playful accompaniment

In ensemble playing with less firm, differentiated roles (while still maintaining asymmetry in responsibility), both patient and analyst play together, at times in a mutually interactive way, elaborating each other's contributions. There is more anxiety and uncertainty for the analyst here, requiring spontaneity, improvisation, and risk-taking. Miles Davis created an interactive group conversation on *My Funny Valentine—Live at the Plugged Nickel*. Here, an attentive sharing of the creative movement requires the drummer Tony Williams's moment-to-moment responsiveness all the while maintaining the rhythmic framework. Williams sometimes solos and the group accompanies *him,* a beautiful trade-off of roles, though Williams's beat, his responsibility for the beat, is never lost. He offers the possibility of mutual play and interactive soloing. In my experience, it takes a while for most patients to make use of this kind of accompaniment, only after the establishment of trust and tolerance of separateness and dissonance.

Barry, a middle-aged male architect, brought in endless obsessional accounts of his work. He could not produce the necessary drawings for his projects. Marking our time together was a mechanical, machine-like beat that he set. I had the sense that either creating a strong counter pulse or being quieter and more receptive would not alter his driving rhythmic obsessions. He would either graft his rhythm onto mine or power through a more nuanced background.

Instead, I wanted to find a way to catch his interest in another, different rhythm that we possibly could share. I really did not know how to do this initially, nor where that sharing might lead, but I had faith, not certainty, in a sense that Barry could tolerate the space of interaction, if I could do this. However, I had to live within this mechanical rhythm until a genuine source of accompaniment organically emerged in me and with us. I let go of attending to his rhythm in order to find an embodied place for both of us to begin. This letting go expanded my sensorial consciousness, allowing me to become more alert to sensory aspects of our meetings: the light of a particular time of day that brought out different colors and moving shadows on the walls, the way the sound of our voices echoed in the room, the smell of coffee, and fragrances from outside, and so on. *My attention had widened and I found life in the surrounding world we shared.* Then a slow accompanying rhythm started—a way I wanted to speak that had more fluidity and depth. I pointed out sensory aspects of the office; he would then comment on what I said. In the give and take about the sensory surround, something was building in our interactional rhythms. Unlike a mechanical beat, these rhythms varied in cadence, tone, and intensity, interweaving in something like a fugue: two rhythmic figures, two motives, that are in conversation while developing independently.

In one session, while listening to the nice sound and pattern the rain made one late afternoon, I said: "Listen to that rain". "Yeah", Barry said, "It reminds me of the sound of sailing" with vitality and feeling—far from mechanical. Barry went on in an enlivened way to vividly describe the sensory qualities of sailing and sense of movement. In one moment, a few sessions later, after a period of relaxed silence between us, he casually got up from the couch, sat next to me, and showed me pictures he had taken with his phone. The pictures were street scenes, glimpses of people in motion. In contrast to many of his dreams early in the analysis, which were devoid of people and involved desert-like landscape, these pictures had life. I did not know of his interest in photography. As he described the pictures, and I responded with lively associations, he noted how important this activity was to him: "It brings me into the world of people".

Over time, we were able to build on these experiences. At times he would be the one to offer some meaningful observation, to which I associated in response to what I saw, adding something of my own sensibility to the conversation. I definitely felt the risk involved in this playing, the real risk of mis-attunement, or a feeling I had taken over something of his, or had used it for my own purpose. At times I could see when I went too far and backed off. But more often he was energized by the interaction and continued to bring in new aspects of his life and interests. His greater sense of creativity—in himself and interpersonally—also enlarged the space for me to respond from my own experience. A shared conversation ensued: our mutual interest in music and art as the vehicle for enjoying the vitality in each other. I did not lose track of who was responsible for the beat and accompaniment, and who was meant to develop and grow, though there was no obvious demarcation of soloist and rhythm section as in the previous examples. The accompaniment shifted back and forth, finding myself in a clearly supportive accompanying role as either the steady pulse or providing the unobtrusive rhythmic fabric of support. I found that what Barry needed was a partner in improvisation rather than a participant supporting his emotional elaborations. To do this, I had to interest him enough in a world outside himself to join me in creative dialogue.

Clinical illustration: Joan, with enlivening accompaniment

Sometimes the analyst needs to break out of deadening rhythms and take the lead, though a lead that should eventually engage the patient in his or her own experience. This might be like an extended drum or piano solo that invites the soloist to engage and eventually take the lead.

Joan was a woman in her 40s who sought treatment for marital difficulties. She was highly intelligent and had an elegant and erudite way of speaking, though the stories she told were intensely disturbing. Often the scenes she relayed involved sadomasochistic sexual experiences with her partner. She could not organize a thought that would have disapproved of her partner's behavior because she did not experience it. She was not there.

Initially, I was so caught up in my own emotional reactions that I could not appreciate Joan's empty state of mind. I tried to control and understand my sense of outrage on her behalf, caught up in her stories that left me silently cut off from her. I became a silent witness to a disturbing primal scene. Gradually I returned to her and the way she related to me, encountering something strange and disorienting. I had the uncanny feeling that Joan and I might as well be Skyping: there was a glass wall or screen between us—we were not sharing an embodied space. I started to have overt de-realization experiences. Her mouth would move but there was no intelligible sound. At times I felt as if I was watching a movie without sound or in a foreign language. Her movements lacked meaning. There was no way to join her without entering this deadened pantomime. This shared disembodied world was important for me to know about, but I had to do something with it, disrupt it by changing this rhythm by offering something that brought us back to two bodies together.

I would have to try to provide a pulse by improvising, becoming the soloist-accompanist, providing the pulse, tone, and narrative to see if she could join me. To do this, it was crucial that it did not come from my anxious need to connect and for her to comply, which would duplicate the exploitation she knew well. In one session, after she spoke in her usual way, I started to narrate how she came in the room that day, how she moved and looked, her facial expression and tone of voice. I tried to do this not as a distant observer, but someone close-up, as someone might lively narrate in their own mind what they are doing—the basic *fact* of having a body, relying on my embodied experience of her.

A: I heard your light footsteps coming up the stairs and saw you smile when you came in to see me. Maybe happy and a little nervous.

P: You noticed that?

A: Yes, and how your voice started strong but then got quiet. Now it sounds quiet but I can still hear you. (*I think at this point I'm injecting more feeling. I'm telling a story about the two of us. I am not sure if she will join me.*)

P: I'll speak louder.

A: Do you want to?

P: Hmm. I don't know. I didn't notice my voice. Now I do. It sounds scared maybe ... I remember going to a lake for summer with my family. My younger brother was fearless and would take a canoe way out there. I would be on the shore looking at him and not being able to say anything, but I was scared.

A: (*I sensed real feeling as the story unfolded. There were many ways to interpret the memory she described. Had I left her behind by initiating a story between us, as she watched me like she watched her partner, doing his own thing? She was experiencing something, not detached, relating to me in a way I felt. I thought it best to stay with her fear of separation and abandonment. The connection was delicate, I hoped to maintain it and not go too far beyond her. So, I chose to emphasize my continued presence.*) We don't have to be that far apart. I won't drift away.

P: I want you to stay with me ... tell me more what you see. (*This request that I tell a story about her or about our relationship was surprising and became more frequent going forward. The stories were actual descriptions of what I experienced, staying in an embodied register. I rarely suggested motivation and or wondered about complicated feelings. The form of request, the wish for a particular sort of accompaniment was important: "Tell me what you see", a request for recognition, a description she can also observe, finding her way back to her body and her experience.*)

A: I hear a soft voice but with more feeling.

P: Yes, I do, too ... hear my voice, and feel more.

This exchange went from dissociation to the emergence of her voice in response to my soloist-accompaniment. These exchanges were very important: I would commence with "what I see", then Joan would recognize something about her own experience, become a subject in her story. Eventually, Joan began to take the lead in the conversation, as when she requested that I stay close to her.

Clinical illustration: Deborah, with disrupting and disrupted accompaniment

This case will illustrate the fluidity of varying forms of accompaniment, from disruptive, to unobtrusive, to echoing and reaffirming the patient's solo expression in shared emotional time. This last form of accompaniment is not "I am with you" but "*We* are in this together".

There are occasions when the analyst disrupts the patient's rhythm, creating a freer, unstructured form that may lead to stronger self-experience in the patient. Sonny Murray's rhythm with Cecil Taylor was disruptive and rhythmically dissonant, with the aim of searching a new interaction. Over time a heightened ensemble experience is reached. An example of this is his work on *Lena*.

In our first meeting, Deborah announced, "I don't really know who I am". She was a high-powered executive who ran at 78 rpm. She spoke so rapidly I often asked her to repeat herself. One aspect of her history stood out: when she was eleven she underwent surgery following a traumatic injury. She presented this history casually despite the fact she had what must have been a frightening several months in hospital. She was facing the loss of important capacities for the rest of her life. Fortunately, she did fully recover physically.

I interrupted her with questions and clarifications meant to disrupt her rhythm. I chose this path from experience. When I *observed* her relentless pace, my comments hardly altered her breakneck cadence. By disrupting her, she eventually was at a loss of what to say: "I realize I'm just filling space … what I'm saying has no real meaning to me". My interruptions were an attempt to empty space of "filler", to see if, in an open space, she could find real emotional experience. Lengthy silences ensued that I did not interrupt. I thought this was uncomfortable progress for both of us. In the disquieting silence, Deborah worried the impact she was having on me: "You must be so bored". I had faith that this could evolve productively if we both had the stamina. She eventually settled down and verbalized feelings of emptiness and hopelessness that occasionally broke long silences. I provided an unobtrusive accompaniment, careful not to take the lead, wanting to communicate patience and acceptance of what she experienced. We both expressed hope that something will come of this new and painful experience.

But what happens when the analyst is disrupted and drops out as accompanist or is inadvertently disruptive? How does the analyst re-emerge as accompanist in that situation?

An unexpected event occurred. We had a flood in our office building. Big dryers were placed in the common areas and the place was in shambles, with the rugs torn out exposing unfinished flooring. I was discombobulated, anxious, distracted. Should I even be seeing people in this shabby space? The noise of the heaters was distracting. Aside from having no carpet and the hardwood floors exposed, my office was much the same—enough so that I did not feel completely at sea. At least I was making that case for myself, that I had enough in me to attend to my patients. But I certainly was not the calm unobtrusive analyst now! Nor the deliberately disruptive accompanist. I was in fact taken out of any obvious accompaniment mode.

When Deborah arrived, I expected she would have a big reaction, as most of my patients did. Instead, she casually moved to the couch and continued her silent vigil as if nothing was altered. But after several minutes she started to speak about *my* state.

"I can really sense something is wrong in you. You seem agitated, anxious, off, not yourself … Are you OK?… This is starting to really distress me. (*She starts to cry, an unusual emotional expression.*) You are *definitely* not yourself*"*.

This was a crucial moment. She sensed and was affected by my agitated rhythms, which I internally, unsuccessfully, attempted to damp down. I was tempted to interpret her attributing her own distress to me. There was some truth there, and hostility, too, because her safe environment had now been shattered. I did not make that interpretation because it would have been defensive, and she was having *an experience* of me that was accurate. This was the main thing. So, I listened and encouraged her to go on. In listening, I found a way to be present and tolerate my sense of exposure and guilt, until I could find the right way to accompany her and what I wanted to say. I wanted to do this in a sincere way, not denying her observations and not providing false security or false calmness, but an honest, vulnerability account. The accompanist was having trouble and that truth needed to be acknowledged for an authentic rhythmic connection to begin. I found this by verifying her perceptions of my inner states in an affirming way.[5]

A: You're right. I'm unsettled and distracted by my office—because of the flood.

P: I assumed that. I wanted to ignore what is going on here because I assumed *you* would have it all in hand and it was not a big deal … that sound is actually annoying and distracting. (*She starts talking about the environment more strongly, much more intensely.*) I hate this! I should just ignore it!

A: It's pretty hard to ignore it. I'm having a hard time ignoring it.

P: It's strange how I never had a sense of you in this way—you're not your usual calm voice—now it's your whole anxious self! You're moving a lot back there. Your voice isn't normal.

A: I'm not in my normal state of mind because of all this and I'm worried about how this affects you. Now I see it is my state of mind, my nervousness, that's affecting you more than the office … You sound different too. Your voice is really strong, certain, distressed. Present.

P: (*After a very long silence*). We are really together in a different way. You're not just a talking head and I'm not either … this place is a drag really. But I feel a bit freer.

In the following sessions, we discussed the office scene and how we both felt about the dryers, the floors, the smell, and future construction. As she took in more and more of the external reality, asking me detailed questions about the office and my state as well, which I responded to openly, she made contact with herself and me in an embodied way. There was a true pulse in regular time, not double-time. Due to her traumatic experience in hospital, this aspect of her inner world and relation to her body had been severely attenuated.

Out of the despairing, empty silences in which I accompanied her unobtrusively, I sensed a new beginning. This period lasted a few months. With the office flood, she had direct access to my embodied state in a realistic way. The way to her body then was through mine: she would first find in me a preliminary container for her own physically distressed state. My role as accompanist was to reaffirm her experience of me and its impact on her, the way the rhythm section reinforces the soloists statements.

Eventually, associatively, the time in hospital entered our conversation. She went over the physical aspect of her hospital room in great detail and the terrified expression on her parents' faces, before touching on her fears of her own body and what was happening to it. In this phase, I was again in the position of the unobtrusive witnessing accompanist. But there were moments when she sensed my anxious or disturbed reactions to her narrative that was correct and shared. This was a kind of booster that allowed her to continue being emotionally present because the sharing of emotional-physical states was essential to her finding a way to experience her trauma. The establishment of this connection eventually opened up the "residue" of the associations to the flood: her traumatic stay in the hospital that she had not experienced until now: the panic in her parents and her own fears of losing bodily integrity.

Conclusion

This chapter extends Knoblauch's work by arguing that improvisational accompaniment is a primary mode of embodied analytic attention and action. Accompaniment is not blending, merging, or doubling the patient's voice, or an easy way of "mirroring" the patient, nor is it symmetric mutuality. Rather it is offering varying modes of embodied attuned presence that is emotionally hard-won; our internal work is required to find the right form of accompaniment by tolerating discomfort, uncertainty, and unpredictability. It involves our internal struggles to remain receptive both to our and the patient's disturbing, disruptive bodily experiences that often come from suffering and trauma.

Accompaniment marks one important area of creative engagement. Currently, embodied awareness is usually not taught or considered in supervision, case conferences, or written case histories. Yet, the training of embodied attention and internal perception allows one to grasp essential information about the pulse and affective form of the relationship, increasing awareness of two bodies together in the language of movement, tone, and rhythm. This awareness opens up a novel, potentially transformative realm of analytic accompaniment.

Musical references

1. John Coltrane, *Impressions*, The 1961 Complete Village Vanguard, Impulse, 1997.
2. Paul Motian, *River's Run*, Mark Copland New York Trio Recordings, Vol. 2: Voices, Pirouet, 2007.
3. Miles Davis, *My Funny Valentine*, Live at the Plugged Nickel, 1965.
4. Cecil Taylor, *Lena*, Nefertiti, the Beautiful One Has Come, Revenant, 1962.

Notes

1 I am very grateful to Sam Klein-Markman and John Schott for their insights into jazz communication and improvisation.
2 See, for example, Elise (2017) and Rose (2004).
3 In *Forms of Vitality,* Stern (2010) considers vitality forms the substrate of all experience.
4 These questions involve the content of our relating but not its embodied *form.* It was not my *first* priority to communicate content in the form of action and interpretation derived from metabolizing and symbolizing non-represented states in the patient or living out unconscious object relations.
5 For reasons of space this passage is a condensed version of the interaction.

Chapter 7

"One-sided analysis is no longer possible":[1] "mutual analysis" as the analysis of mutuality

> The general feature of human life that I want to evoke is its fundamental *dialogic* character. We become full human agents, capable of under-standing ourselves, and hence defining an identity, through our acquisi-tion of rich human languages of expression.... Our identity requires recognition of others ... formed in dialogue with others.
> —Charles Taylor, *The Ethics of Authenticity* (1992)

We know ourselves in dialogue with others. This is the basis of mutuality from which all else evolves. When we engage with another we have the opportunity to see ourselves from another perspective, as others see us. This truth pertains to therapists as well. I believe knowing ourselves in the relationship with our patients, in real time, is essential to therapeutic action and the best safeguard against im-passes.

Our conversation takes place in a historical and cultural surround. The relationship can be impinged upon by realities that both thera-pist and patient share. All of us know this now, going through the pandemic, climate change, and political upheaval, which makes the acknowledgment of *mutuality* all the more relevant.

Robert and I

Suddenly Robert urgently pressed me, "What is going on! Why am I feeling this way? ... I feel like I'm falling apart." I was completely caught off-guard and confused, not knowing what was happening or what to say. One moment we were relaxed together and the next he

DOI: 10.4324/9781003208518-7

was in free fall. My first reaction, reflex really, was to make sense of it, to give him an interpretation, an understanding of why he is feeling this way. I had my theories. At the same moment, I ignored other things I really know. Like being emotional *with* the patient. I *am* committed to viewing the clinical encounter as experiential first and foremost. What happened?

Something in me was off. I spoke calmly to him as an insight-giving analyst, but my words sounded abstract and lifeless to me. Robert says, "You don't know what to do with me, do you? ... I've totally confused you but you're pretending you know what's going on. And that's not helping. You don't seem real".

I was invested in helping Robert, but this frequently ran with feelings of ineptness, confusion, and helplessness when he fell into states like this one. I did not know what to do as the usual interpretive tools were useless. But, instead of being with him in his emotional turmoil, I withdrew in a way familiar to me, through understanding and surety. His state made me feel quite vulnerable and I protected myself, but in doing so, left him. This realization only made me feel worse. As I sifted through my feelings in the moment and tried to slow down, he continued to describe his sense of me. He was particularly angry with my lack of self-awareness and directness in communicating. "I can tell when you're not there. Where are you?"

I had a mixture of reactions to being pressed like this: irritation, frustration, and embarrassment—that is to say, Robert's reactions at first intensified concern about myself, and in so doing, distanced me even further. Eventually, I surrendered to feelings of helplessness and confusion. I started to relax and observe myself in relation to Robert. I could see how I was trying mightily to be a "good" analyst, one who would not let him down and always knew what was going on and what to say.

I said, "You're right, I'm confused by what is happening, so I tried to appear like I understood ... I don't really know what to say ... but I can feel with you the anxiety you have now and the trouble I'm causing you by the way I am acting".

Robert got that I was struggling with my reactions and that what I said to him felt sincere. Simultaneously there was a freer feeling between us and something to be curious about together. "Now I feel you're being real with me and that helps a lot". Not so paradoxically, by witnessing my struggle and vulnerability, Robert had more trust in my capacity to help him. He said, "When I know what's really going on in you, and you see it too and tell me, it is a great relief. You feel stronger to me rather than weaker and in need of my support".

I want to explore clinical situations like this one with Robert, when our way of engaging and our emotional attitudes toward the patient are known and problematic. The clinical questions are: What do we do in this situation? How do we respond to what the patient sees and reacts to? What is therapeutic?

As with Robert, patients can perceive what is going on in me and the way I am relating. Depending on what they see, it can make me uneasy. Aspects of my personality, ways of working, things I reveal that I thought were concealed or unknown, are uncomfortable when seen. Exposure is not a pleasant thing and it often takes me by surprise.

If I don't shift the spotlight back onto the patient, I have to contend with something I said or did, or revealed unconsciously, that I would rather not have on view. What is seen can be problematic to the patient—all the more so if I am not aware of it, and even worse if I deny it or put it back on the patient. I am grateful to my patients—for their courage and tenacity for the truth, going against the implicit authority of my position in the analytic setup. Especially those patients who are natural caretakers and so not inclined to upset the relationship, they still take this risk.

Mutuality and mutual analysis

Almost 100 years ago Sandor Ferenczi, dealing with the same issue I am exploring here, tried something bold and many thought mad. In an impasse with a patient (RN), an impasse they both agreed was created by Ferenczi, RN insisted on a mutual analysis in order for Ferenczi to work through his obstacle to analyzing RN. He alternated patient-analyst roles to get at his unconscious negative countertransference, while also continuing to analyze the patient. He called this "mutual analysis". He felt that in order to analyze this patient, he needed to be analyzed. Ferenczi turned to the patient who saw something in him that was not dealt with in his personal analysis with Freud, nor his continuing self-analysis. Ferenczi came to understand through this process of mutual analysis that his excessive caring for patients hid dark negative feelings toward women that related to his own childhood sexual trauma. Coming to terms with this in the mutual analysis allowed for the analysis to proceed. Contrary to expectation, it did not lead to chaos or a *folie a deux*, but a productive analytic process.

An important clinical fact is RN's history of horrible abuse in childhood. Ferenczi was very interested in trauma and his theories about it are still very alive and clinically useful. The point here is that by using mutual analysis with RN at her insistence, he let her regulate the interaction in ways that brought out her traumatic history, with Ferenczi as the re-traumatizer. Owning his part in the re-traumatization through mutual analysis was therapeutic.

Ferenczi's voice and the implications of this experiment vanished from the analytic conversation for over 50 years. The term "mutual analysis" elicited rolled eyes and knowing looks; it did not lead to the engaged discussion it deserved. It was only in the late 1980s, with the publication of his *Clinical Diaries*, that certain analysts experienced a shock of recognition. Elaborations of his major themes in the *Diary* entered the analytic conversation and vitalized it.

Ferenczi eventually abandoned the explicit application of role reversal in mutual analysis. Yet, out of that experience, he came to important realizations. He wrote in his *Clinical Diary*:

> An attempt to continue analyzing unilaterally. Emotionality disappeared; analysis insipid. Relationship—distant. Once mutuality has been attempted, one-sided analysis then is no longer possible—not productive. Now the question: must every case be mutual?—and to what extent? (p. 213)

My aim is to illustrate the Ferenczian spirit of mutual analysis and show that, in fact, *every case is mutual* and that "One-sided analysis is no longer possible". For me, this means that the analyst explores with the patient, in plain view of the patient, the clinical consequences of the mutual relation in a therapeutic way, within a living relationship. The analyst's subjectivity is made accessible to the patient. The analyst then interrogates within the relationship his or her contribution to impasses and obstacles.

Mutuality means that we recognize our impact our patients. If this dynamic of mutual impact remains unacknowledged, we may assume that we are stirred up intentionally by the patient, or that the patient's reactions are strictly transferences, or solely communications and not reactions to real aspects of our personalities. The ground is laid for repetitious cycles, bastions, impasses.

As with Robert and RN, the recognition of our own part in the interaction can begin with the patient's insights. The patient and analyst are revealed and known to each other. The depths of one's personality, anxieties, wishes, intentions, feelings—whether analyst or patient—are not fully hidden but are revealed in the encounter, in dialogue. The analyst is not in a privileged, safe position with regard to knowledge about the state of the relationship, nor about what is going on within the dyad, even the way he or she is participating in the relationship. Interpersonal knowledge is democratized. This is the bottom floor of mutuality: intrinsic mutual recognition, democratization, and interpenetration.

The emotional consequences of mutuality for us are not easy: shame, exposure, confusion, instability, loss of authority, and the negative feelings that come from being put on the spot. But if we accept that we may act in unconscious ways that the patient picks up, recognizes, and is affected by, we are open to view these experiences in a fresh way that helps the patient develop a stronger sense of self and perception of reality.

Concerns about mutual analysis

I will address two concerns now. One is whether mutual analysis will lead to a narcissistic misuse of the patient by making the patient the analyst's therapist or confessor. Second, when the patient's reactions come from a strongly transferential place, does confirming their perceptions rather than interpreting them lead to supporting *their* narcissistic misperceptions of the world?

What constrains us and holds us back from using the patient in various ways, is the absolute asymmetry and ethical position we hold and the *fidelity to interrogate our own actions and states of mind as our own responsibility*. Aron (2007) stresses that mutuality is not symmetry. The analyst tries to never abandon the asymmetry that is crucial to the analytic encounter. This asymmetry comes from the analyst's ethical stance of caretaking and responsibility for the patient and responsibility for the analyst's intended or unconscious failures of attunement and care. This is where we start from and is the basic ethical orientation of mutuality that I am espousing. Responsibility for our experience extends to our actions as well. We are never off the hook, and this is a good thing.

When as analysts we start with our experience as our own and claim responsibility for it and do the emotional work to free ourselves from our own transferences, expectations, cherished theories, this is a protection against imposing our most valued ways of understanding. This move, then, is one of humility, of being in a position of curiosity and not-knowing, of primary concern for the patients' realistic experiences of the way we are with them. This shift in our analytic attention takes us as an *objective* object in the patient's emotional world, de-privileging our first-person authoritative perspective.

I ask myself, though, where *do* the patient's transferences come into the picture? This question involves sharpening our sense of the origins of transference, especially with patients who have a history of trauma. In that situation and with many of the people I see, the patient's transference is triggered by real aspects of the analyst's personality and behavior that need to be owned. I've come to approach the problem this way: Given that I am never sure of my own contribution to the patient's reactions, I start there, making space in myself for the possible truth of the patient's perceptions. I give myself over to *his or her* emotional truth in the moment. I have found that this does not close off the possibility of understanding the transferences and traumatic repetitions. Rather, it allows for transference expression through enactment that is vividly lived through and eventually available for understanding. The more fluid, spontaneous, and emotionally open we are in the interaction, the more possible our unconscious desires and transferences are *overtly* played out with the patient. Enactments are another form of dialogue, always occurring (see Grossmark, 2012). Playing out our unconscious attitudes with the patient helps bring to light our transferences, as it does for the patient. Interaction and dialogue are the road to self-knowledge.

By engaging with the patient in a non-skeptical and accepting way, many patients have the freedom, some for the first time, to consider that their emotional states and perceptions as real responses to what is going on with another. This gives them a self-affirming and reality-affirming experience.

Our emotional involvement and expressivity

What is most crucial in our engagement in mutual analysis? How much, and when to self-disclose, to reveal our internal world to the patient? There *is* a basic ethic I use to guide myself. Patients need to feel our human qualities, our struggles, and authentic commitment to them and to the emotional truth of what is happening. Who we are emotionally—our struggles with openness and honesty—will ultimately be more important than what we say or reveal. What the patient needs from us is our basic attitude of love and care that is expressed by our pursuit of the emotional truth at whatever cost to our own stability and comfort.

Here is the main point: *What needs to be witnessed by the patient is our struggle with a difficult emotional truth. The patient needs to feel the analyst's emotional involvement in the problem the patient is presenting and needs to sense the analyst's emotional work to show that the message has been seriously taken in.* This experience is what fosters intimacy and trust: that the analyst is working with, really taking up, something in themselves that would naturally be resisted. Do we have skin in the game? Are we personally involved and affected?

Then, what I say depends a lot on the relationship and my sense of what would be helpful for the patient to know. The clinical examples later in this article illustrate a variety of responses. There is always risk and uncertainty. Mutuality is messy. Nevertheless, I do need to say something. I try to avoid making a confession. This has many obvious problems, including a subtle plea for forgiveness to be let off the hook. I strive to avoid burdening the patient with my negative reactions to the situation because many patients assume that they have provoked it and are responsible for it. I try to contain my feelings and reactions, metabolizing shame or guilt, and moving into a position of seeing myself through the patient's eyes. For me, this is an iterative process, not a once-and-for-all thing. I am continually learning how to do this each time it comes up with a patient—as it often comes up in unique and surprising ways. It is always work met with resistance. This makes the encounter a personal and intimate one.

More often than not, I confirm the patient's observations if I find some truth in them. If I cannot find that truth, I say that I will consider seriously what they noticed. There may be things I cannot know that they can perceive. How much I say and elaborate depends on the level of their experience with me, and whether they can hold onto their own mind in the midst of regression.

The patient's necessary contribution to our self-awareness

The gist of Ferenczi's paradigmatic shift is a rejection of an analytic enigmatic attitude. The analyst becomes ordinary and human, a caring yet contingent person, as much victim to unconscious forces as the patient, as much affected by the surround of culture and historical events.

We as much as the patient repeat early object relations and may be as averse to novelty and the unknown as the patient. These are not only object-relational attributes but unconscious aspects of our personalities--our level of narcissism, insecurity, reparative strivings, and need for knowledge and control, and so on.

Finally, and this I want to emphasize, strong feelings and reactions arise from the *novelty* of contact with another person who is *not a transference figure*, who is a foreign presence ultimately unknown. This causes further disruptions. This core aspect of the relationship Berenstein (2001) calls "subject relations" rather than object relations. This means that the other person is experienced as a subject in their own right and not an object for study, resisting our need to understand and, in a sense, possess the patient through knowledge.[2] This important element has been given a lesser role than it in fact deserves. This "space between" that Berenstein theorizes is an area that cannot be symbolized; the patient cannot be fully grasped by our empathy and identification because there is a private and foreign part of him or her. If the space or gap is bridged, it is through the patient's willingness and capacity to communicate the hidden dimensions of his or her personality. But there will always be a remainder, a sector of personality that cannot be symbolized and communicated. This is an important reality we need to live with and not collapse out of our need to repair or to know. Subject relations is important because it theorizes an immediacy, nowness, and novelty to the interaction between us and the patient.

Given these challenges, how do we come to know ourselves in our analytic relationships? A useful concept that illuminates relational understanding is Aron's (2000) idea of "Self-reflexivity". Aron draws from James's (1890) designation of the self as an "I" and a "me". The "I" is the subjective experiencing self, engaged in pursuing desires and needs. The "me" is the sense of myself seen as an object in the world, among other objects, the kind of person others see us, from their perspectives. A fuller way of knowing oneself comes from managing the tension from two perspectives as a subject and as an object. *But it necessitates an interpersonal context.*

I must emphasize that this is not primarily for the analyst's benefit, though increasing self-knowledge does make us better analysts. What is important is how this openness to self-knowledge through dialogue with the patient helps the patient. It is this process that allows the analyst to uncover dissociated or repressed aspects of feeling and relating that are part of the relationship with the patient that can be problematic and block communication and receptivity. This view helps us be open to the patient's reactions and perceptions, not as projections but as possible realities in the analyst.

We then learn the hereto unconscious feelings and attitudes toward our patient that we were unwilling or resistant to see. And this dissonance between our conscious intentions and attitudes and our unconscious ones creates difficulty and stress for the patient. It does not inspire trust and openness, but compliance or silent resentment and fear—or defensive idealization.

I am advocating that our efforts, in pursuit of truth, start with an interrogation of the quality of *our* engagement. Creativity has to do with our flexibility and willingness to imagine ourselves as active objects in relation to the patient.

Mutuality and regression

Regression in therapy has important clinical implications for mutuality. Our obligation is greater if we offer the patient a place for regression, dwelling, and a potential "new beginning". The patient then "knows", "sees" the analyst not from the position of a mature adult but as a child in relation to an adult—with all the traumatic vulnerability and adaptions of that particular individual. Winnicott (1955) theorized this in his concept of "regression to dependence", as did Balint (1968) in his concept of therapeutic regression to the basic fault. Regression is meant here as the possibility of finding alive being-ness, the emergence of a True Self that emerges early in development but was thwarted early on. If the conditions are supportive, the patient lets go of the "mature" and precocious aspects of their defenses to put themselves in the care of the analyst, but only when there is a real sense of safety and reliability. It is in this state of "regression to dependency", owing to the analyst's warmth and sincerity, ordinariness, honesty, and presence, that the patient is then most vulnerable as well as most sensitive to subtle lapses and shifts in the analyst's investment and engagement.

In these periods of heightened vulnerability, it is all the more important we embody the values of mutual analysis. By this, I mean that I try to avoid placing the patient in the precocious role as analyst to the analyst. *Yet it is very important to appreciate the patient as knower, as sensitive perceiver of the sort of environment in which they find themselves.* Is the environment safe, reliable, responsive? Many patients coming from developmental trauma are vigilant and at times very suspicious of our intentions. This is natural and expectable. It is part of how they survived. If the patient comes from a challenging childhood, regression allows for this experience to be told and the perpetrator to be named and confronted.

There are times when the patient is regressed and needs our separate presence much in the background, in a quieter, though still present way. We are functioning as an embodied holding environment, as an "unobtrusive analyst" (Balint, 1968). In these moments, care is given to how much to offer when there has been a lapse on our part. There are many times when I will help the patient turn back toward themselves rather than explore the interaction in a more collaborative way. The analyst is saying, in effect, "I am here, back on track. You are the important one here. Let's get back to you". When done at the right moment, when we understand what the patient needs at that moment, this is not avoidance of the negative transference or an infantilization of the patient. It is strengthening the patient's developing self, by giving them the freedom to turn toward themselves. Generally, in periods of dependency, which are in fact late occurrences in analyses after much work has been done to create a reliable and safe setting, it is a developmental achievement for patients to turn away from the analyst, but they need our support to do this.

Mutuality in regression is not symmetrical collaboration. The analyst finds, often without the patient telling us, where we went wrong and how to right the situation.

Mutuality and the analytic frame

Nacht (1962) says that "... it is what the analyst *is* rather than what he *says* that matters ... what the analyst genuinely and fundamentally is matters more than what he rationally decides to be in regard to the patient" (p. 207). What the patient is looking for is a genuine engagement, a living relationship in which we are willing to face our own emotional obstacles and limitations in order to welcome the patient and be available, to achieve *presence*. In Nacht's words, the analyst's "*inner state of being* ... can be the decisive factor" (p. 209; Italics in original). For Nacht, it is that

> No one can cure another if he has not a genuine desire to help him; and no one can have the desire to help unless he *loves,* in the deepest sense of the word. (p. 210)

For me, the deepest sense of loving in my work is the desire to recognize another in his or her own right and to be a part of their emotional growth and development, despite the emotional discomfort I will endure along the way. This is an emotional struggle that arises from the mutual relationship, as I have emphasized. That struggle is a crucial part of the loving commitment to patients that they can feel.

I propose that the analytic attitude Nacht proposes is the bedrock of the analytic frame, an *internal* dynamic frame that contains experience in the conversation. The patient gets to know and depend on this from us. How each of us brings this forward in our work is unique and particular to us, based on all sorts of internal ways of experiencing and regulating our self. This basic way of being present looks different with each analyst. But importantly, *the boundaries of our way of being with the patient are not fixed.* I mean this as much in terms of action, as in words and attitudes. So, in the process of a living, growing, evolving analytic relationship, we have the occasion to go beyond our previous point of safety and surety. We might experiment, be spontaneous, improvise. We might be pushed by the patient beyond our comfort levels into new spheres of emotional experience.

If we maintain an asymmetric relation and what Neri (2008) calls "relational authenticity", where our freedom to be authentic is bounded by the care for another, then expansion can enhance the possibilities of experience for both analyst and patient. He elaborates the balance by saying that:

> ... giving a degree of free reign to one's feelings ... is not spontaneity tout court, but a *"special spontaneity"* that involves tolerating powerful feelings and not evacuating them. The responsibility involved is one of "taking responsibility for one's relationships and becoming aware of the effects of one's words and actions on the other." (p. 336)

The analyst, then, is *"saying things that correspond to the reality of relationship"* (p. 335, my italics).

The frame then broadens and deepens. Sometimes when the patient senses our struggle with the tension of freedom and safety, they may take the risk that widens their subjectivity as well.

This is not all smooth and easy sailing. The truth we both seek, the relational truth, though beautiful, is painful. The patient is a witness to our struggles and humanity that can be hurtful and disappointing. Yet we offer the patient a real experience, the reality of a "living relationship between one human being and another". Then our emotional work to recognize this and take responsibility can be extremely reparative for patients who have not encountered this before, and instead have protectively assumed or been forced to assume the blame for all relational disappointments and hurt.

Clinical illustration: Tom

When I returned to work a week after my father died, Tom said, "You seem off. Did something happen? Is that why you took off? Did someone die?" I replied that my father had in fact died. I had missed several meetings in the preceding months due to his illness and Tom knew that there was an illness in my family. Tom was silent for a moment, and then replied in a surprised tone, "Why did you return so soon?" Tom had asked many questions about what was going on in the months that preceded this conversation. I tended to respond directly to his questions. His curiosity developed and deepened in our relationship as he overcame an inhibition about learning about me, directly from me—an inhibition not uncommon in many people we see. For Tom, free-associating about me had a feeling of compliance and so he pushed to express his curiosity more openly. I had not sensed nor interpreted greed or intrusiveness, and my responses often brought out his feelings in useful ways.

I responded to Tom that I returned because I wanted to be back at work, that it helped me deal with my feelings because I felt closer to my father while working (he was a dedicated pediatrician), and I thought I could be fully attentive to him. Tom pointedly commented, "I don't believe you. You're not grieving but pretending to. Grief does not sound like that".

I was startled by the forcefulness and truth of his comment. I think he was troubled to hear how I spoke. Tom had suffered serious losses of his own in childhood and knew something about what grief sounds like. I reluctantly conceded to myself that there were false notes in what I said. In reassuring Tom, I was also reassuring myself. I then questioned whether to say anything personal at this moment of heightened vulnerability for me. Would I covertly be seeking an empathic listener? Or be surrendering to a masochistic impulse? I held back, not knowing what to say in the moment. I told him, "I did not know what to say or how to respond. I will think seriously about what you noticed". I then assented that what he said sounded true to me and added that this is a vulnerable time and I feel a bit private and careful what to say.

Over the next few days, I contended with this uncomfortable realization about myself, and negative feelings toward Tom for exposing this. His confrontation felt intrusive and disruptive at a time I was more vulnerable than I knew. I felt persecuted and self-protective, and so was unable to see things from Tom's vantage point. In that state, I remained relatively quiet. Strikingly, perhaps intuitively, Tom did not press me further and seemed able to accept my reticence. Tom could feel I was working through something. Gradually over a couple of sessions, I calmed down and could face more directly my sadness in Tom's presence. I could then be more fully open to the truth of his insight—the denial of my grief. Tom's insight was helpful to me in considering the reasons I chose to return to work so soon. I had overestimated my real capacity for work. I am not usually forced by a patient to face this. An important point here is that, though I understood this aspect of myself through my personal analysis and subsequent ongoing self-analysis, and also understood its origin in my childhood experience, when I was faced with this again in the interaction with Tom, it felt new. So, we discover ourselves anew, in facing emotional truth, as does the patient, in the distinctness and richness of the relationship.

I eventually told Tom that his perception felt true to me. I said this not as a fact, but as an emotional truth. I *was* out of touch with my grief in giving him that explanation. I also said that it must have disturbed him to witness that I was out so of touch with myself and my loss.

I think this felt real to him. He took it seriously and calmly. This exchange did not prompt more questions from Tom. Instead, he considered what this meant to him. In subsequent sessions, he brought up his lack of trust in me. How could I help him get in touch with painful parts of himself when I seem unable to face my own? How could he feel confident that I could have sincere feelings for him? Was I always disguising, unknowingly, my true feelings? Am I pretending with him as well? I followed him closely. I clearly got his point, which called not for reassurance but acceptance of the real emotional dilemma I put him in.

Though what I said was true—my identifications with my father intensified after his death—I had been a bit dissociated in my work, trying to do too much too soon, and I was out of touch with Tom. I simply said, "His death is having an impact on me. I was not fully here the way I can be and how you need me to be, and I'm sorry for that". This statement communicated that I had returned in a more real, though imperfect way, and was present with what was going on between us and the impact I was having on him. I could take that in and be with him as fully as was possible at that moment.

Instead of feeling dropped in the presence of someone not emotionally there, now Tom seemed to have more trust in my presence. In part, this was because I admitted my vulnerability and blind spots, that I make mistakes, that my mistakes affect him, that I am not always at my best. Tom said, "I'm glad you said that ... you must feel it's okay to share that with me and that feels good". Tom's comment was not an expression of forgiveness. I think he was glad that I could be open and human with him, that I did not keep him at a distance for my own self-protection and that I confirmed what he felt was the truth.

There was a tender mutual recognition as he began to talk in new ways about how long it took him to face losses in childhood. Maybe he is only beginning to do so as well. Memories come up of the terrible pain he felt living with parents who were lost in their own world of alcohol and society, and who left him before any possibility of repair occurred. We were two sons who lost fathers, and simultaneously a father-therapist now caring for his patient-son. This circular interaction involves the way my capacity to self-reflect in his presence led to a lessening of similar defenses in him, and a mutual recognition of the power of grief shared between us, in a personal way.

Clinical Illustration: Anne

Anne told me toward the beginning of a session that I seemed withdrawn. She thought I was lost and distracted. I seemed awkward and off-balance. After getting more of a feeling of what she sensed and how it affected her, I acknowledged that she was right: I was more low-key than usual. As we began to discuss this, both of us immediately became much more alive and engaged. This is a common occurrence in my experience. When the dialogue enters into an immediate and personal realm, enlivening immediacy occurs in tone, rhythm, and gesture as we made more contact and things felt more vital and personal between us.

I said that because we had missed several sessions over the last few weeks, and that I had not seen her in over a week, this may have contributed to my less engaged state. Her response was very common for many patients and is an important opening for therapeutic action. "It was not only my fault I missed some of the sessions", she said, "You did, too". She felt blamed and took responsibility for my state of mind. Here I had the opportunity to tell her in a firm way that my comments were not meant to blame her; I take full responsibility for how I am with her. I was the one not able to fully hold onto her in my mind during the disruptions, some of which I had caused. It takes time for me to settle back in and that is a problem that affects her. She then said angrily that I am not supposed to flake out on her in sessions, especially when we've had so little contact recently. She was right. Her reactions signaled a shift back to her own experience when relieved of the burden and blame of my emotional state.

I imagine some concerns raised here. Am I burdening the patient with too much information about myself? And is this information likely to hurt her more? Could she feel that I did not keep her in mind because she is so easily forgettable? In fact, the opposite occurred. She was relieved because what I said was believable and jibed with her *actual* experience of me. She has noticed that after long breaks it does takes me time to resettle in and reconnect. (This is not my version of Bion's eschewing memory and desire, by the way.) The therapeutic moment here is how she can begin to differentiate from me and her internal object world in ways that strengthen her sense of self and reality. That is why patients often do not collapse when they hear something true about us, even if the content has negative and disappointing aspects. This patient's evolving sense of herself was progressively stronger the more her perceptions were confirmed. This was my immediate therapeutic aim in this period of the work with Anne.

Clinical illustration: Brian

Brian is an academic I've seen for many years. I have mostly a fatherly attitude of care and admiration. He is something of a star in his field and his achievements have evoked pride in whatever part I've played in his development, as he moved from an insecure graduate student to an established professor. One day he was recounting his recent success at a conference. He spoke on a topic I have a keen interest in and with which I have some familiarity. I was marveling at his insights. He paused for a moment. I commented on some of his ideas and the exciting effect he had on his listeners, consciously feeling admiration. Manifestly, I intended to strengthen the powerful force of his ideas. But I noticed, and I could tell by Brian's reaction, that I wasn't making a lot of sense. I was rambling and vague. Brian looked confused and asked what was the point I was trying to make? At that moment the session ended.

The next day Brian went right to the end of the last session. He commented, "What were you getting at? I couldn't follow you. I had the sense something was bothering you—you're usually more clear". When I tried to connect what I said to my feelings of taking pleasure in his success, he looked dubious. "Is that really it, because you were flustered. It didn't seem so straightforward?"

In going over my feelings in Brian's presence I could find something quite different from the benevolent father I wanted to be and how he often felt me to be. Instead, I felt competitive and surpassed by Brian's way with words and ideas, how he poetically delved into exciting and difficult ideas that were wonderfully creative. It's an important, maybe obvious point that a benevolent and loving analytic attitude, though therapeutically essential, can hide problematic feelings in the analyst. So I realized that I tried to enter the conversation by saying something, anything, that showed I was with him and at his level. But my words lacked real meaning because I felt something so entirely different. This was hard to admit to myself. Nevertheless, I sensed that I needed to say something genuine about the reasons I interrupted his narrative and interposed myself in the story of his accomplishments at the conference.

At that moment, though, I wondered if Brian could come to this realization on his own. If I entered too soon here, I would be repeating a different version of the day before, this time as the self-aware analyst who can admit his feelings and be generous with his self-disclosures while maintaining my position of authority with him. The crucial emotional moment was really whether *he* could imagine that I was competitive with him, that he could stand surpassing me, even if he knew it was difficult for me. This would disrupt our often-comfortable way of being together. So, I asked him whether he had an idea of why I acted that way. "I can barely think this, but it might make sense you were competing with me ... is that so?... yes, I do feel that's a real possibility, that you felt competitive ... well?"

"Yes", I said, "I did feel competitive with you and your real talents that go beyond mine". There was a long pause. Then, "I had the feeling that if I brought this up with you, you'd work with it. You wouldn't deny it if it were true. I wasn't sure where we'd get to or how I really felt about it. I feel now, sort of anxious and excited...that ultimately saying what you did means you are actually OK with my success ... that it is beyond you in this area". "And other areas as well, perhaps", I affirmed.

This is a small fragment of mutual analysis. I must leave out many things not relevant to my main point here, which is to show that mutuality doesn't always mean immediate self-disclosure. Nor is there a safer road of non-responsiveness. In the interplay here, giving Brian room to find the truth of his own perceptions still requires that I acknowledge what he sees in me, that I can live with it, even while struggling with the emotional truth of what's going on, even at the cost of my comfort and easy position I established with him. It's much more acceptable emotionally for me to be the kind and loving father than the competitive and envious one, facing the loss of a son going forward in his life with all his capabilities and future possibilities. This is a developmental trajectory that both son and father need to traverse in ways that don't damage either of them, and that enhance the experience of being a father and a son.

Concluding thoughts

Mutuality is not only a sensibility; it is a reality: two contingent human beings trying to create enough of a shared experience, in which solace, peace, and shared emotions are a possibility—no, a necessity.

A crucial curative factor in mutual analysis is the possibility for a non-repetitive, novel experience. The unknown becomes a palpable, welcome presence in the analysis, bringing a sense of hope and discovery, not only of the past but the present and future. In this spirit, mutuality entails an appreciation of what cannot fully be known about oneself and the other, what is a potential, and what resists knowing and may always remain unknown.

This brings us back to the first sentence in this paper, that we "know ourselves in dialogue with another". Both patient and analyst depend on interaction for growth, recognition, self-awareness, and a cultivation of what is important to us. We are bound by our appreciation and need of others, our need for dialogue, and our tolerance of difference. The fundamental experience of mutuality—why we risk it—is not to gain power or love but for recognition and emotional truth. Both of us in the conversation need this. Self-definition and elaboration come into being in dialogue. And this is the core value and emotional significance of mutuality.

Notes

1 Ferenczi, S. (1988). *The clinical diary of Sandor Ferenczi* (J. Dupont, Ed.) (M. Balint & N. Zarday Jackson, Trans.). Cambridge and London: Harvard University Press (p. 213).
2 This is an important reason Bion turned toward "negative capability" and "O", moving beyond "K".

Chapter 8

The radical uncertainty of psychoanalytic practice

When the object is perceived as particular and unique and not merely the member of a family, when it appears independent of any general notion and detached from the sanity of a cause, isolated and inexplicable in the light of ignorance, then and then only may it be a source of enchantment.
—Beckett, *Proust*, 1931

[A good picture] takes away our certainty because it deprives a thing of its meaning and name. It shows a thing in all its manifold and significance and infinite variety that preclude the emergence of any single meaning and view.
—Gerhard Richter, *Text: Writings, Interviews and Letters, 1961–2007*, 2009

It is true
The wind blows terribly here—
But moonlight
Also leaks between the roof planks.
—Izumi Shikibu, *Of this ruined house*,1990

Disrupting certainty

Shikibu's beautiful ancient poem paints moonlight entering a house wrecked by wind, summoning a mind exposed to whatever comes, whether turbulence or illumination. A breakdown of structures occurs that are meant to keep the elements out. What comes in? The windy turbulence exposes the self to a less protected and organized frame of mind, but also one open to the glow of moonlight. Beckett invokes the same experience. When freed from paralyzing habits, we have fresh perceptions in the "light of ignorance". Richter also

DOI: 10.4324/9781003208518-8

connects "taking away our certainty" to behold a widening significance of the world. "Moonlight", "enchantment", and "infinite variety" emerge from strong winds shaking our certain and safe abode.

Another wonderful poetic voice: Paul Éluard, the French Symbolist, wrote (at least these words are ascribed to him) that "There is another world, and it is this one". This "koan" plays with the sense that what is before us, the world of ours we think we see and know and live in, we actually don't—unless knowledge of our ignorance opens our eyes to "another world" that has always been here before us and now comes forth.

These revelations from Beckett, Richter, Shikibu, and Éluard are relevant to our clinical work. They all point to the fruitful impact of disrupting our sense of certainty. Uncertainty is a psychological concept—a state of mind. When we undergo and live with uncertainty (letting go of what we rely on to feel we know), fresh feelings and perception arise—another world that is this one. In this chapter, I describe my experiences of uncertainty and its therapeutic potential, using clinical material, a metaphor of musical dissonance, and the contribution of two analytic theorists' views on uncertainty that have had a major impact on my thinking.

Why "radical" uncertainty? Because seeking uncertainty is clinically non-intuitive. Aren't we trained to possess knowledge about the mind, what can go wrong there, and how to intervene therapeutically? Yes, what we know about development and the impact of the environment is crucial, as is an understanding of psychic conflict and defenses. Yet, how we go about our interventions and what state of mind is best in the work of helping others is not so straightforward. Contrary to expectations, living in and tolerating uncertainty pays off clinically—as a therapeutic sensibility (an analytic attitude) and as an ethical position. So what makes uncertainty "radical" is that it is a state of mind that goes against our natural, protective inclinations and the role ascribed to us—by ourselves and our patients. It is of course true that we understand and have convictions about things that may be very useful, and the understanding about this that we communicate is helpful. But our *desire* to know that is motivated by anxiety and insecurity—something we all know about—actually limits what can be known through being in experiences that are less formed and more inchoate. Our desire to know constrains the possibility for a richer and more meaningful engagement with our patients.

Living in uncertainty with Mr. P

During the course of an analysis, Mr. P presented a dream that triggered a shift in me from consonance and habit to dissonance and openness. This dream occurred during a period in which he was mourning the loss of his father who died many years before:

> *I was standing by a body of water when I noticed two beautiful dolphins swimming together. They were black with white spots and I began to imagine, in my dream, the genetic pedigree and similarity between the dolphins. Then, to my horror, the water began to swirl like a vortex, pulling the dolphins under while they struggled against the current. I felt terrible despair as the waters calmed and I saw that the dolphins were gone.*

Mr. P associated with great sadness to his father, who abruptly left his life when he was a child. Mr. P's life was a story of loss, deprivation, and, ultimately, triumph of a certain kind. He grew up extremely poor. His mother had many affairs, which led to the divorce from his father. She remarried a man who was alcoholic and abusive. His father then disappeared and remained out of contact until just before he died. Mr. P recalled few moments of warmth or guidance from either parent. He emerged from this environment self-reliant and intellectually precocious—an example of a "successful" false self that saved his mind but left him emotionally constricted in relationships that limited real intimacy and aliveness.

In surprising contrast to the lack of depth and intimacy he described in his relationships, I felt a particular easy connection, an especially good attunement with Mr. P—which he also felt and commented on. I was moved by his stories of loss and triumph as I was by the dream, swept into his narrative current. His life in certain ways improved though the analysis in that he felt freer to be creative, but satisfying intimate relationships remained unattainable. His current romantic relationship was full of strife that he presented in a way that evoked my sympathy. All the while, no real insight was gained into his contribution to his relationship difficulties. This lack of progress was confusing, given how related he seemed to be with me. He appreciated my help and worked hard in the analysis. I felt that I understood him, could follow him easily, and often had something to say in response to the material he presented.

As time went on, I began to fill a disquiet that I could not sort out—an agitation that flickered at the edge of our relationship. Although my reactions to the dream went along with his associations to his father, a restlessness persisted and then a subtle claustrophobia emerged. The comforting way we related—I often sensed immediately where he was going with the narrative—started to feel shallow and stale. Something emotionally shifted: I no longer felt in synch with him.

This was the beginning of dissonance between us. The harmony of sympathetic and easy relating dissipated, leaving me dismayed and lost. I tried without success to find something in me, some counter-transference that blocked an empathic connection, to restore our prior ease. There was a heightened, uncomfortable vividness now—in perception and feeling—that went along with the loss of our easy sense of sharing. I was confused and found little to say. What was this shift about?

As I listened to Mr. P in the hours following the dream, I found myself more disturbed, not by the loss of his father, which was certainly where his feelings were, but in the image of the identical dolphins dancing toward death. Though the narrative content of the hours focused on the absence of his father, now I could see that the dolphins were in fact the two of us, indistinguishable, pulled into something annihilating. There was no father/analyst. This emotional truth was ironically opposite to that of the feeling of the narrative, and seemed obvious only when I was out of the pull of the vortex we had created. I let a deeper melody take hold of me. It was a shift into atonality and fragmentation—a "ruined house".

My emotional shift changed the atmosphere between us. Subtly and suddenly, I no longer was his emotionally predictable partner. More anxious, Mr. P became obviously controlling of what he said and how I should respond. When I did not respond in my usual way, he became angry and critical. His grief about his father passed surprisingly quickly, replaced by a vague sense of being wronged and unappreciated. He did not immediately connect these feelings to me just yet. I was able to talk to him about his irritation with me—his disturbance that I was not appreciating him in the way he had grown used to. I acknowledged my former contribution to the "dolphin dance".

He started to feel empty and alone in a new way. Memories flooded in: reading alone in bed, listening fearfully to every sound in the house, walking alone to kindergarten, knowing no one, focusing only on winning over his teachers. He had no friends and recalled feeling completely unprotected, relying on his precocious intellect and ability to sense the needs of others in order to survive. I cannot over-emphasize how opposite this was to his conscious experience of always feeling in control and triumphing over every obstacle. I now sensed his fear and vulnerability at a level not touched on in the previous period of our work. His sense of ease—telling a story, winning me over—was gone. We were entering a new current no longer as twins. This was the most difficult phase of the work for him: the painful recognition that we were not the same and that he needed me not to be the same, or he would be lost. During this period, he had this dream:

> I am sitting at my desk at work, feeling in control, on top of my game. Two students enter—typical types, work shirts, casual. I know them. I ask what they want. Without saying anything, they both grab me by the arms and pull me over the desk. I had the terrible feeling I could not overpower them, I am losing my footing, even though they are smaller. I am terrified.

His associations subtly would lead me to make the obvious interpretation: he no longer is in control; he is more vulnerable. This time I wait. I am thinking about pairs again, pairs of students. He starts thinking about K in Kafka's *The Trial*, and here I see how truly persecuted he feels by me, by my lack of involvement in the narrative. The two paired students were the ones who took Mr. K away. In this state of mistrust, Mr. P courageously continued to come to his sessions. He would often turn from the couch to look at me. Many hours were filled with long silences. I was present for him in a warm way, but that did not ease his fear. He was often at a loss for what to say, as he became more aware that every effort, every gesture, was meant to evoke a particular and predictable response in me in order to feel safe. I could point all this out him—especially his need for safety—but this would not allay his persecution and probably would have added to it. These hours were painful for me, too, in different ways: watching him suffer, I wondered whether he could bear it. I wondered what I was inflicting on him and whether I should relieve him of these feelings. Yet, I managed not to reassure him, not to change the dissonant music we were in—though I was often tempted. Nonetheless, I had no idea how we would go forward. It was not a static state but a painfully uncertain one, for both of us, especially when his persecution turned to rage and attacks.

Like Mr. P, I had to let go of my need for comfort—the good feeling that I knew him and could tell that things would turn out well between us. I now wondered whether hatred and persecution would prevail—something I truly dreaded. But I was beginning to let go. For me, there is faith in the containing and nourishing power of this specialized conversation. But faith is not a certainty, though it helps us keep going in the face of uncertainty.

How did Mr. P and I come through this? Mr. P came to believe we could both bear his persecution and rage, which he tested out each session. Although many sessions were filled with vicious attacks and fears of me, something began to strengthen in his trust of the setting. We were witnessing—he articulated this—something very real in him that had value for that very reason, a part of himself that was hidden away until then. Crucially, he was allowing this to happen in himself and with another person.

The course of treatment was now uncertain for both of us. Over time, surviving this protracted period of paranoia and hostility opened up a space for something new to happen in him and between us. He recognized the enormous, constant effort he made to organize the people around him that left him feeling empty and out of touch with himself. Now, he felt a stronger sense of something real in himself, and this greater sense of himself was held by the form of the analytic conversation, however painful. This form was ultimately sustained by our joint efforts. But both of us had no clear sense of how long he and I could bear his suffering, or whether he could establish and maintain a more solid feeling of trust in me and (simultaneously) a sense of well-being in himself.

"The emancipation of dissonance"[1]

What does it mean to tolerate uncertainty and what do we gain by it? As clinicians, we resist uncertainty because we put ourselves in the position of knowing and helping. Yet, in my view, bearing uncertainty *makes space for*, allows for patients *to be*—to be in their own right and to be recognized for who they are becoming.

In teaching a course on Bion to candidates, I created an experiential situation to explore visceral reactions to undergoing uncertainty. I analogized openness to uncertainty to listening to dissonant music. Dissonance is another way of talking about uncertainty. By dissonance, I mean the way sounds don't harmonize and fit together in predictable ways to form familiar, expectable patterns. I found that students took in Bion's early work on projective identification and containment much more readily than his later contributions involving letting go of what we know or expect and experiencing and "being-with(in)" the emotional situation—a new orientation toward the way we receive and make use of the patient's communication. This analytic position was spelled out in Bion's iconic-koanic paper, "Notes on Memory and Desire" (1967). I studied this paper with my students as a starting point for approaching his way of cultivating a tolerance for uncertainty. I focused on one line: "What is 'known' about the patient is of no further consequence: it is either false or irrelevant" (p. 17). What then? How to engage when what you know and what you aim for in your technique "is of no further use"—an altered and altering way of listening and taking in experience.

The music ranged from Schoenberg and Debussy to more contemporary composers like Cage and Ligeti. We also listened to late John Coltrane and Ornette Coleman—so-called "free jazz". My idea was to approximate what listening without memory and desire *feels* like—the disruption of expectation, habit, and familiar comfort. Musical dissonance seemed to be a good model for that and I wanted to emancipate it. After listening, we each gave an account of how this musical experience affected us.

Most students found the experience troubling and quite un-comfortable. Time went by very slowly even if the piece lasted but two to three minutes. Some were angered by the music ... and by me. At first, many could not settle into the music nor be open to whatever would come next. They looked forward to the piece ending. I knew something of their experience from my own first encounters with free jazz and contemporary classical music. It does require a different form of attention, more free-flowing and present-centered, free from expectation.

At first, some thought this exercise rather sadistic on my part. Most eagerly shifted when I moved our focus to Bion's late work—only to find the same feelings of irritation and confusion come up there as well! As we continued to focus on Bion, I persisted in this musical exercise at the beginning of each class over ten weeks. I noticed a definite change in the candidates' reactions. Year after year, I would notice this evo-lution happening. Gradually, they accepted the unpredictable, at times jarring, listening experience. Their comments focused less on their distress or irritation and more on certain qualities in the passages of the music and the variety of feelings the music evoked—by letting go of their need for predictable form and familiar experience, the students noticed the sensorial and emotional texture of the passages. They be-came *attentive* and open to what comes, "waiting on" not "waiting for". Some even started to enjoy this experience of finding new musical elements and looked forward to the next piece of music that changed each week, that opened up new sounds.

This musical exercise illustrates the experience of inhabiting a place of uncertainty that Keats (1898) calls "negative capability":

> I mean Negative Capability, that is, when a man is capable of being in uncertainties, mysteries, doubts, without any irritable reaching after fact and reason ... (pp. 193–194)

How can we, in following Bion and Keats, receive from the patient the lower and less audible registers of communication? Noting our responses to challenging, disruptive music, I recognize that negative elements of "countertransference" can arise from reactions to un-certainty, and not only from the patient's projections or our transferences.

Expanding the musical metaphor to grasp the clinical implications of dissonance and uncertainty, dissonance can be liberating for patient and analyst. Analysis offers an opportunity to leave the safe confines of a "tonal center" (habit, familiarity, what is already known) and move into tonal realms uncomfortable for both analyst and patient—what in the present moment is most difficult for both of them. Dissonance is about gaps, otherness, and the unknown. It is recognizing that change is extremely difficult and resisted and prey to great pressure to maintain the status quo of familiar harmonies.

The progression in Western Music is toward an increasing inclusion of notes, of suspended sounds, and of lack of resolution—dissonance and atonality. This means that a greater range of sounds entered into the musical experience. Schoenberg in the early 20th century invented the 12-tone series—his aim was for the "emancipation of dissonance"—in which every note is considered equal. The formal/structural strategies changed significantly, leading what, in Hall (1996), Benjamin Rattle calls "present centered listening". But this change also creates considerable insecurity and anxiety in the listener that sometimes leads to rejecting the music outright.

A similar evolution has occurred in psychoanalysis, in which analysts have become open to hearing more in the analytic hour, including new vibrations outside speech. Our theories have evolved to allow for and capture new phenomena, perhaps even calling for a paradigm shift in our listening position (such as Bion calls for). And, our theories have evolved to allow more dissonance, shifting our attention, allowing for the register of new tonalities. Bion, our Shoenberg, was at the forefront of this radical paradigm change.

Uncertainty as a sensibility: Bion

Bion was at the forefront of emancipating dissonance in psychoanalysis. His late work insists on this radical openness. He privileges receptivity over interpretation.[2] With a fine sensitivity to the obscuring effects of habit, narrative, and causal connections (the "why" of the matter), Bion demotes the importance of content or a search for unconscious fantasy as a structuring element. In contrast, he particularly attends to the unfolding nature of (unformed) experience. Bion normalizes uncertainty, confusion, indeterminacy—making analysts more open to it.

Bion (1967) states that a moment in a session "shares with dreams the quality of being wholly present or wholly absent" (p. 18), capturing the fluid, contingent nature of language. The metaphors we arrive at do not represent the Truth or express the Truth. Rather, they are tools to carry us through the momentary ebb and flow of the evolution of an aspect of the patient's personality or relationship. In *Los Angeles Seminars and Supervision* (Aguayo, 1967/2018), Bion says, "Something pushes out towards you, you begin to notice it, and then an interpretation will come with it" (pp. 10–11). "Something pushes" is the opposite of "reaching for", "finding", or "gaining" insight. We are taken by something that captures our notice, as a beginning, and an interpretation that "comes with it" is not in us. "Truth happens to an idea. It is made true by events", as William James (1907) observed.

As Bion (1967) states oracularly, "Psychoanalytic 'observation' is concerned neither with what has happened nor with what is going to happen but with what is happening". Thus, we are led to perhaps his most powerful pragmatic idea, derived from Milton's description of Genesis in *Paradise Lost*: "Out of the darkness and formlessness something evolves" (p. 18). "Darkness" and "formlessness" are necessary areas of ungraspable experience to be protected and endured in order for form to evolve. An interpretation arises out of the matrix, out of formlessness.

Bion's confounding concept of "O" turns the analyst toward this unarticulated, "invisible" register. To do this, he proscribes for the analyst a radical openness to uncertainty, a stance that forsakes memory and desire: "… when you have a particularly dark spot, turn onto it a shaft of piercing darkness" (Bion, as quoted in Aguayo, 1967/2018, p. 8).

What does it mean for the analyst to work this way? From a pragmatic point of view, it alters the analyst's attention, moving it from what can be known and legible in words, to what is outside language and representation. Only "being" can reside in the realm of this non-symbolized undifferentiated register. So, in order to have contact with this realm, a new way of being present (being-with) in the sessions is required. A different, state of mind is needed.

Bion's contributions are therapy for the analyst as much as for the patient. His sensibility of transience and temporality:

Leads to attention to the fluid nature of subjective experience

Leads to an understanding of the limits of language

Leads to being (in/with) rather than knowing

Leads to a focus on the unformed, unrepresented

Leads to fear, confusion, disorientation, uncertainty, and decentering

Leads to the appearance of new forms of emotional truth.

Bion (1963) also has something important to say about the emotional consequences that follow from this sensibility. By asking this crucial question (he does have a way of getting at the heart of the matter):

What elements in a session (considered an emotional experience) must be selected to make it clear that the experience has been psychoanalysis and could have been nothing else? (p. 13)

Here is his answer, with my emphasis:

At no time must either analyst or analysand lose the sense of *isolation* within the intimate relationship.... *Detachment* can only be achieved at the expense of *loneliness and abandonment*. The detached personality is in a sense new to its job and has to turn to tasks which differ from those to which its components are more usually adapted, namely scrutiny of the environment excluding the self; part of the price paid is *insecurity*. (1963, pp. 14–15, italics mine)

In this complicated quote, Bion is doing two things. He is emphasizing that what makes an analytic conversation analytic is separateness-isolation (dissonance). Bion is sensitive, from his work in groups to the power of group mentality—a pressure to merge into non-thought and habit that collapses reflective, potential space. This collapse is also a form of emotional (false) security. He argues here for an emotional analytic stance that is alert to this collapsing pressure to return to comforting melodies. But this stance has the emotional cost of *loneliness, abandonment, and insecurity* in order to face what has not been faced before. These emotions—the hallmark of uncertainty—are what Mr. P and I felt when our analytic conversation allowed for dissonance between us.

Yet, when a space is maintained between patient and analyst, a space of formlessness and the unknown, creativity and symbolization arise from this disjuncture and disruption. Bion called these disruptions "caesuras"—or breaks. These caesuras engage us deeply because they are transformative. They are moments (or longer) of fragmentation and disentanglement—that "sense of isolation" in our ruined house. For the analyst, the patient is "isolated and inexplicable in the light of (*our*) ignorance"—harkening back to Becket. Then, some disentanglement, a reordering—an emerging form of insight out of what preceded that moment—gives us a sense of awe and beauty. I felt this strongly when Mr. P came day after day to live with me in a terrifying world. Mr. P's presence came forth.

Uncertainty as (also) an ethical position—Berenstein

Isidoro Berenstein (2001, 2012), an Argentinean psychoanalyst, meditates on the ethical implications of uncertainty and dissonance by exploring the idea of "subject relations"—extending Bion's perspective. Like Bion, his work is dense and full of paradox—but well worth the effort. Coming from a Latin American psychoanalytic culture, he nonetheless arrives at insights harmonious with Bion's, but his view of the analytic setup is more deliberately intersubjective.

Berenstein works in the tradition of Pichon-Rivière's (1998) link theory.[3] He distinguishes "object relations" from "subject relations"—two models of the analytic meeting. The first is based on the dynamics of object relating involving projection, introjection, and unconscious phantasy that leads to a pressure to repeat. Berenstein's model of "subject relations" is based on the *vinculo* or link—for Berenstein, a dynamic structure that defines a relationship between subjects. He writes (2012):

> *Vinculo* generates a virtual space (with real consequences) of radical difference between people. We call this space the *in*

between, and emotional events and effective actions unfold in it. This *in between* creates new possibilities for exchange. (p. 571)

By "exchange", Berenstein means that, in giving to another, one is offered a space in return. In analytic terms this applies to both analyst and patient, each offering a psychic space for the other.[4] This thinking takes us beyond Bion. Berenstein writes (2012) that the link produces:

> ... an expanded, modified, renewed subjectivity that *makes it possible to negate the ego's (narcissistic) confinement* in its identity and to establish this subjectivity as novelty. The couple has its own life as aggregate ... which is ceaselessly being constituted in each of the numerous "nows" they experience together. (p. 573, italics mine)

He is saying a lot here. Berenstein means by the "ego's narcissistic confinement" the way one subject confines the other by possessing them through a knowledge that defines them. The link "negates" this confinement by offering the possibility for another, as subject, to be novel and unknown. This possibility then allows the couple to have an evolving life "ceaselessly constituted" through shared experience. Berenstein calls this negating enlivening process "interference", in contrast to "transference". Thus, *vinculo* interferes with identity relations, the way one subject possesses the other. In contrast to transference, which is about creating-updating-re-creating existing norms and patterns, interference is "produced in the space *in between* as a result of there being two or more subjects *whose presence generates something new and unknown*". This dynamic allows for "... a *becoming* based on difference while dealing with the uncertainty about what they may be able to achieve" (p. 576).

Berenstein's model is profoundly meaningful and clinically ethical. The *vinculo* of subject relations is betweenness and difference that resists—works to negate—our ego's desire to "confine" another by knowing them. If, according to Bernstein, "object relating" involves an imposition on the object of our ego identity ("I am me and you are it"), "subject relating" dissolves that confinement and opens one to the subjectivity of another, freeing another to be. *I believe this is an ethically therapeutic offer analysts can extend to their patients.* As with Bion, we must deal with the uncertainty, loneliness, and abandonment that arises in subject relations—and the uncertainty of what might be possible. Mr. P and I were in the midst of this for the later part of the analysis.

Transformation and uncertainty are essential elements in subject relations. The transformative effect of subject relating is based on the idea that the other is foreign and *resists assimilation and identification.* If object relating is an "I–It" relation, subject relating is an "I–Thou" relationship. Here, we see clearly the ethical dimension in Berenstein's clinical approach. This new sort of analytic-ethical relating by "interference" is not about working through, as is the transference, but about making room for the other as a different subject who is:

> ... generated by the *irreducible specificity of the other subject* that cannot be represented, and therefore leads to an ongoing work of inscription and *making room in one's mind.* What is foreign, strange, new, radical, different about the other emerges out of the construction of the *vinculo* itself. (Berenstein, 2001, p. 574)

Conclusion

Berenstein and Bion share a vision that embraces uncertainty—with deep therapeutic-ethical implications for us. If we embody the position of "interference" and "subject relating", if we allow the patient to be unknown in their "irreducible specificity" in each session, if we allow the "in between" and "formlessness", then we give space and freedom for the patient to be and develop. The analyst is also changed in offering this, as well. When Mr. P and I allowed for *vinculo,* tolerated uncertainty, and did not collapse it, we were both altered. He encountered a fuller sense of himself, a sense of self-possession and realness not possible when we engaged exclusively in transference-transference living. I changed as I worked through my own needs for understanding and certainty that "confined" Mr. P— as it "confined" me as well.

Notes

1 Schoenberg (1926) wrote this phrase to mean, according to J. Samson (1977) "As the ear becomes acclimatized to a sonority within a particular context, the sonority will gradually become 'emancipated' from that context and seek a new one" (pp. 146–147).
2 See Markman (2015) for a discussion of Bion's late work.
3 I will discuss Pichon-Riviere's work in more detail in Chapter 11.
4 Gabriel Marcel's (1933) idea of presence to the other is this kind of offering.

Chapter 9

Modes of therapeutic time

> A sufficiency of going on being is only possible at the beginning if the mother is in this state (of primary maternal occupation) ... that is a very real thing.
>
> —Winnicott, 1956

> ("Now moments") are unfamiliar, unexpected in their exact form and timing, unsettling or weird...The therapist must use a specific aspect of his or her individuality that carries a personal signature.
>
> —Stern et al., 1998

Two modes of therapeutic time

Patients change through experiences with us that occur in subjective time. There are two therapeutic modes of time in analysis. One mode Stern et al. (1998) describe as "now moments". This mode is a discreet passage of time in which there is a heightened sense of living and perceiving internal and external reality. It comes from a disruption of the status quo of each subject's relationship to another and the world. The other temporal mode is "on-going-ness", a way of living in which time stretches out to a distant horizon. Like Winnicott's (1960, 1963) notion of "going-on-being", experience is flowing, neither punctuated nor disrupted, and a subjective light is cast around the person.

There is an important dynamic interaction between these two modes. Moving from "on-going-ness" to "now moments" can be developmentally enhancing, although "now moments" can also be simply traumatizing. Re-traumatization may remain repetitive or lead to emotional growth. Both of these dimensions of time matter in

DOI: 10.4324/9781003208518-9

analysis and come up differently with different patients or shift within the same analysis. While promoting change in different ways, these two temporal modes of experience have different phenomenological qualities and clinical significance. In "now" moments of import and heightened intensity, the patient and his or her relationship with us are disrupted from a stable state, opening up an alive and vivid passage of time. Tumult, turbulence, novelty, and surprise add to an intrinsic heightened awareness that we are going through something that is ours. There is a felt sense of something happening in which each member of the analytic couple is the experiencer, now, and what is happening is meaningful to each of us, now.

The ability for the dyad to weather and fully undergo these un-settling "now" moments depends on "going on-ness", which builds trust in us and the setting and leads to self-establishment. The patient is supported and accompanied by our presence as we remain in the background in an unobtrusive way. The dyad is not just passing time waiting for the "now" moments. Going-on-ness is a fundamental and therapeutic domain of treatment in itself for most patients. I believe transformative "moments" would not occur unless this mode has been established. Without this background of safety, "now moments" are more likely to be traumatic otherwise.

The way people change in these temporal modes depends on our way of engaging. In both domains of time, we are talking about shared experience, though in the going-on-ness of time, there is also a limited sense of our separateness and subjectivity.

Another important way time is experienced[1]—really not-experienced— is a diffuse out-of-time "non-experience", when the person moves through time in a disjointed, dysregulated way from one impression and feeling to another without a sense of continuity, containment, or awareness. These are trauma-related states. They can arise on their own or when a now moment's rupture of the analytic relationship sends the patient there. These states are part of the fabric of analytic phenomena but fall outside of subjective time and feel oppressively endless and static.

"Now moments": Lena

My patient, Lena, and I had the sort of experience in therapy that arises from a disruption of the status quo that brings a vivid passage of living. In a confident and assured voice, Lena called me asking for analysis, saying, "I think this is the best treatment for my problem, my intimacy problem". At our first meeting, her image matched the strong, direct voice I heard on the phone. She was tall and wore a beautifully tailored suit. She was graceful, professional, and corporate. I was surprised to learn she was a graduate student in philosophy, writing a thesis applying linguistic philosophy and philology to ancient texts. In a different, less assured tone, she vaguely described having trouble with men: "I get involved with men beneath me, so it's pretty unsatisfying".

Over the next few weeks, I witnessed a dramatic transformation in Lena. Her professional suit gave way to T-shirts and sweatpants and she became quiet and diffident. Instead of brimming confidence and independence, Lena turned into a shy graduate student with a deep sense of inadequacy. She now spoke tentatively and softly. It turned out she really sought therapy for brief, submissive experiences with men that were at times sexually masochistic. "I'd do anything to keep it going". More relevant, she felt there was something very bad and damaging in her that made others reject, mistreat, and abandon her. She sensed something violent inside her that she had to keep out of view, so she was on continual lockdown in the presence of other people. Lena had few friends or relationships because she knew she would drive them away or they would mistreat her. And when she tried to be in a relationship, she did indeed seem to drive people away—by her withdrawn, inaccessible presence. At times, she evoked sadistic treatment from the other person. Now, she never "did" anything. She lived a solitary life.

In analysis, she was demure and compliant. There was a striking absence of any sort of tension between us. But she was not boring. I found myself interested in the way her mind—or rather her intellect—worked. She came from an orthodox religious background and preserved some ties with that community. Although she had no passion for religion or religious experience, she had a deep understanding of religious texts and their history. She was passionate about ideas. She had a subtle and incisive way of forming questions and could turn over problems or issues in ways I found very interesting. This was the bond between us. She gave mini "lectures" and I listened attentively.

All the while, she described herself as "an alien"—"really strange and different from others"—with "something deeply wrong inside me" that had to be hidden. I wondered how we would find out about that hidden part of her that I had not sensed yet.

Gradually her life consisted exclusively of her intellectual work and her analysis, without any other contacts. I was worried. What was I missing? What was she doing with me? Was I meant to be her only companion in life to soothe her loneliness? Was this the only "relationship" she could manage, one safe and interminable?

Lena seemed perfectly content with me and the analysis, even when vacations and breaks disrupted our meetings. She had no obvious ambitions in the treatment, only to be in analysis with me. She settled in and filled the sessions with her thoughts about literature and philosophy and translations. I was the only person she talked to, except for rare contacts she had with her advisor. Because she was writing her thesis, that contact was minimal.

Lena became distressed whenever I disrupted the flow of the session and her musings by searching for something more personal and emotionally meaningful. It was strange though how undisturbed I was by this situation—only mildly frustrated and perplexed. I would describe my state as being partially drugged by the monotony and impersonal nature of the conversation. I did have the thought, "Life is but a dream". After a year of treatment, she had this dream:

I moved into the same apartment building you lived in, in a different flat that connected to yours. We visited each other in the evenings after work. There was a doorway between our flats, and we shared a wall.

This was a "simple" dream in her words. Her recounting of it was bland with no associations. It was as if she was telling me a fact and not a dream, something that was true and is really happening, like describing a trip to the grocers. In that matter-of-fact way of telling the dream, it brought out vividly the way she actually lived a symbiotic relationship with me.

This realization gave me an eerie feeling. There was something disturbing beneath the blandness in her telling, something a bit menacing in the way she moved in next to me in the apartment building and had full access to me. The physicality of the dream weighed on me. I didn't feel her dream was a symbolic expression but a picture of her living reality. In her mind, in her belief, we lived together, and we were psychically and physically connected.

Finally, I came awake to what was going on between us. I wanted to say something about her reality that analysis was about sharing a life together that satisfied all her needs for a relationship without difference or separation, and that she believed that I was content with this arrangement as well. I wanted to convey something of my understanding about this arrangement that in fact disturbed me. Its eeriness plagued me. I wanted to wake us up, not from a dream but a delusion.

But sometimes events (or an actual waking dream) do the talking. The arrangement of my office at that time helps to situate what happened. I had a small cottage behind my home where I worked. In my usual routine before seeing my first patient, I would go into the office to prepare it for the day. I'd then go back into my home and have my coffee and breakfast before returning for my first patient.

One early morning, following my usual habit, I entered my office to arrange it. I was startled and frightened by a dark form with their back to me, crouching in the corner near the bookshelf. I gasped— Oh!—and then Lena turned to look at me. I then angrily shouted, "What are you doing here!?" I was totally in an experience of fright. Immediately, I could see the impact my words and facial expression had on her. She cried, "I was just looking at your books", and ran out of the office.

A "now moment" often begins with a rupture—not one always so harrowing—when a disrupting event shakes up habitual ways of relating between analyst and patient. The dream was a hint, but then Lena unconsciously created a moment in which so many elements of what was transpiring between us became vividly manifest.

As I collected myself, I began to put together what happened and my reactions to it. I still had some time before seeing her in our session. I was trying to regain my balance. This moment of confrontation exposed feelings I had only partially known but were lurking at the fringe of my consciousness, gathering momentum after her dream. I never expected such a dramatic way of knowing of her, knowing her in such a physical and alarming way. Her intrusion felt violent. She did something to me in a real way—the intensity of my experience was beyond the actuality of the event. I was disturbed all the more by her blandness and innocence. It was clear she believed that my office was open to her, was her office, too, to enter any time she chose. I would never have entertained this idea as a possibility.

Yet, it was Lena's belief that she had access to my office and me at will. There was no divide. We shared a wall. Now I took in the concreteness of her belief that this was so—that her dream was not dreamt but a bit of materialized psychic reality. What seemed so truly strange was the simultaneous feeling of her innocence (her conscious experience of "I'm just looking") and her violent intrusion into me (unconscious, certainly for me, until that moment). The office we "shared" (this world needs to be qualified) was no longer a bland and tranquilized space but a dangerous one—for both of us, as my re-action had violence in it, too.

I knew that my anger and blatant revulsion at being so invaded were directly and forcefully expressed. I felt I had direct contact with what she described many times as her strangeness and weirdness. She felt like an alien and I felt her to be one. Now she painfully knew I encountered that strangeness and violence in her and I imagined what that must be like for her.

When we met an hour later, she was clearly shaken and tearful. My heart, too, was racing and I did not know what would happen. I knew I startled her as much as she startled me. I didn't lose sight of that. But I was emotionally, physically revved up in anticipation of seeing her. As we talked, I calmed down and took an interest again in her experience. I came to understand that what was foremost for her was the *anticipated* confirmation of her "alienness". The shock of my expression, though disturbing, made sense to her. She anticipated this clear recognition on my part. In the mix-up of experience and phantasy, she felt my anger was aimed (appropriately) at something deep in her. Her experience began with my face and angry words that matched her sense of herself in the eyes of others—a perfect fit.

The session began as follows:

P: I see you're not angry now. That is a relief ... I can't say what I was thinking today. I wasn't thinking. I don't think you know this, but I've gone into your office many times before our session to look at your books, even to lay on the couch. I liked being there very much. It's quiet and peaceful. That seemed OK to me—right?—better than waiting in that little room that is so cold and neutral—there's nothing of you there. I never thought it was wrong. But I never imagined you'd see me there because I arrive so early for my appointment ... Maybe I did have a feeling it was crossing some line but, somehow, I could ignore it. I sort of had to ... this is weird, but it mattered a lot—I was getting a lot from it, as if you were there ... I feel I've done something to end things here ...

A: No, I don't think so. But it was a real shock for me to find you there. You believed you were doing something natural. Now I see that you were really living here with me, deriving sustenance from that. I just didn't know that. But when I saw you there, it shocked and scared me. You saw that shock and anger, even fear ...

P: That I'm despicable and parasitic!

A: I don't feel that way. But I have the feeling that how I discovered this is important—that your reality is very different from mine. I have strong reactions hearing that you come in here unannounced, making yourself at home here. I see now and had inklings that you were making our relationship and the analysis your whole life. I guess it's not so extraordinary that you would do this, or at least want to do this, to have that sort of experience in my office.... It might even be easier to get what you need here when I'm not physically present. But the way it happened is important. It really woke us up!

P: I feel so bad, it's scary seeing you act that way ... I never thought you'd mind, but then I never thought ... you'd know. I never imagined you had that in you—toward me—I feel strange. Something *déjà vu* in this. I mean, I usually can manage to be cool with you but underneath.... And I can get people to be very angry and hurt me. And that happened with you.

A: Today, for me to know your need to live here, to actually live here, and that my separate existence is not registered—this is important for us to see. You had to show it, live it with me, communicate this to me.

Even though Lena knew her intrusion caused my reaction, it still startled her because she was doing something that flowed naturally from her sense of the reality of our symbiotic relationship. Her world bordered on a delusion. In the following session, she asked herself how could she assume that forays into my office were OK with me? How could she assume she knew how I'd feel about it? Why hadn't she mentioned it? Whatever had been my interpretations of what happened at that powerfully disruptive moment, it was her curiosity about my reactions that ruptured, for her, the delusional dream she was living in. The reality of our separate existence could be denied until that moment.

I subsequently learned that there was a considerable amount of physical abuse in her relationship with her mother. This fact in her life had not previously been important enough for her to relay to me. It was more accessible in our conversation when she realized that she lived this out with men. She recalled some violent experiences that were similar to what occurred with us, where she evoked rage in a man while feeling innocent and oblivious.

Lena continued to be distressed by the look on my face. This was a portal into more embodied memories. We came back to this image many times before she recounted memories of her mother's rages, how her face looked, and how she learned to provoke them, even when quite small. It took some time to have another image of me than my angry, frightened face. Previously she saw my benevolent, warm presence as giving her permission to have access to me in any way she wanted. She believed that I would completely give myself over to her, and she to me. My entire attention would be devoted to her and her alone. She did not question this. It was a fact. And this way of being together repaired what she felt was so damaged in her.

I will not go into all the rippling effects of the "now moment" in the vignette and how dramatically the flow of an analytic relationship can change in such a moment. At the core of this shift was the revelation of an emotional truth, in her, and between us. She slowly grasped her intense need to get inside of and merge with me. In that effort, she could rid herself of a sense of her own separateness and the fear that comes from a separate existence. For Lena, feeling psychically separate meant being in danger. She might be seen and attacked.

In her mind, the merger with me allowed for a place of safety and protection—something absent in her childhood. She believed I would allow for this merged life, in the space (body/office) I provided. Of course, she did not articulate this or be really conscious of it. She just knew it to be true and what she needed.

With this delusion disrupted, a different emotional field evolved. We were both roused from our shared waking dream, and there was a palpable sense of strangeness and separateness between us. Even the sensory qualities of her presence and the office changed. The objects in the room appeared more defined (or I was there to notice them), and her very being seemed quite childlike, like a young girl coming over for a sleepover. But that seeming innocence covered the "strangeness" and "eeriness" of a psychotic delusion of merger that now made me very uncomfortable. I felt strongly that I did not know her—that the fabric of our relationship before this shift was very thin and colorless. Although she referred to herself as an alien and strange from the beginning, I had not wanted to see or feel that in her, and had interpreted these feelings away as a horrible internal object persecuting her. Although there was some truth in this, this view protected me from the impact of a psychotic presence within her. I was not ready to live out or take in it. In a moment of mutual shock, I could no longer deny this. I took it in, bodily registering it, and was disturbed by her invasiveness that she lived out in a secret world before each session. Making it actual gave me access to the emotional current between us that I had shut off.

Lena was now lost with me with no sense of what analysis was really for—if not to provide a complete world in which to live and be provided for and made safe as an end in itself. She eventually recognized and could put into words her wish to merge and cease to exist as a separate person because being separate and noticed was so dangerous. Over time, we understood that any sense of separateness had been extinguished early on in her childhood, as she made her way into the mind and body of another person. Perhaps now, separateness and development might be possible. For that to occur she would need to experience "on-going-ness" and my unobtrusive presence in developing a sense of herself.

Theories of "now moments": Donald Stern

Encountering Lena in my office began a heightened passage of living and perceiving internal and external reality within the relationship. The moment was tumultuous and completely surprising (to our conscious minds).

In his book, *The Present Moment in Psychotherapy and Everyday Life* (2004), Stern creates a typology of shared experience within a temporal framework. He presents the language of subjective time in the "present" and "moment". For Stern, an experience only can happen now. Yet, he says, "It is remarkable how little we know about experience that is happening right now" (p. 3). Stern has a lot to tell us about what an experience is by looking at what is happening in the "now"—the present moment: "We are *subjectively alive and conscious only now* ... now is when we directly live our lives" (p. 3). I would add that when we feel alive in an "experience", a present moment, it brings us to an awareness that we are living *and* that we are aware of living and that we exist. Note the linked terms of vitality and conscious. A present moment engages our awareness and brings our *self* onto the stage: "It is me going through this". This also contrasts with dissociated or habitual states that do not entail the subjective sense of a present moment.

Stern uses the Greek word *Kairos,* for now moments to refer to an intersubjective moment of opportunity. He writes,

> The central idea about moments of change is this: During these moments a *"real experience" emerges, somewhat unexpectedly.* This experience happens between two (or more) people. It is about their relationship ... This jointly lived experience is mentally shared, in the sense that each person intuitively partakes in the experience of the other. (p. 22; my italics)

Stern puts in quotations "real experience" to indicate a real happening between two people that each is aware of, something concretely happening that each can refer to, such as the encounter Lena and I had. What occurs concerns each in a relationship that is shared; each *intuitively* (i.e., through "implicit relational knowledge" and non-verbal communication) knows something of the other's experience in a mutual way. I had a vivid sense of Lena's emotional state, as she certainly did of mine. This is not the run-of-the-mill occurrence in analysis—having such immediate access to another.

Stern believes "now moments" form the axis of change. He theorizes that intersubjectivity "is a condition of humanness", where "patients want to be known and to share what it feels like to be them" (p. 86). This need aims to define, maintain, or reestablish self-identity and self-cohesion—to make contact with or strengthen a known part of ourselves. Following Stern's line of thinking, perhaps Lena found a way to tell me about herself in a way I could not ignore (as I had been) in the unconscious intersubjective matrix of understanding. Stern observes that, "These special moments, when they suddenly arise, threaten the status quo of the relationship and challenge the intersubjective field" (p. 208). In spite of our defenses and inclinations to collude, Stern believes, and I strongly agree, that we are always also pursuing an enlargement of subjectivity in relationships: a greater sense of self-awareness and self-possession—when we find the right partner. Stern beautifully describes the therapeutic process this way:

> A therapy session (or any intimate dialogue) is made up of a series of present moments that are driven forward by the desire of this sort for intersubjective contact and an *enlargement* of the shared intersubjective field. Intersubjectivity is a primary motive in this movement. (p. 207)

We seek sharing our minds with others in order to expand a sense of who we are, and we are willing to brook the tumultuous uncertainty of present moments for that opportunity. In that light, it is not so surprising that Lena grasped the opportunity for emotional growth despite the degree of pain and possible re-traumatization involved.

Unexpectedly encountering Lena in my office before the session began a heightened passage of living and perceiving internal and external reality within our relationship. The moment was tumultuous and completely surprising (to both of our conscious minds). That one intense moment became a vital source of disruption that we worked with over and over. There was first shock and disruption for her. This gradually gave way to acceptance, curiosity, and surrender rather than traumatic repetition. She could apprehend her way of living out a non-existent life, especially if she could, in her words, "find a host". When thrown out of that world, there was nothing to replace it. And this was the tough, ongoing work of analysis. Both of us had to be aware of this as an opportunity and to resist falling back into our prior ways of being so that the possibility for real existence for her could be seized.

Going-on-ness: David

David was a 50-year-old man who started work with me, suffering from incapacitating anxiety. In his younger days, he was a successful athlete. Now, he organized his life around strenuous competitive exercise, spending many hours before and after work and on weekends running, swimming, and lifting. He was always preparing for the next challenge—like (in fact) riding over the Alps from Switzerland to Italy on a mountain bike. He would say, "This is the only thing that makes me calm … otherwise I'm pretty much a wreck". He could not pinpoint the source of his anxieties although he struggled with this most of his life: "I'm just agitated whenever my mind is free". He seemed successful in most of his endeavors because of his intense competitive nature and capacity for work. But he drifted uncomfortably as he moved from job to job, relationship to relationship, endlessly searching for something better. "When I walk into a restaurant I immediately scan for the best table. But, even if I get it, I'm looking around to see what I might have missed. I do that with everything". Not surprisingly, he suffered from insomnia. He dreaded the moment when the lights go out and his mind lights up.

David watched me like a hawk. He needed to locate me and know what I was thinking most of the time. He plied me with questions on a wide range of topics: what I thought of his symptoms, his mind, his background, and my background, interests, and family. He interrogated my thinking in the moment: "What are you thinking?" "What's on your mind now?" Though the answer to some of these questions mattered somewhat, the point was for me to do a lot of the talking to fill the space. He would have liked to make the analysis about me in order to know me, where I was coming from, who I am, while feeling relief from introspection and living within his own mind.

But watching me closely had another meaning as well. He needed to reassure himself that I was here with him and had not left him. Organizing the sessions this way gave him the only safety he found, at last in the early phase of analysis. I could not discern anything that evolved because every session was like the last. It was about survival from moment to moment, session to session. Ongoing time was compressed into moments of anxiety and the momentary relief he found in locating me.

I tolerated this mild interrogation. I did not experience it as aggressive or intrusive. I could sense the extreme level of anxiety that this was meant to contain. I was not too bothered by this setup and in no hurry. He did allow me to speculate on his world and his worries, but I had to do the talking. I don't think it was what I said that mattered as much as that I said things to him in an actively engaged way. Over several months, in an almost imperceptible way, moments of silence began. When his speech trailed off into momentary silence, I felt a palpable sense of calm in the room. These silences stretched out but would eventually be broken by self-castigation: "I'm doing nothing here", "You must be so bored". I responded that I was in no way bored and that what I thought was happening was very important. I did not ask him what was happening in the silences, which would only be a demand on my part for him to do something in response.

I don't want to paint a picture of a clear and easy path toward a therapeutic regression and going-on-ness. There was a lot of back and forth, from his questioning me to falling into silence. Yet, things moved in that direction in such a subtle way that some long periods of time would stretch out before I noticed that he was in fact silent. I felt in good contact with him and content during these silent periods. Eventually, he would remark that "I never could be with myself before like this"; or "I'm assuming you're there". I felt like a parent watching over a child heading toward sleep and their dream world.

How had David's internal world become tolerable and his anxiety lessen? David could arrive at "going-on-ness" because a great deal of analytic work had been done. His felt sense of my being with him and tolerating his anxiety furthered the work. He used me—my non-demanding presence, my relative openness, and adaptation to his needs—to start to live within an atmosphere of safety. To turn his attention inward and outward to a subjective world, he had to have a sense that I would be there interested and attentive, without needing to work at it or keep track of me. He could take my presence for granted.

Going-on-ness requires the analyst's provision of a facilitating or holding environment. For the analyst, there is strain in containing emotional states, so as not to intrude one's subjectivity on the patient. It is not a constant state either, as there are times in these regressed states that David needed to make direct contact with me. This contact momentarily opened up a more mutual, though curtailed, interaction, as in rapprochement: "Are you still here? Good. I'm off again".

Theories of going-on-ness: Winnicott and Balint

Winnicott's work on the development of the True Self relates to the experience of going-on-ness. This area of experience precedes object relations, meaning the analyst is in the position of a "subjective object" and not experienced as having a separate existence. In infancy, to paraphrase Winnicott (1986), the mother *is* so the infant can *be*. "Is" means a present adaptive relatedness without sharp personal boundaries. "Be" means being. In this mode, time and experience are open-ended and non-intrusive, as the analyst provides an atmosphere or "medium" of non-impingement for the patient's self to emerge and develop. An emergent self is protected by the "holding environment", a metaphorically physical offering. In analysis, Winnicott describes a "regression to dependence", a return to this developmental state, a timeless experience with a subjective object.

The therapeutic action in this mode allows for the building of a stronger sense of self, self-presencing, the first gestures of creativity, play, and spontaneity. It is an amazing moment when the patient becomes aware that they are not occupied with the state of mind of the analyst and not responsive, but turned toward their own self-states, desires, and feelings—the beginning of going-on-being.

There are long periods, as with David, in which the patient is neither in the first nor second temporal mode of experience. In this fragile state, every moment is treacherous and precarious, like beads on a string—the string representing periods of anxiety and non-existence. If this can be managed the patient slowly begins to build on moments of going-on-ness, and the spaces in the string get shorter and shorter, as happened with David.

Balint's (1968) work focuses us on the analyst's personal qualities required to sustain a patient in a state of going-on-ness. He emphasizes the need for the analyst to be unobtrusive and ordinary. In addition to "unobtrusive and ordinary", the analyst "must do everything in his power, not to become, or to behave as, a separate-sharply contoured object" (p. 167).

With this provision the patient can then, according to Balint,

> ... develop a primitive relationship in the analytic situation corresponding to his compulsive pattern and maintain it in undisturbed peace till he can discover the possibility of new forms of object relationship, experience them, and experiment with them. (p. 166)

In order for the patient to find these new forms, the analyst is then willing to "accept the role of a primary object whose chief function is recognizing, and being with, his patient" (p. 172). Balint clarifies what he has in mind:

> Emphatically, this does not mean that in these periods the analyst's role becomes negligible or is restricted to sympathetic passivity; on the contrary, his presence is most important, not only in that he must be felt as present but must be all the time at the right distance—neither so far that the patient might feel lost or abandoned, nor so close that the patient might feel encumbered and unfree—in fact, at the distance that corresponds to the patient's actual need; *in general the analyst must know what are his patient's needs, why they are what they are, and why the fluctuate and change.* (p. 179; my italics)

I italicized the final phrase to show how words can fail in this temporal mode. We have to intuit the patient's experience and *act* rather than interpret. Why? Balint argues that in regression to the basic fault, "words have become unreliable" and the analyst should act "by sincerely giving up, for the time being, any attempt at forcing the patient back to the verbal level" (p. 177).

With David, that was very important. His silence *was* the eloquent communication of the way he was living at that moment. He did not need understanding or interrupting.

For Winnicott and Balint, the object-relational and intersubjective dimensions are less important. Both theorists focus on patients traumatized in early development by various forms of environmental failure and impingement and fracture of the infant's ongoing sense of self-experience. The analyst's presence is required and could not happen without it. But the space is not "two minds sharing", but, rather, one mind at the service of the other, such that the patient can eventually take the analyst's mind for granted. This analytic way of being allows for and enhances the experience of selfhood. For example, David's subjectivity in the first part of therapy is not enhanced through "now moments" but through going-on-ness. The analyst role is not one of a passive bystander, as Balint emphasizes. The work of accompaniment and attunement, finding the right way of being with this particular person at this moment, is a creative, playful, and improvisational activity. So, I agree with Balint that the presence of the analyst in holding is "felt", does not disappear, is never not relevant, but it is secondary.

David had long periods of analysis in which silence and a sense of peace reigned in the session—as long as I did not disrupt him. He seemed to be able to manage the separations because I really didn't exist for him outside of our time together. Inevitably, the process of entering into and maintaining states of going-on-ness is disrupted, as previously dissociated aspects of experience, a sector of non-experience comes to be experienced with the analyst in "now moments". The patient becomes the subject rather than the observer of what happened to him. This can be extremely disorganizing and involve great suffering, demanding reliability and consistency and self-containing on the analyst's part.

Here is how this happened with David. Through the long period in analysis in which silence was the main event, David cultivated a stronger sense of his self and existence. But then something turned. Once in a relaxed state in the silence, memories emerged. Until then, the facts of his early life were a matter of facts and not feeling. Now was different. I learned in an emotional way, as David did in the act of telling, that his mother had several bouts of major depression beginning in David's early childhood. She was hospitalized on three occasions, once for at least six months. The father was a busy businessman who traveled a lot, so during two bouts of David's mother's depression, he was sent to live with relatives. He said he'd never really let himself think about—feel through—these events in his early childhood. As this part of his life come up in him now, he would become more anxious with me. We went through many cycles of this. He would live through traumatic abandonment experiences as "now moments"—"claimed his history", as he put it—but then fear my disappearance. Once he re-established my presence, he would calmly sink into silence, a return to our way of "going on ness", only for this cycle to begin again.

The analyst's participation in two modes of time

In conclusion, I will now step back to consider the analyst's way of engagement and mindset in order to be present in each temporal mode of experience. The analyst's basic attitude and way of being with patients maintain and support the dialectic between "now" moments and "going on-ness".

There are particular challenges in the mode of "going-on-ness". The mindset and personal qualities of the analyst are presence, availability, and attunement at the bodily level, in order to find the right form of accompaniment to the patient *senses*. This is an active process. Also involved, as Slochower (1996, 2013) emphasizes, is the analyst's capacity to contain his or her emotional responses, work through painful, confusing, and uncomfortable states, and, often, to endure emotional deprivation and loneliness. We may be tempted to use the patient to contain our discomfort (through interpretation or excessive self-disclosure), or to shut down in ways that emotionally abandon the patient. Finally, we need to surrender to the particular and intense needs of the patient that may feel self-depriving, even masochistic. Having a view of the course of treatment and an accurate model of the interaction is necessary.

During disruptions caused by "now moments", another set of qualities is needed in us. In these moments, when we as well as the patient are implicated, it often becomes very personal—in ways opposite of "on-going" time. We may feel exposed and vulnerable. Our capacity to receive the patient's observations and reactions in a nondefensive, open way is essential. This may not be pleasant for us. It is most challenging when we are implicated realistically in the disruption and the suffering of the patient. Our knowledge, acceptance, and ownership of our actions are especially crucial at these times. As Stern writes, these moments require "a response that is too specific and personal to be a known technical maneuver" (p. 911). It requires "a personal signature that shares the analyst's subjective state" (p. 912).

Notes

1 I discuss this subject further in Chapter 11, "Process and Non-Process".

Chapter 10

Moments of transformation and beauty

There are memorable moments between us and our patients that transform each of us. The asymmetry of care is maintained but there is an interpenetration of feeling and deep rapport that widens and deepens our sense of self and how we know each other. Subtle transformation occurs that makes us ready for the "moment" of concrete, vivid, transformational experience. To do this, we become available when we come to inhibit the world of the patient, or have the patient's world live inside of us, however difficult.

Previously, I described two modes of experiencing time and the potential therapeutic experiences that can follow. Now I will discuss an intense transformative experience that goes beyond "now moments" in several important respects. The experience involves both participants in an interpenetrated way. This kind of moment involves a deep rapport that transforms the self and expands the experience beyond the present moment because of its enduring effects. And the quality of the experience—or whether it is possible—depends on experiences in early childhood. These moments harken back to experiences of attunement and understanding and sharing between child and parent before words and concepts. One analytic aim with certain patients is to revive these feeling-states of this earlier time or to initiate this for them for the first time.

Psychoanalytic and philosophic writers, including myself,[1] have thought of these transforming moments as "aesthetic experiences" and "moments-of-beauty". Later in this chapter, I will bring in this language to describe these transformational experiences, offering a richly poetic language for its phenomenology and the emotions

DOI: 10.4324/9781003208518-10

involved. This perspective also draws on experiences of union and rapport in early childhood between parent and child relevant to our work with adults.

What do I mean by a transformational experience? Both subjects are altered in lasting ways so that their subjectivity is widened and enriched. There is a sense of shared emotion—perhaps a "communion"—when both analyst and patient are vitalized, destabilized, and there is an intensification of feeling and imagination and a loosening of the boundaries of self and other. There is a letting go of ways that hold the self together defensively and protect us from the emotional influence of others. As both analyst and patient have established conscious and unconscious defensive ways of distancing and self-protection in engagement with others, this transformational experience loosens or breaks this down. Hagmen (2002), in writing about beauty, describes moments when both are "known, found, penetrated, and recognized" (p. 670). Something powerful comes together between us, a deep intimate connection that has staying power. There might even be sense of something basic and primal that is re-found in the current relationship recalling earlier life experiences. At that moment, we might say to ourselves, "This feels beautiful", or "This really is beautiful".

For these moments to arise, a change in the emotional field has already occurred. We are available and make space inside us for the patient, which requires emotional work. The patient may already be benefiting from this openness in us. When the transformational moment occurs, it gathers together elements of preconscious and unconscious experience in the form of vividly lived experience.

The effect of these moments lasts—perhaps because of the internal changes that preceded it—and are internalized as a creative source of inspiration and vitality. Because passion, love, and curiosity are part of this, it is pursued by both patients and ourselves. It may be the inspiration to live more meaningfully and creatively. We pursue experiences that alter us.

There are particular, consistent sensorial aspects of these moments that I am familiar with. I notice vivid perceptual and somatosensory qualities, like a radiant quality of light, a sense of warmth and well-being, a freshness and feeling of renewal of thought and emotion, a greater fluidity of my movements and gestures. These emotions coexist with the disruption and turbulence that attend the loss of protection that habit provides. The content of these moments may involve loving images or painful memories and scary impulses and fantasies, while the overall feeling is life-affirming. It feels real and creative. As this palpable world is shared with the patient, one senses a shift in the flow of relating, a greater sense of intimacy and closeness in the common shared current of feeling. I am giving myself over to something new in myself and toward the patient, as is the patient, and we both implicitly acknowledge this.

Transformational experience with Barry

Barry is the patient I described earlier regarding mutual play. Here, I want to go more deeply into the sudden emergence of a transformational moment between us to show the unexpected way this arises and, with it, sensorial vividness, feelings of aliveness, curiosity, and wonder. I also want to show my emotional work necessary for this to happen. By working through emotional obstacles that open me up to Barry's world, both Barry and I are changed.

Barry is a male architect who sought treatment for his inability to be productive in work. It took him a long time to produce drawings. The few dreams he brought in featured inanimate objects and impoverished landscapes. In one dream he wandered along the side of a dry creek picking up and carefully examining stones as he went along, then putting them down—not to collect, only to observe. He was absorbed in this activity.

From the beginning, I had a feeling of deadness and hopelessness in his presence. I noticed how I anxiously moved things along, asking questions, bringing things up—trying to bring to life the desolate landscape of dry stones in his dream. I was trying to revive someone who seemed barely alive. Eventually, I commented on the nature of our interaction, noting his lethargy and need for me to invigorate him. Whenever I would mention the atmosphere he lived in and perhaps his wish for me to enliven him, there might be an initial moment of aliveness, an association to his past, or to his fear of boring me, but the pattern invariably reverted to a pallid stasis again. There might be a novel sense that there was more to him and to life than tedious and odious burdens, but this, too, would recede back to a familiar place in him—and me. My own state of mind oscillated between hopelessness, frustration, and boredom—with spurts of hopefulness that dried up only to repeat this cycle again. This is not a productive passage of going-on-ness but the opposite—stasis and impasse. I was caught in my own need to change the situation and so I was blocked from being available and allowing for an open circuit of emotional communication. I could not take in, live within his internal world. I was impervious to him. This kind of internal impasse comes from many sources—my transferences, my inability to experience and contain shared emotional states, and an overlapping of our defensive object-relational patterns.

I began an internal process of surrender and mourning. I recognized my transference to him: my need for repair and a familiar sense of futility. I could also recognize certain states in me that were a reflection of his internal world of paralysis. That is, what he did to his objects he also did to himself, and I began to empathize with him— really share the same emotions. However, these insights did not fully alter my agitated, constrained way of being with him because the intensity of his deadness overwhelmed me with such a strong sense of hopelessness and withdrawal. I often found myself doodling random images on a pad with no clear value or meaning. I might characterize this cycle as founded on a *shared* unconscious assumption that we enacted based on feeling that contact with another person would never last or matter and a deadening stasis must always be. But, I also had to face that I contributed to the agitated, frustrated atmosphere, recognize this, and accept it.

As time went on a shift occurred as a result of my surrendering to my experience of frustration and agitation. I gained more capacity to bear it. This began, as it often does, with me asking simple questions to myself, such as, "What makes this deadness and hopelessness so unbearable?" I found myself more alert to sensory aspects of our meetings: the light at a particular time of day, the way the sound of our voices echoed in the room, , and so on. I did not know exactly why this shift occurred. I felt internal emotional work going on in me that shifted my embodied state and widened my attention into a new register. And something was developing *between* us. I want to emphasize that had I urged myself to practice "free-floating attention" or to "eschew memory and desire", I would not have arrived at this place of widening attention and surrender, which cannot be willed.

To paraphrase Heidegger, I moved from "waiting for" to "waiting on" the experience between us—an indication of surrendering to my agitated state and to his feelings of deadness.

Borgogno (2014) refers to Ferenczi's idea of the analyst needing to "become the patient" in order to cure him, that "transformation of the patient depends unequivocally on the willingness of the analyst to be *transformed in and by the analytic process*" (p. 303; italics in original). Part of my transformational process is allowing myself to be inhabited by Barry's world and to let go of my need to know, even feel like the analyst I want to be. In this regard, Borgogno emphasizes that

> ... the analyst must be an individual able to take upon himself and to contain the patient's most primitive qualities and, in so doing, *disidentify* himself with his identity as an analyst in order to make space for the other. (p. 307)

Bollas (1983) makes a similar point:

> Provided the analyst can tolerate the necessary loss of his personal sense of identity within the clinical situation, I think he is more able to achieve the necessary *process identity* which allows him to receive and register the patient's transferences. (p. 5)

Both writers focus on the analyst's process of change through the loosening of boundaries through , in effect, to "become" the patient. This transformation is necessary for the patient's transformation. With Barry, I tolerated and inhabited feelings of agitated deadness—*paralysis agitans*—where I feel a sort of illness take me over. This makes room for something new in both of us to emerge in the relational field.

It did not seem to matter what Barry talked about or what his affect was, all of which usually lacked much variation. The heightened sensory experience was enough: I felt content just as things were. As I went through this —surrendering—I felt a receptivity to what *is*, a hospitality even, which felt, paradoxically, as Bollas and Borgogno describe, a loss of my sense of purpose as an analyst.

Nevertheless, this was an indication that I was now present and available to him. What I let go of was my need to enliven, to be an enlivening object. I also accepted the real possibility that the patient may not come alive in my presence. Simultaneously with this internal process, the sensory qualities of the room continued to become more vivid. Acceptance led to aliveness.

Then a transformational moment arrived unbidden. The session began in the usual way, with Barry telling me about some concerns for his sons, and his worry that he was growing older and had not been a great model for them. This account was not without interest. Yet, it felt like a diversion from something more primal, elemental, something occurring in the embodied register. It was a stormy day outside, bouts of heavy rain alternating with silence. I noticed toward the end of the session a particularly heavy downpour. As I relaxed back in my chair, I heard the rain tapping on the window. The patter made a nice sound with its irregular soft rhythm. I was captured by the sound that I knew Barry could hear as well. Was he affected? I felt content and the office seemed to me a safe, warm, and lovely place for both of us. I said, "Listen to that rain". My comment was spontaneously given.

After a few minutes' silence, Barry said:

> In ninth grade, I built a sailboat … and I was so proud of that boat. I raced it on the lake nearby. It really planed, keeled, and I was so excited. It had yellow sails and a red spinnaker too... I loved that … I felt so free … It took most of a summer to build it and some kids I knew at the lake started coming around to watch me or help. I was no longer an outsider. Up to that point in my life, most of what I did I did alone—my reading, my science projects, my drawing. And I never talked about what I did. This time I had help and companions. The main thing was the feeling of sailing in my own boat with my new friends.

I was startled by his comments in this new emotionally metaphoric register. I had never heard him express anything like this—its content, its dream-like presence, or its aliveness and vitality and connection to others. His response to my observation about the rain was entirely unexpected.

Up to that moment, I had never felt so "with" him. I could feel the wind, the flow of color of the sails, the angle the boat took in the water. His picture was alive in me. I felt deeply, tenderly for this creative and lonely child who finally found companionship and aliveness through his own creative efforts of building and skill with the boat.

I sensed a similar feeling in Barry. He was opening up a part of himself to me, to be "known, found, penetrated, and recognized". There was a palpable sensation of sharing emotion—his emotion and my emotional response.

It is difficult to parse who started what between us. Before my comment about the rain, I was pervaded by a feeling of warm intimacy, coziness even, and well-being. Did this just come from my world or was there something we were quietly sharing together deeply? Even before this session, I had worked through some of my constriction with him that, by doing so, was an invitation into a shared world metaphorically pictured in the office-boat. If the subtle shift in key went from my availability to a shared emotional atmosphere, then that sharing allowed for my spontaneous comment. In giving myself over to this spontaneous gesture, I had a feeling Barry would understand it, feel it at many levels, and do something with it. It was not a non-sequitur. That confidence meant we were already approaching a moment of unison. We could speak in a concrete and symbolic dream language. In retelling this now, I feel the limits of language to grasp this experience.

Although the sailboat was not referred to directly, the following sessions felt alive. His narrative came from a more vivid core inside him. What changed was not the content of his narratives so much as their emotional texture and the atmosphere in the room that we lived in, and that was in us. He communicated his inner world colorfully. A desolate landscape changed to one that was full of color, water, movement, companionship. He noted that something felt different inside. In one session, when he felt particularly excited, he said the couch was "like a boat—we're sailing together", he laughed. I felt this, too, that we were together in a different world, that my experience with him was brimming with life, movement, and connection. In this period of shared transformational experience, what came up between us was compelling and worthy of careful attention and was sustained.

I considered whether to comment on the companionship he found with me. This question hinges on the sort of companionship we may be having at that moment. Yes, coming out of a schizoid, lonely world into a world of others is such a dramatic part of his boat story, as is building and sailing. But it's really the emotion now in the room between us that is happening and powerfully affecting. So, my comments went to the feeling between us, to the sense of excitement he conveyed, to his keen interest and curiosity in others, and to the way, the sensory feeling in the office brought up this sensory memory—I named the feelings and indicated that I shared them in some way, including the novelty of the moment.

In one moment during this period, after a relaxed silence between us, he casually got up from the couch, sat next to me, and showed me pictures he had taken with his phone. Again, this took me by complete surprise. Barry generally moved little on the couch. His gestures tended to be curtailed and his body rigid. This spontaneous gesture flowed from him. The pictures he showed me were of street scenes, glimpses of people in motion. In contrast to many of his dreams early in the analysis that were devoid of people, involving desert-like landscapes, these pictures had life. I did not know about his interest in photography. As he described the pictures, and I responded with lively associations, he noted how important this activity was to him: "It brings me into the world of people".

For a few weeks, the pictures became a focus, often leading to playful exchanges between us. Not only was a creative side of Barry available to him, but the two of us, in our exchanges, were creatively, playfully interacting. At times he would be the one to offer some meaningful observation, to which I associated in response to what I saw, adding something of my own sensibility to the conversation. He was energized by the interaction and continued to bring in new aspects of his life and interests. His greater sense of creativity—in himself and interpersonally—also enlarged the space for me to respond from my own experience. A shared conversation ensued, with our mutual interest in music and art as the vehicle for enjoying the vitality in each other.

In these ways of being together, sharing emotional states, and riffing off each other, the relationship itself was not a focus. It was a shared play that evolved from that first transformative moment—solidifying his creative ways of making and seeing, and, eventually, being.

How had Barry come to live in such a barren internal landscape? Why were dimensions of his vitality atrophied? Barry's early life matched his dismal internal landscapes. His father was a successful lawyer. Barry's primary memories of him were that he was either locked in his study working or frequently traveling on business, scarcely seeming to notice Barry and rarely sharing in family activities and vacations. Barry's mother was a high-strung, over-burdened obsessional woman who joylessly performed her tasks as mother and homemaker. She constantly complained about her husband and her life situation and the work at home. Barry remembers no warmth or pleasure in interacting with her, and no joy in her experience of him. He was part of her work and burden.

In this desolate childhood, Barry found respite in solitary activities: particularly drawing and building. He often took solitary walks in nature, taking a keen interest in the processes of the natural world. There was life *out there*—but it was beyond him. He enjoyed rare moments—like the sailing story—of pleasure and exploration and wonder with another. I think that a dearth of shared experiences, along with his identification with the deadness in his mother, led to a lack of vitality and bareness in him that profoundly affected his life. His experience shows, by its lack, the crucial importance, starting in earliest infancy, of a companion sharing emotion. But importantly, these emotions can be found in the analytic relationship.

Transformation and beauty

A shared aesthetic experience of beauty occurred in the analytic transformation initiated by the sound of rain and wind, when Barry and I became simultaneously alive, infused with each other's states and the world around us, equally penetrated by sounds and visual associations, living in the office-boat that continued beyond that moment into new ways of creative relating. The aesthetic perspective is rich in poetic, evocative imagery that comes close to capturing what eludes us in words. It also importantly grasps the sorts of emotions that accompany transformations. And, from a relational perspective, it emphasizes companionship. Primal aesthetic experiences form a foundation for future such experiences.

The emotional experience of beauty has been described in philosophy, psychology, and psychoanalysis. These endeavors illuminate aesthetic moments like those with Barry. In having an experience of beauty, we feel the mind cleared of haze and habit and the world arrives fresh, clear, and compelling. We feel deeply engaged, arrested, in a way that alters the "humdrum" or static world into one alive, rich in meaning, and full of possibilities. We experience a heightened sensory-perceptual awareness and expanded imaginative freedom. We lose our hold on the expected and the status quo, which can then turn traumatic, deadened, or dissociated states and shallow ways of living into something more integrated and vital. Many writers on beauty use words like "freeing", "destabilizing", "surrendering", "wondering", "challenging", "enlivening", "more than can be captured by concepts", "rightness", and "truth". As we go through such an experience, we might then use the term "beauty" to describe it, label it, and contain its intensity, such as, "That's really a thing of beauty!"

As Anne Carson (1965), an expert on beauty as well as on ecology, writes,

> Once the emotions have been aroused—a sense of the beautiful, the excitement of the new and unknown, a feeling of sympathy, pity, admiration, or love—then we wish for knowledge about the object of our emotional response. (p. 49)

Carson's description rings true to my experience with Barry when he began to speak about sailing. Yes, the excitement of the unknown was certainly there, but I also felt admiration and love and sadness (for the lonely child), and a strong wish to know more about this part of him.

This moment with Barry heralded a shift in the emotional climate moving forward beyond that moment, beyond that "now moment". American philosopher John Dewey (1934) in his *Art as Experience* uses the term "aesthetic experience" to describe a heightened, enlivening, and meaningful passage of living that transforms the self. His way of understanding this transformation is relevant to clinical work. When habit breaks down and we "undergo" (an important word for Dewey that captures a letting go and surrendering) an experience, there then follows a reorganization of the self. Dewey writes that

> ... "taking in" in any vital experience is something more than placing something on the top of consciousness over what was previously known. It involves *reconstruction* which may be painful. (p. 41; my italics)

In his picture of the evolution of self-establishment, Dewey provides a clear, overall theory of how emotional growth happens:

> Life itself consists in phases in which the organism falls out of step with the march of surrounding things and then recovers unison with it.... And, in a *growing life*, the recovery is never mere return to a prior state, for it is enriched by the state of disparity and resistance through which it has successfully passed. (p. 14; italics in original)

We are jolted out of a routine way of living, and in the process of reestablishing ourselves, we find new ways of being. The sailboat memory did not stop there with us. It set us on a new enlivened path, as Barry brought in and shared more of his creative experience. I was his companion in this and became more active with him as time went on.

The contemporary American philosopher Elaine Scarry (1995) also describes the transformation of self in the language of beauty:

> The beautiful thing seems incomparable, unprecedented, and that sense of being without precedence conveys a sense of newness and newborness of the entire world. (p. 22)

Although Scarry is not using Dewey's word "aesthetic", when she speaks of her "beautiful thing", she is describing transformation—when the world, both internal and external, is enlivened, born anew.

This moment is the "beautiful thing". She states in a more poetic way Dewey's idea that "the conception that objects have fixed and unalterable values is precisely the prejudice from which art emancipates us" (pp. 100–101). It is not only art that does this but psychoanalysis as well, emancipating both patient and analyst from objects "fixed and unalterable".

Continuing this perspective, Armstrong and Detweiler-Bedell (2008) elaborate the phenomenology of emotional transformation by focusing on beauty and its relationship to learning and truth. The authors write,

> Beauty presages understanding before one's cognitive faculties can be certain that an object or experience will yield any coherent conceptual representation. (p. 305)

> ... beauty is an exhilarating feeling that something complex, perhaps to the point of being profound, might yield to understanding. (p. 312)

This is an important statement. Transformational experience exceeds our cognitive understanding, but a new form of understanding might arise. They continue:

> Instead of protecting one's knowledge against the threat of inconsistency, one welcomes novelty for its promise of yielding understanding ... in ordinary cognition, one smothers uncertainty with a familiar concept to avoid confusion. (p. 320)

Psychoanalytic writers provide a developmental-relational perspective, bringing us back to early transforming experiences of union and attunement with the primary object. For example, Rose (2004) writes:

> Where does aesthetic responsiveness arise? A prototype may well lie in the nonverbal emotional rapport and empathy of the earliest infant-parent interplay. (p. 1)

What is laid down and inscribed in infancy becomes the substrate for our capacity to experience the emotions of beauty later in life.

Authors from different analytic theoretical perspectives speak of unison, union, rapport, and oneness in the original dyad as the enduring wellspring of aliveness and creative living. These early transformative experiences establish a rich well of emotional memory inscribed more in the body-mind than in mental representation.

Klein (1957/1975) sees the mother as an active participant in providing intuitive understanding and care. She emphasizes the mother's emotional provision that powerfully affects the young child, offering love, understanding, unity, and, ultimately, happiness. In a remarkable passage, Klein shifts Freud's metapsychology from instinct to love, from physical satisfaction to emotional bliss:

> Freud described the infant's bliss in being suckled as a prototype of sexual gratification. In my view experiences constitute non only the basis for gratification but of all later happiness and make possible the feeling of unity with another person; such unity means being fully understood, which is essential for every happy love relation or friendship. At best, such understanding needs no words to express it, which demonstrates its derivation from the earliest closeness to the mother in the preverbal stage. (p. 188)

The infant's needs and states of mind are understood by the mother in communion without words. This is bliss. Mutual love comes from this way of understanding and being understood, forming a basic connection in an ever-deepening way. From this mutual love begins the drive for the child to know the love object more fully, especially the mother's body—the object of the child's phantasy as well. Klein stresses the profound importance of this infantile experience, as "the basis of all later happiness".

Bollas (1978) emphasizes the primary object's *active* rapport as a real presence. He goes to the roots of transforming experience. For Bollas, in elaborating Winnicott, the "aesthetic moment" is a "deep rapport", a "generative illusion" of fitting with the object that lays down existential rather than cognitive memory. Bollas's emotional descriptions of unison are "uncanny" even "reverential", and "outside cognitive coherence". They are "registered through the experience of being, rather than mind". Bollas, like Klein, focuses on the transforming aspect of maternal care:

The first human aesthetic, characterized by deep rapport of subject and object, underlies all aesthetic experience where the subject feels captured in a reverential moment with an aesthetic object. (p. 20)

Bollas believes these experiences are instantiated in existential memory and are the font of later emotions of beauty. He vividly elaborates upon this, saying:

The mother's idiom of care and the infant's experience of this handling is the first aesthetic. It is the most profound occasion where the content of the self is formed and transformed by the environment. (p. 386)

Clinically, Bollas's emphasis on the transformational action of the mother's care and holding are relevant to both therapeutic action and what can go wrong in development. Like Klein, these transformational aesthetic experiences form the basis of later happiness and the ability to surrender—even seek—reverential feelings of wonder and awe.

The clinical relevance of this developmental-aesthetic perspective is several-fold. First, aesthetic language gets at the profound experience of the "bliss", "awe", "wonder", "excitement and vitalization", and "reverence" that arise from the transformational effect of deep emotional rapport with primary objects—feelings that go beyond Stern's description of "now moments".

What do clinicians see in patients when this "basis of all later happiness" did not occur. How do we help them? Writers emphasize the determining effect of this experience on later development, in positive and negative ways. We see people who lack the capacity for this emotional experience or are highly defended against it. As a result, their life is limited. Experiences of renewal and creative inspiration may be curtailed. Perhaps, the tumult and instability are too intense and threatening. Perhaps, there has never been another person to share and help them through these choppy waters. Perhaps, there has been a lifelong pattern of damping down excitement and curiosity—emotions that were not crucial to their survival. Knowing something about the development of the capacity to experience beauty helps us to identify specific sorts of interferences and to find ways to participate in sessions that might give the patient a chance to experience this emotion and develop. My work with Barry is an example of the way he recovered these essential alive parts of himself through the intimacy and rapport we were able to share.

I conclude this discussion of aesthetic experience, beauty, and transformation with Carson (1965), who writes:

> If a child is to keep alive his inborn sense of wonder ... he needs the companionship of at least one adult who can share it, rediscovering the joy, excitement, and mystery of the world we live in. (p. 44)

I want to underscore Carson's noting the "need for companionship" as a necessary element in the continuing development of feelings of beauty. Not only do we need this companionship throughout our lives, but the analyst may offer this companionship for the first time in some patient's experience. This relational dimension opens the possibility for transformation in the analytic situation, in which the analyst actively participates in interactions and in an intersubjective matrix that allows for the unexpected moment and a feeling of interpenetration and surrender, and vitality. This participation is necessary with all our patients.

Varieties of transformative experience

The two examples that follow show ways transformations can emerge in different forms. One is that of companionship in a shared world—what happened with Barry and me—and here with Anna. The other way is within the interaction itself when habitual ways of relating and managing the relationship are disrupted. That happened with Don.

Entering Anna's world

Anna, a precocious female undergraduate student, requested analysis because she could not fall in love—could not really feel romantic love. She ended her romantic relationships when they inevitably began to feel superficial and hallow. The relationship between us was like a father doting on his lively and clever daughter. I presented her

to colleagues and they all had the same reaction: she was very enjoyable and they looked forward to the next installment, which always brought fresh and interesting material. Over time, however, I
began to recognize that our conversation never went anywhere deeper
but remained at this enjoyable and comfortable level. I began to
sound repetitive to myself. I felt sleepy and inpatient for the session to
end—a dramatic shift in the way I had been feeling. Oppression
seeped in. I was curious about this change but could not let that
curiosity fully develop.

At that time, I made a premature, aggressive comment to Anna
about a feeling of repetition and familiarity in our work. The shared
feeling of enjoyment—which had already changed in me—collapsed
almost instantly. My comment jolted her and sent her into a panic.
Inadvertently, I had created a rift in our way of relating that had been
absolutely essential and protective to her.

This shift catapulted us into a phase of hopelessness. A striking
feeling of impoverishment marked our time together. Anna began to
drink and act out in various ways, missing sessions, coming to sessions high, and the like. I become quite anxious about her, yet I
noticed that any expression of concern or encouragement to make the
appointments only made her more avoidant..

When Anna did make the sessions and was not in an altered state
from alcohol or marijuana, I could sense that we were palpably
submerged in an atmosphere of menace that was difficult to name or
tolerate. I noticed my desire to grasp the situation, to make sense of it
in a way that would have restored a feeling of separateness and my
safe role as an analyst because the asymmetry between us felt dan-
gerously collapsed. I struggled to admit to myself that I felt like a
frightened child.

In one moment in a session, I had the image of two frightened
children hiding in a closet. This was not just an image but a complete
sensori-perceptual world. The consultation room was dark with
weird shadows. The building was uncannily silent. And my body felt
rigid, and I had to hold myself still. I had no words for this at first. I
did feel a sense of relief and curiosity mixed in with the terror: "This
is the truth: this is what is happening", I said to myself. I allowed for
this experience in me which I thought might embrace her as well. I

knew somehow that this was something to live through and explore. I made no mention of this shift in my world.

Such shifts often announce a transformation—however dark and menacing. However menaced, I noticed my imagination intensify, full of possible stories. My curiosity also intensified about Anna and her world. I felt I could enter it now.

Then Anna started to come more regularly. The sessions were mainly silent. If I intervened out of any sort of anxiety or need to help on my part, Anna's anxiety would visibly rise and she would disappear for a couple of sessions. Then things would settle down again in a silent way during the hours. The following exchange shows a turning point.

P: (*After a twenty-minute silence*) I don't know ... we can't do anything about this but stay quiet ... I'm so scared and I know sometimes you are, too. And can't help me.

A: (*What I had to work through here is that I felt that I actually could not help her*, and *to think that I could help would paradoxically abandon her*). Times when I'm anxious or need to explain something, times when I can't deal with what is so terrifying in this room. We are in it together with no one to help.

P: (*After another long silence*) At first, I was afraid of *you*—you were some kind of monster. That's when I drank the most in order just to show up. But then I felt that you were scared, too, and I started to remember some things ... and when I remembered, I wanted to come and be here ...

This sequence in the work and what led up to it is highly complex. The shift came from the disruption of my comments about the repetitive nature of our conversation. This opened up an atmosphere of fear and menace that I in fact could not contain, but tried to stop, only escalating her sense of danger. What began to shift in me (and her?) was the possibility of imagining and living through this as a pair of tormented children hiding together. This image which came up spontaneously helped contain my experience of what was going on and also allowed me to give up control of the sessions and of what she was doing. As we discussed, this is an emotion of beauty, when we surrender to something deeply interpenetrating and shared. I became absorbed in the image of two terrified children and the sensations in the hour—without verbalizing it. In the exchange above, Anna put this into words, but I believe it was a shift in her sense of my availability that allowed her to speak.

We did manage to tolerate the experience, and an emotional transformation and beauty—a terrible beauty—emerged. What transpired, over several months, was a recounting, at times a reliving, of physical abuse by her mother when the father was away traveling for work. The mother would drink, which resulted in violent, out-of-control states. Her reliving this—or rather "experiencing" it for the first time and describing to me this most tragic aspect of her life—was moving to both of us. When she was in this trauma, I was often experienced as the father who was away while in the room, though at times I could be the terrified child that she had been and was embodying now. Only rarely did I represent her mother, and that would occur when I happened to make casual remarks that missed her. She then worried that my mind was gone and I could act in impulsively and a frighteningly . Yet, even in those moments, her ability to convey her state of mind signaled that a fundamental aspect of our relationship was intact, one in which she could feel that I was available to her.

Her fear gradually diminished. We both experienced what is possible in an analytic conversation—a transformative shared experience out of the reality of our meetings, however difficult. Her life began to make more sense to her, and a feeling of an unpredictable yet hopeful future opened up. We arrived at a sense of reality she had avoided since childhood. She understood her lifelong pattern of being appealing, precocious, and nonthreatening, but also empty.

Don and the beginning of curiosity

Curiosity comes from ignorance. One is not curious who already knows. Don came to analysis at the urging of his wife. "She feels she doesn't know me", he said. Immediately, he idealized me and our relationship, which I found aggressive and paralyzing. He expressed his confident belief in our mutual regard, caring, likeness. and understanding and had an uncanny way of picking up my expectations and fulfilling them. I had to constantly fend off a sense of invasion and cultivation of my feelings for him.

This defensive posture had the effect of leaving me quieter and more constricted than usual. I had the sense that I could not say anything novel or truly add anything of value to the conversation—all was already known by Don. I had difficulty finding a way into his speech to disrupt his seamless narrative about the two of us. This paralysis in his presence would overtake me. We were trapped in an idealizing, seamless narcissistic dyad in which no real contact occurred. The power of this kind of relating lay in creating a sense of falseness that could not be named or disrupted for some time. I could not find a way to be creative to go beyond my narrow way of thinking, which meant I could not make contact with the emotionally protected part of him. I was more concerned with escaping his constant barrage (I am putting this experience in terms more conscious than those available to me as I experienced it).

At some point in the analysis, I was about to move my office from a downtown financial district high-rise to a cottage behind my home. The cottage was small and intimate, and aspects of my personal life, including my family, might be on view. Don's intrusiveness and inquisitiveness made me anxious in anticipation. I noticed how the anonymity of the business arrangement at my current downtown office was protective. His reactions to me were "projections" and not really about me. Though I tried to take up his idealizations in many ways, there was something a bit half-hearted in my attempt. What was I afraid of? It seemed we both needed the distance of "projections" and "transference interpretations". And, we both were untouched by this. Why did we need this?

These early questions were the beginning of a shift in my relationship with Don. As the office move approached, a slight sense of freedom began to grow in me. I could detect my need for protection and anonymity and could gradually begin to give it up. I had access to a metaphor—a space between us—in which I could more easily expose and tolerate my vulnerabilities and our differences, and, I hoped, contain his anxieties.

When he first entered my very modest cottage, he said he was moved by the "grandeur of its simplicity", the "exquisite taste", etc. This did not put me off in the way such comments had in the past. I tolerated my exposure and resistance to intrusion, which earlier would have felt persecutory. As a result, I could sense, in a new way, his anxiety with me. I could speak to this in a fresh way—there was something more alive in the dyad. I conveyed the newness of this situation to both of us. I said things like "Yes, but it's disorienting a bit to both of us"; or "We don't know how this will feel yet"; or "This is very different from downtown or from what you might have expected". I offered my sense of the novelty of the situation, perhaps the surprise, and how much he was having to absorb. I noticed how simple and obvious and human my comments were. I could make empathic contact with the vulnerable part of him that had eluded me before and so I could speak simply and in a more embodied way. We were in a different world now, which prepared the way for transformation.

When we moved to the new office, I felt more open and available. I felt present for him in ways I had not been able to until then. My shift in internal states—intersubjectively constituted by both of us—was necessary for something new, for the experience of beauty to occur. The following session shortly after the move illustrates the emergence of this experience.

P: It's nice to ride BART, much more relaxing than going downtown, and I get a chance to read. I'm mostly too agitated to read but I can on BART ...

A: (*I detect a nervousness underlying this peaceful state, even though the metaphor of entering a new and calmer space is significant. I am concerned he will keep going on with his narrative to calm himself, to make the new space a habitual one like the previous one, and to try to restore his equilibrium. I interrupt:*) The book you were reading ...?

P: Oh, something I picked up. It's current. I like history. Passes the time. History—you probably know what I'm talking about, takes us out of our limited place and we get a sort of vacation, even though history can be grim, mostly is, really ... so I have a pile of history books on my shelf, just picked this one. The writer is English I think ... anyway, this is neither here nor there. My wife and I are having a tough time of it.

A: (*I note the phrase "takes us out of our limited space". "Yes, we are being taken out", I think.*) So, what's the book?

P: (*Irritated*) I told you. Some history book by an English fellow.

A: (*I tolerate the tension because I know we're in a new place. I can speak simply and freely to him.*) You don't want to tell me?

P: (*After a long pause, in which he seems irritated, and seems to contemplate whether to tell me or make up some other story.*) Well, it's a story, a Nazi story, or rather, okay, a Holocaust story, about, ordinary people who carried out Hitler's plan.... There was one story I was reading today about a low-level clerk or a prison guard, who enjoyed raping Jewish women in the camps. This weird mixture of ... this man then went home each night to his wife and children ... this kind of split is terrifying.

A: That part of him could be so detached. (*As I said this, I could feel a need in me to back off a bit—to identify with the detachment rather than the act.*)

P: (*Interrupts*) No, well yes ... and I got kind of stirred up reading it and felt afraid. (*A long silence unusual for him*) I realized that I'd been having some weird feelings since I came here, to this new office, especially the couple of times when I've seen a woman that I take to be your wife. I don't think I can tell you more right now.

A: All right. (*I feel calm again in the sense of being receptive and not needing to direct the conversation away from something terrifying or toward something known.*)

P: (*Again, a long silence*) I have had some fantasies of doing something bad to your wife, and it was exciting and horrifying. I can't believe I'm telling you this. Can you hear this? What must you be thinking of me? It's horrendous! I've never had this sort of fantasy ...

A: This isn't just any woman, she's my wife, she's with me, we're together. And you see a part of my life that separates you and me. It feels too much and it's terrifying and enraging. And so, it's exciting to possess someone I have.

P: It was such I shock to see her, that you have her in your life, true. But that I would have such intense ugly feelings ... I wanted to, and in such a terrible way ... the power, I think, to just take it.

Although the material is horrible, it is also a transformational moment between us: the emergence of emotional truth and realness that my patient felt, an authentic expression of his desire. There must have been subtle unconscious work in him to know he would not destroy me, and for me to know I could push him in ways that I did not previously. This allowed for greater aggression between us at that moment. It followed that Don was confronted with his own need and greed to possess my wife, but more intensely, to have me exclusively, in a terrible form. The experience arose from the patient's grasp of our separateness—that he did not "own" me.

The level of his violence toward me tortured him for some time. That he could eventually face and share that part of himself, which he had split off into others and expressed in attenuated form by his intrusiveness, was a transformative "moment of beauty": an emotional truth, no matter how difficult, that can be sought and expressed in companionship. And hidden in this for a time but eventually emerged was his intense curiosity to actually know me as someone he desired and yet was someone separate and different from him in so many ways. I was an unknown.

Ironically, but not surprisingly, his first real human contact with me was through a feeling of hatred, violence, and separateness. Don could feel now how much my wife and others were an intrusion into the special symbiotic relationship we had. He had a disparate need to possess me and not suffer separateness and loss—the prime target for his hatred was the existence of others who threatened our exclusive special bond. It was not long before his hatred turned on me with his recognition that I want to be involved with others as well as with him.

Don would refer to that exchange around his BART reading as a moment when, unexpectedly, he felt "real". The sense of what it is to feel "real" became a guiding experience in our work together and a state we could come back to.

How can a person's capacity for alive, authentic relating and creativity be thwarted early on, as was Don's? His childhood revolved around a special relationship with an adoring, idealizing father. Don excelled in everything to the absolute delight of his father, who had a serious medical condition that limited his life in many ways, particularly in sports—an activity cherished by the father. So, his father lived a vicarious athletic life through his son. Don's mother and sister took no part in the family dynamics—at least as Don recalled. Nothing should disturb this special relationship with the father. Nonetheless, throughout his life, Don could count very few moments in which he felt alive and real. He lived primarily through the regard of others, particularly men who recognized his special talents.

Again, as with Barry, Don lacked a sense of his own vitality. He was a one-man show, imprisoned on stage, without lines of his own. Through our experience together, he eventually came to feel a longing for his mother, who was relentlessly devalued by his father. Later in our work, his deeper, early emotional needs for a loving maternal experience were recaptured in our relationship.

Conclusion

My concluding comment is really a question. Where do these moments of transformation fit in the overall process of an analysis? How do these experiences deepen and build over the long run? In the next chapter, I will discuss the model of an analytic process that integrates these transformations with mourning surrender and presence.

Note

1 Markman (2017). Presence, Mourning, and Beauty: Elements of Analytic Process, *Journal of the American Psychoanalogical Assn.* *65* (6), 979–1004.

Chapter 11

Process and non-process

What is an analytic process and what causes periods of "non-process" when movement is halted? These basic questions will give me an opportunity to integrate the elements of creative engagement as it unfolds in time over the course of an analysis. In this chapter, I hope to show how the emotional work of surrender and mourning gains analytic presence that then allows for open communication, creativity, spontaneity, and the possibility of transformation. These elements of creative engagement are crucial in establishing an analytic process. They are also at play moving the analytic dyad from "non-process" to "process". I will present forms of "non-process" and illustrate these forms with brief clinical examples.

Dynamics of analytic process

The theories of Pichon-Rivière (1998) are fundamental to how I think about the analytic process. His groundbreaking contribution to Latin American psychoanalysis (and eventually beyond)—on which Berenstein bases his ideas on *vinculo*—led to major innovations in the way the analytic set up is theorized: from "dynamic field theory", to revisions of a theory of countertransference, to "social psycho-analysis". These theoretical developments bring in culture, class, and ethnicity as crucial dimensions in making up who we are. Pichon-Rivière advanced the view that subjects are embedded in the world, influencing, at times determining, the analytic relationship. The depth of his vision is revealed especially in his view of the analytic process.

What defines an analytic process? Process is movement and flow

DOI: 10.4324/9781003208518-11

and evolution, created by what Pichon-Rivière (1998)[1] calls "an open circuit of communication" between patient and analyst that transforms each. The evolution is a "dialectical spiral" created by this communication. Pichon-Rivière (1998) writes:

> All unconscious mental life, by which I mean the domain of unconscious fantasy, must be considered as the interaction between internal objects (internal group) in permanent dialectical interrelation with the objects of the external world. (p. 42)

In Pichon-Rivière's model of analytic process, change occurs through interaction with real objects that change the internal world for both participants in a dynamic that depends on an open circuit of communication. The open-circuit of communication—feeling states passed back and forth—is the hallmark of the quality of connection Pichon-Riviere calls *vinculo*.

Pichon-Rivière's term, *vinculo,* or "link", as translated, theorizes this type of constitutive, meaningful connection between analyst and patient. When the dyad meets and relates, each brings in a whole singular world of his or her own. The existential encounter of two individuals "produces" (more accurately, "there arises") a unique dynamic structure, the *vinculo. Vinculo* can be thought of as the quality of connection—for example: alive and evolving and richly communicative versus struggling and conflictual or static. One radical aspect of Pichon-Rivière's theory is that our sense of self and experience is strongly affected by this link.. As emotions are passed back and forth, each in the dyad is affected, which in turn affects their connection, or link, in a moving circuit. Essentially, each subject's experience is contingent on the nature of the link that arises between the two.

Pichon-Rivière (1998) describes *vinculo:*

> ... as a complex structure that includes an individual, an object, and their *mutual interrelation with processes of communication and learning* (p. 10, my italics)

This "mutual interrelation" is determined by communication in various registers. Pichon-Rivière believes the basis of human relationships is the drive to communicate by all means of expression—from words and actions to intromission, to projective identification. It is through communication that learning about oneself and the world takes place. The link evolves because of that learning process.

It follows then that the analytic situation is, according to Pichon-Rivière (1998):

> ... [a] new situation of two, who are permanently working to modify a specific structure, [that] configures an alive and permanent process in the action of the dialectical spiral. (p. 94)

This vibrant sentence needs unpacking. First, analyst and patient are in a *new situation*, not repeating, but in a new world (which each may try to pull down into habit and ritual). In this new venture, the unique dyad is driven to work on the nature of the link between them that then is constantly revised and reestablished as more understanding is brought to bear. This evolution of the link alters the couple in turn. Taken as a whole, this work frames an alive, permanently driven analytic process of deconstruction as well as revision, rupture, and repair. As the link is revised, so the emotional experience of each in the relationship is affected and, at times, transformed.

The analytic process Pichon-Rivière describes signals a sign of health in the analytic dyad. Within the dyad, communication and interaction "function as ... an open circuit, one of spiral trajectory" (1998, p. 11). Here, the metaphor brings both a visual and energetic—electrical—meaning to it. The open circuit especially depends on the analyst's receptivity and capacity to contain unwanted states and disruptions of his or her identity—to keep the circuit open. A signal is sent and it is received. Its reception is acknowledged (in itself, a communication) and may be given back to the sender in a different form—empathy, interpretation, "mentalization", "alpha-function", embodied accompaniment. But what is communicated to the analyst can be hard to bear and often comes in forms unsymbolized and unmentalized—causing uncertainty and anxiety. Nonetheless, if we do not block it and we receive it and enter into a dialogic circuit, an analytic process is established.

A useful metaphor for the movement of an analytic process is a classical musical form. If things are going well, the analytic pair establishes a *home* key, one in which the patient is accompanied, held, and contained, and communication is passed back and forth. This is "going-on-ness". In this stable tonal-emotional area, mutual trust and the opportunity for the patient to "go on being" in a holding environment is possible. When the analyst successfully contains deposited elements from the patient, this also solidifies and enhances the home key. The movement of the analytic process in containing and holding is in a deepening direction. These quieter moments in treatment are crucial for establishing and securing a home key. It may take a long time to establish and depends on the analyst's capacity to be available and receptive, making room for the patient internally and finding the right form of accompaniment.

Then, as in a musical composition, there is disruption, and the pair modulates to a new tonal-emotional area. New experiences create tension within the participants and between them. Movement from this home key to new tonal centers involves a sense of excitement but also turbulence and anxiety. In a spiral process, in a period of disruption-modulation, there is transformation if these new tonal worlds can be held and worked through, and communication remains open, so that upon returning to the home key both participants have been changed by what they went through on their journey of modulation. The home key feels and sounds differently, is experienced differently, as both participants view and know themselves and each other differently— perhaps more fully and more realistically. However, when the dyad or one of its members blocks the open circuit, or external factors impede (such as psychoanalytic institutions and training styles, theories, political upheavals, and social catastrophe, etc.), there is a breakdown—"a closed circuit degraded by stereotypy", as Pichon-Rivière calls it (1998, p. 11). "Stereotypy" means habit, collusive institutional rituals, or dogma that "degrades", takes apart, undoes analytic process. *This is called "non-process"*.

Problems that people bring to therapy result from a lack of a therapeutic spiral process in their relationship with themselves and the world. Learning from experience does not take place. If new experiences are resisted or closed off, this is what reoccurs in the analysis, and "non-process" prevails. When an "open-circuit" of communication is established or re-established, the link between patient and analyst can transform each in new, evolving ways. In this model, self and other and the third (link) are not so easily separated phenomenologically because they are living in a dynamically related matrix.

Barry's move from non-process to process

I want to return again to Barry from another perspective, to focus on elements of process and non-process. When Barry's world—which he intensely communicated—overwhelmed me, the open circuit of communication shut down and no movement, or "non-process" occurred. There was no vital "link" in Pichon-Rivière's sense. In order for a process to begin, I needed to surrender and mourn my attachments to certain emotional states and my identity as an analyst in order to be receptive and to bear what he communicated. I could then be in Barry's world, not mine, or rather be in a shared world we both were living in, in the river of shared emotional experience.

Important also is the role Barry played in this process. As Barry and I existed within and in part are constituted by the "link", I believe he sensed subtle shifts in my emotional states: less anxiety and agitation; more calm and ease. This shift made Barry more available to me and himself as well. Perhaps, this happened simultaneously. Or, perhaps unconscious shifts in Barry's state opened up a new horizon of freedom for me that then led to my availability. Whatever its source, we began an "alive and permanent process in the action of the dialectical spiral" (Pichon-Rivière, 1998).

Gradually, I was able to open myself to his dead and deadening world—and live with it and in it. This cleared the way for me to notice the sound of the rain with him, which brought Barry more fully into our process. We then shared an open circuit of communication in the link and the therapeutic spiral began. Living within his world changed the link too. Unconsciously, we both worked on being together and communicating and sharing emotional states. From my side, I felt peace and comfort, particularly sensorially, despite the continued deadening content of his speech. The words did not change but the music did. Something crucial had changed in me, in him, and between us. There was a feeling of "going-on-ness" and a deepening unspoken intimacy. I found myself more alert to sensory aspects of our meetings, such as the cast of light at a particular time of day, the way the sound of our voices echoed in the room, the smell of coffee, and so on. This indicated my widened attention in a new register and a sense of going-on-ness. It did not seem to matter what he talked about or even his affect, which usually lacked much variation. The heightened sensory experience was enough: I felt content just as things were, being in this world with him in a relaxed way. These sensory changes let me know we were in something new and that we were also moving toward something new.

This period lasted several months and established a home key of going-on-ness. I believe Barry sensed calm and acceptance in me. Although he spoke less, "produced" less, it did not evoke a sense of urgency in me to move things along. A calm settled feeling reigned. I had a slight indication from him that he was less agitated and tormented in the work. All of this could not be communicated through a transcript of words and the exchange of comments but existed as a lived music between us.

My comment about the rain initiated a transformational moment. There was an intensification and enlivening of the link and much more life was directly communicated through an open circuit. As writers on aesthetics describe, I had a sense of wonder at his response. How had we arrived at this intense moment together from a "simple" comment about the rain?—the feeling of wonder I call *relational aesthetics*. Two people can sometimes create a transforming mode of contact that involves feelings of deep rapport, harmony, resonance, and perhaps, at-one-ment.

With Barry, a passage of intense meaningful living followed, of creative play between us. Eventually, this period of time ended in a calm state again—the home key, now enriched. The climate between us, the "link", had changed. He no longer filled me with deadness. Other conflicted elements eventually came up as he felt more alive— which would eventually lead to disruption and further revision of the link. But the open circuit remained. Both he and I had changed.

This is Pichon-Rivière's view of analytic process that I want to focus on. Barry and I start off *in stasis*, or "non-process". We are not living out something that is growing. We are constricted. My work is to be present in a way that releases the constraining elements of my engagement. Then, the dyad shifts toward communication. This period of vitality is not permanent, but it does leave traces for further development in our work. The link has been modified and, from this point, there is no real return. There were other impasses to get through, as the constellation of my and Barry's transference evolved and interacted in different ways. Also, importantly, you just can't go back to what happened, even if it is significant, because it is no longer emotionally relevant in the same way. One has to look forward, not back, and let go again of what one had—at least consciously.

The *vinculo* structure evolves through complex forms of communication drawing on both of our histories, ethnic and class backgrounds, and present life situations. Though I can't possibly include what is going on in each of our lives outside the sessions, nor our particular histories, it is relevant. For example, in the early part of treatment, Barry established metaphors with me that were quite communicative and intuitive. Though we came from quite different circumstances, his reliance on visual metaphor—he was an architect after all—jibed with my own visual way of taking in and relating to the world. So, in addition to the somatosensory communication of deadness, one that was at first very difficult for me, we shared and elaborated visual metaphors as I learned more and more about his internal world, and as he learned about me, from the times and the way I immediately picked up his metaphors. I think we both sensed we spoke the same language at times. This must have gone into the beginning of my imperative statement about the rain—"Listen".

I believe we arrived at transformative emotional experiences because *both* of us were "permanently working to modify a specific structure"—the "link" established between us—actively trying to participate in an "alive and permanent process" of communication.

The concept of the therapeutic spiral suggests that, though we are trained to see the epiphanies, it is also true that "life is what happens when you are busy making other plans", as John Lennon sang. I don't think we can overestimate the work the patient is doing to communicate and modify the link between us, even (especially) when we are encumbered by our own difficulties. Or, to put this more accurately, even during what looks like land-locked periods, there may be constant interaction and communication that is changing the internal worlds of both analyst and patient. But this happens only if the analyst is available for it. The moment of transformation, then, is the result of real "alive and permanent process" happening all the time during an analytic process. It breaks through as a result of some shift or disturbance in the field, and within the dyad.

Forms of non-process

Baranger et al. (1983) call "non-process" a non active vinculo at work—no open circuit communication. Another way of putting it is that there are forms of being together that resist thought, communication, and emotional growth and that constrict the emotional freedom in both participants, thus creating "non-process". This aspect of our work is very important and not rare, and the recognition of "non-process" is crucial for the analyst to recognize and work through. The particular forms of "non-process" that I will describe will further help us recognize the various *types* of "non-process". These types have particular recognizable qualities and ask for different emotional work on the analyst's part.

As a model of "non-process", we can begin with the perception of a closed circuit of communication—the basic cause of "non-process". Following Bion's (1961a) theory of basic assumptions that stifle thinking, growth, and learning in groups, I propose different forms of "negative links" (-link) between analyst and patient, or forms of "stereopathy", that have the same effect. The various forms of "non-process" -links are created by different sorts of basic assumptions. Each has a different gradient of intensity and fixity that determines the quality of non-process.

I have discussed how Barry and I worked to establish an open circuit of communication, an alive *vinculo* that I call an "aesthetic link". The link is structured by a shared search for emotional truth and a wish to face it—actively modifying the link in order to grow emotionally and learn. That defines an analytic process.

I propose three non-process "-links" of varying degrees of entrenchment. Each of these is determined by a shared basic assumption arising out of a particular -link or "*anti-vinculo*". What follows are some clinical examples of these forms and ways of recognizing and working toward an aesthetic *vinculo* and the establishment of a therapeutic spiral. They are shown going from greater to lesser flexibility.

The -link of avoiding emotional truth

Ed had been complaining for weeks about the way I related to him in a critical, imperious way, just like his mother. I felt, however, that I understood him and was in tune with him, and I could appreciate in an emotional way his reaction to me (as transference), tolerate his hostility and disappointment, and put into words how hard this made it for him to trust me. I did not feel critical or imperious, but caring and concerned. My comments were quite sensible and, if read in a transcript, pretty accurate and attuned to Ed's state of mind. But as he went on and on with this complaint, and as I continued to offer the same comments, I became bothered by my complacency with what I understood and offered interpretively. In a moment in one particular session, I was startled to hear in my voice a tone of self-contentment and calmness. I suspect, in a subtle way, it had always been there, in my voice, with him. Indeed, I apparently *was* the very figure of the mother he railed against—impervious and self-satisfied. Ed was attempting to communicate to me plausible aspects of my way of relating to him in an attempt to be understood. When I communicated that I understood what he was saying about me, Ed felt relief. Even though the way forward also brought up anxiety for him, as the nature of the relationship was now more uncertain, that anxiety was tolerable and was expressed directly in dreams and his associations.

To translate what happened above in terms of non-process: a "-link" was formed by an enactment that provided mutual emotional stability to each participant. This is the messy, common, and ordinary business of doing analytic work. It is not necessarily uncomfortable because it avoids disruptive moments of transformation. Habit dominates. It is not primarily destructive. There is communication, but it is meant to stabilize the dyad. Signals are passed back and forth that form unconscious collusion to avoid certain areas of conflict. It is dynamic, with the potential to go into and out of an aesthetic link. The analyst participates in this through complementary countertransference.

The - link of intolerable deadness and dissociation

Jake's mother was seriously sick throughout his childhood, often in bed for long periods of time. He was left to the care of various nannies because his busy father traveled frequently for work. It was a lonely, barren childhood. Jake made every effort to engage me, with constant stories of his exploits, but I somehow could not respond or feel his presence. He seemed to be talking behind a thick panel of glass. I felt like I was watching a video when the image and voice are out of synch. He would say the same of me—that I seemed distant and inert and not real. There was a no-contact zone between us. He finally gave up and lapsed into depression. During this period, I was subject to the most unbearable states of emptiness—as I am sure he was. At times I could articulate something like, "This is what non-existence is like". If Jake was distressed by my "inertness" in the first phase of treatment, my current vacant state made his negative feelings much worse. He finally said to me, "You're dead to me", which brought him to the height of despair in the treatment. He fell into an almost catatonic state of silence.

For a significant time, I could not really find my mind with him. My efforts felt fake and flailing, to me as well as to Jake. This fakeness was caused by my attempt to remove myself and Jake from unbearable feelings of deadness.

One hallmark of a dynamic field and *vinculo* is that outside the field, out of contact with Jake, I re-found an aliveness and active imagination with regard to him. But the moment we were in each other's presence, we were drowned in a monotonous thick atmosphere of emptiness. For incredibly uncomfortable periods of time that felt like an eternity, I could not form distinct thoughts. I had nothing to say. Paradoxically, this was the hardest, most hopeless part of the work but a sign of progress. Prior to this experience, a falseness in both of us paralyzed the work. We both pretended that everything was ok. This is an aspect of this form of -link, and, if it remained, a rather permanent non-process would have been established. But when we both entered into the horribly stagnant waters of dissociation and trauma, and I could tolerate this and my guilt for abandoning him, there opened a possibility for movement. I had to recognize though how deeply down a well of empty despair we had both fallen. Although there were no ready means of escape, a gradual feeling in me and in Jake started to emerge that we were together facing difficult experiences in it together, suffering together, as two separate people.

Eventually, I could put into words what it "feels" like to not-exist or feel real, when no one alive appears on the scene to help. I noticed that whenever I could find some words for what was happening, I felt immediately more embodied and Jake seemed to experience the same thing. This was a beginning.

To translate this clinical experience in terms of non-process: there was a constant dissociated "-link" of deadness, thoughtlessness that we both needed to escape. There was no contact between me and Jake or the contact was symbiotic. The "space between" was represented by falseness. There was a shared unconscious basic assumption that separateness and experience was catastrophic. What *is* communicated are states of deadness and emptiness that eventually can be received. But a "-link" such as this is extremely hard to bear, especially if our preference is for symbolic expression. At times like this, the place to enter into some sort of contact is at the level of the body, body rhythms, and gesture, to attempt to initiate what Trevarthen and Malloch (2002) calls "communicative musicality"—an emotional sharing at the embodied level that potentially gives a feeling of companionship and eventually vitality. This often moves very slowly, requiring the analyst's active presence and activity to initiate.

The -link of hatred of growth

I supervised an analyst who was treating a male middle-aged patient with whom he was constantly and very subtly embroiled in masochistic surrender. The patient changed times, requested fee reductions, continually brought up doubts about the value of the analysis and the analyst's true positive intentions toward him. The analyst felt frustrated and angry about the lengths he was "forced" to go to keep the patient involved. These interactions were very subtle but constant. The patient's true need for the analyst, even his loving feelings, were funneled into this destructive field. The analyst could not get out of the feeling of resentment and surrender; the patient was compelled to devalue and push the analyst around. In consultation, the analyst had some clarity about what was going on and the need to interrupt this sadomasochistic dance, but, in the room with the patient, he repeated it and did not have emotional access or words to reach the patient while immersed in the field.

On one occasion, the patient left treatment for a month on business, leaving it unclear whether he would return to analysis. He had to "think about it". The analyst, consistent with the power of the -link, was holding these hours without thought and without clarifying what the patient intended upon his return. However, the physical absence of the analyst brought up in the patient a desire and recognition of his need for the analyst. In a phone session, the patient communicated in several ways his need for the analyst and wish to keep his sessions when he returned. The analyst, still held in the grip of the sadomasochistic field, interpreted that the patient seemed to enjoy that his analyst is left in the dark about his intentions—the analyst interpreted the patient's desire for a sadomasochistic relationship. Although "correct" in the historical sense, what this interpretation did was to reinstate a sadomasochistic world. The analyst was also communicating his hostility, which aimed to make the patient feel guilty. The patient, manipulatively responded, "I had been feeling so good about my decision to return to analysis, proud really, and now I'm feeling bad again about myself. Maybe I'm better off with the earlier arrangement of once a week". There was a subtle mockery and falseness in the "really proud" and "feeling bad about myself". The old order had been instantly re-instated. The analyst felt frustrated and hopeless that he had lost the patient again.

To translate this clinical relationship in terms of non-process: The dyad was trapped in the most entrenched "-link", which expresses hatred of growth, understanding, and freedom. It is extremely powerful, rigid, and enduring. The motive is destructiveness toward meaningful relating, as this threatens the security gained from traumatic levels of anxiety. Words and actions are not meant to communicate but to manipulate and control—both the object and one's state of mind. Holding on to safety is felt to be a matter of life and death. In this case, the analyst, as well as his patient, shared a phantasy that reflection is destructive and dangerous (or irrelevant and impotent), and so they relied on grandiosity and excitement to triumph over dependency and uncertainty.

Conclusion

Our aim is to foster an analytic process that is an open circuit of communication and mutual transformation. This occurs when we are able to be present and available, receiving the patient's communication in whatever form it is offered: words, action, beta elements, or wholesale sharing of an emotional world. When our emotional work achieves this, there is the possibility for both patient and analyst to experience "going-on-ness" and the establishment of a home key, and potentially, moments of transformation. These experiences then deepen and evolve to form a spiraling analytic process.

However, it is also clinically important to recognize elements of non-process, when communication shuts down and the couple is in "stereopathy"—persistent and repetitive action—that is the antithesis of evolution. The three forms of this "stereopathy"—in enactment, deadness-dissociation, and tyranny—when recognized by us afford insight into the particular ways we are contributing to the persistent stasis. The emotional knowledge of our contribution to the forms of "non-process" can lead back to an analytic process. As Bion suggested, changing the "emotional field" (of the basic assumption) starts with the analyst's awareness of the field they are in. With Barry and I, it began with my realization of how I blocked his communication to me of a deadened internal world. Working through this established an open circuit of communication between us. The structure of the link deepened through "going-on-ness", culminating (made manifest) in a simple spontaneous gesture like "Listen to that rain"—a comment I believe Barry could have made as well as I.

Note

1 Translations of selected passages of *Teoria del vinculo* by Glen Gabbard (2012).

Chapter 12

Creative engagement in these times

While writing this book, a global pandemic has engulfed our private lives and our work as therapists. The pandemic has intensified other fears like climate collapse, fires raging through California where I live, and the political threat to our democracy. Every day in every session, we are permeated, at times invaded, by the world around us. Never has mutuality been more relevant. We are immersed in and share the anxieties and fears throughout the course of the day, in session after session. There are days when our containing abilities reach their limits.

What does it mean to be an analytic therapist in these times, without couch, physical presence, visual and physical dimensionality, the time and space between sessions, the coming and goings, the importance of transitions? When so much is altered and lost, what remains that is essential to our way of being with patients? Can something of the source of analytic presence and action be claimed at such times? What would that look like?

Even working by phone or Zoom and with the shared experience of anxiety and sorrow, patient and analyst can still find each other and create what one patient called a "shared psychic space". And this is truly the case: we re-find something essential and vitalizing in the specialized conversation Freud invented. This shared psychic space is a container for big emotions and the possibility for meaningful companionship.

Facing seemingly impossible obstacles such as we currently are, human beings have a deep need to communicate and share emotional experiences all the more. So, we adapt in order to connect. This drive

DOI: 10.4324/9781003208518-12

to connect and create a shared space, whose singular form in each of us can find expression across digital phone or video platforms, remains a therapeutic lifeline. This is especially so for those isolated or dissociated, but also for most of those patients I see.

I have found it is also true for therapists. What drew many of us to this work is a form of companionship that is nourishing even in tough times. This is the symmetrical part of the thing: that we also derive comfort and solace and insight from a conversation designed to find and express emotional truth in a healing way. I believe this is especially true during circumstances of threatening shared realities.

Despite and because of the situation we are in now, elements of creative engagement are even more crucial. The fact of the mutuality of the encounter is brought home in every session by the way we and our patients are immersed and affected by the world around us. At every moment, companionship and accompaniment are woven into our engagement. All the more, our patients need a sense of our presence and availability that we still manage to communicate through Zoom and by phone. Embodied attunement is less palpable and more challenging, though no less important. Our faces and expressions are more vivid. I now sit in a chair that *moves* while on Zoom. My gestures are more visible and available because I actually appear closer. I also move my computer at times to give the patient a sense of the space I inhabit, one that I invite the patient into. The transformational moments still arrive in unwitting ways.

But one aspect of the emotional work of surrender and mourning is challenging. This is the letting go of our usual and preferred way of being with patients, in an embodied way. This really is a loss that both patient and therapist mourn. Many colleagues initially were depressed about our work and what can be done. *It really isn't the same.* It can feel repetitive and thin. The challenge for me in the face of this loss, while being with and sharing what we don't have together at this moment, is a stronger engagement of my emotionally creative imagination. By this, I mean my attempt to internally enhance how the patient lives inside me, how I make space for him or her in a way that requires more of my emotional investment and more interaction to keep the patient and the internal relationship lively. For that reason, I sometimes prefer video to the phone—though of course video sessions hour after hour take their toll. But I am continuing to search for ways to be present and not dissociate or have eye fatigue. I lower the light intensity. I look away into the far distance more often. I tend to be more animated and playful when appropriate. In this sense, mutuality evolves in the shared, active attempt to connect and communicate, while always trying (not always with success as you will see) to maintain an asymmetrical relationship. These are simple ways to try to restore my capacity to be present and creatively engaged.

The following brief clinical examples show how the elements of creative engagement can play out in our work.

Clinical illustration: dark days

The world can encroach and affect the dyad in mutually significant ways. Penetrated by the world around us, my patient Sarah helped me regain my place in order to help her. There was a recent day in the San Francisco Bay Area when it seemed that the sun did not rise and that we all woke up on another planet in a post-apocalyptic world. Everyone was scared and rattled. In a mid-afternoon session, Sarah, who generally is very vulnerable to catastrophic states, brought up the weirdness of the day: "It's all over for us as human beings. We are done for. Me, my children, and my children's children gone".

In the past, when Sarah sunk into despair, I sometimes had a way of helping her out of it. This time something very different was going on. I said, "I know it looks bad and menacing, but there is an explanation. It has to do with the height of the smoke over a layer of fog. This is what creates this darkness. But the air is not so bad". This was an absurd reaction to Sarah's worries, of course—to give a scientific explanation for her expression of catastrophe that she feels externally and internally much of the time. Then again, perhaps not so absurd: I was like a parent explaining the reason for things that make the world less scary, not so unlike the film, *Life Is Beautiful*. But this is *my* defensive way of reacting when I am scared, that I brought in. I may find a reason for what scares me, or I distract myself—as I did this time—with an intellectual solution.

Sarah was helpful for both of us though: "You must be as frightened as I am. Don't you take in how this all looks?" "How does this make you feel?" I admitted I indeed did not want to take it in and explained (which she already knew well) that sometimes my vulnerability is expressed in defensive postures of knowing and an attitude of "I got this". Once this was acknowledged in me and between us and I became present for her, we could both share our sorrow about the potential loss of a California we both loved and our real fears of the climate crisis.

This is how mutuality remains a foundation for me in whatever context but is even more so during the current situation of fear and isolation. There are times we need the patient's understanding to be taken back to our asymmetric role, so we can contain the patient's fears and out-of-control states, not by being distant and on top of the situation, but by actually allowing for shared experiences of vulnerability, fear, and sorrow.

Clinical illustration: a bug is on the wall—and on Pence

On a Zoom call with Steve, my gaze kept wandering to the ceiling. A wasp had just walked into a spider's web. I was marveling at how quickly the spider paralyzed the wasp with a toxin. Steve said, "Your eyes keep moving up. What are you looking at? It doesn't seem like you're thinking—your eyes would do something different".

I described the situation on the wall and my fascination with it. I could sense Steve's keen interest. I spontaneously said, "Do you want to see it?" Knowing Steve, I would need to invite him into my world and take the lead because he is very careful not to over-burden me with his interests, curiosity, and needs. "Yes!" he exclaimed. I turned my computer and moved closer to the dramatic scene in miniature. Steve loved this moment. We both did really. We discussed our nerdy interest in entomology and speculated on the potency of the spider's venom. Steve associated to the fly on Pence's head during the Vice Presidential debate. I remarked that there might be a Sartre play called *The Flies* (thinking about the flies tormenting Orestes, who murdered his mother, Clytemnestra).

This spontaneous interaction illustrates a co-created moment of psychic and sensorial sharing guided by a sense of mutuality and play that I strive to embody—while keeping track of the patient in this exchange. We were not unconscious of the many meanings of this event and explored some of this. We understood Steve's reticence to ask for what he wanted, but, in a way new for him, he did ask about what was going on in me. Underneath this interaction was his ongoing wish, expressed directly and in dreams, to be a part of my family and live in my home.

When I turned the computer around, I invited him into my world. (Don't we do this when patients enter our office, as in Wilson's (2020) metaphor of the analyst as innkeeper?) Steve and I dynamically shared a physical space that had been lost in the pandemic. That sharing was not "virtual" but real. But in the context of the pandemic, that shared space, at that moment, had heightened power and emotional importance.

Then something unexpected happened between us that was completely novel for Steve. He *initiated* contact of with me after this session. Not out of need or a logistical question, but playfully. He emailed me a picture of the cover of Sartre's play *Les Mouches* [*The Flies*]. "Is this it?" he asked. "*C'est ca*", I said. Steve had a wonderful and free response in French which I translate as "This little fly on the white head is perhaps the biggest whistle blower right now".

Steve's expanded sense of freedom, his newfound assertiveness, came out of the spontaneous play between us. The threatening backdrop of the pandemic and the lurking election was palpably there, and, within that context, Steve found humor in reversing the menace (from the spider's venom to the powerful little fly) and intimacy.

Clinical illustration: I know your name, but what's your number

I was having trouble with Zoom on this day. Without realizing it, when I would start a session, the Zoom app would assign me a new ID each time. So, all of a sudden, my patient Ellen could not find me. It took some time for me to realize that in the Zoom setup, I had a choice whether to use my usual ID or a random one, and somehow the setting had shifted to random. I emailed Ellen about the situation and told her that, for the next meeting, we will use my usual ID, which I gave her again.

Unfortunately, I had reversed a number in the ID so that Ellen could not enter the meeting and had to go back to another computer to retrieve the correct ID. When she entered the screen, I had never seen her so distraught and enraged. She started yelling at me that I really don't care about her. She's sick of suffering on account of my lapses and *laissez-faire* attitude. I tried to settle myself down. This was another side of the calm and composed Ellen. Her main complaint was that she must truly mean nothing to me for me to be so careless. I want to say here that I am not the most detailed-oriented person and, at times, reverse letters and numbers. She was quite familiar with my limitations in this regard. This was something much, much more.

I would have liked to think Ellen was overreacting. I did not deserve this assault on my character, I protested to myself. But (and I had to work at this) ... I asked her to tell me more. Ellen said she does so much, works so hard to make contact, is always on time and ready. Her connection to me is urgent and important, a sort of lifeline. And what do I do? I sit back casually in a relaxed way and watch her suffer, offering paltry comfort and thin soup. She suffers and I have an easy life. Again, I thought this was a bit unfair. Aren't we all a bit frayed these days?

I have felt very engaged with her and have spent many sessions listening to the ways she suffers. Her suffering comes from a lack of an internally comforting presence, and externally in her childhood, when she was left alone to understand the confusing world swirling around her. As a result, she is often agitated and in physical pain. Although there was a clear transference dimension to her critique, I began to see that I really had a part in her suffering with me. Not from my limitations around numbers and letters and detail, but from the way I held myself back in a subtle way when I sometimes did not know how to alleviate her suffering and comfort her. I closed off a bit. I became slightly less expressive and kept many of my thoughts to myself, which created an enactment of her childhood situation.

As I worked through the Zoom fiasco, I understood that what she needed was not quiet support or being with her passively (and inarticulately helpless), but a much more active emotional engagement, even if it meant expressing reactions that I thought she would not like. I told her that sometimes I am overwhelmed by her suffering and feel bad I cannot do more to alleviate it. She immediately said, "That helps. I just want to know what is happening between us and I want to feel you're more open to me, giving me your honest reactions. That's what would really help".

The remoteness she felt from me was not a Zoom problem—though it did provide an opportunity for realness and mutuality between us. It was Ellen's longstanding, painful struggle with her fear that I would abandon her or I would be "remote"—not in the technical sense but emotionally, repeating the trauma of her childhood. This was finally brought to the surface by the true emotional catastrophe of not being able to find me on Zoom. She described a dreadful feeling every time she tries to enter our Zoom meeting. I may not appear because the link may not work—so very different from our office days. And I would not care to find her or I may even feel relief if she were not there. Her intimations of my state of mind were true in some sense and inspired me to work with my reactions to her that I did not want to face before.

That I felt withdrawn and hopeless and that nothing could help or comfort her made me lose track of the precious and intense bond between us that she relied on at each moment. Ellen needed to be fed the emotional truth and a sense of real involvement from me. We could eventually talk about my occasional remoteness that opened up new emotional horizons for us. Whatever she talked about, the main thing for her, and me, was the time we had together and someone to listen to her and be concerned—even if there was nothing to be done. Or rather, the doing was in being there, caring, and expressing my emotional reactions to what is going on. As Henri Rey was reported to say in consultation to a student: "Don't just do something. Stand there!" What felt repetitive for me was for Ellen a precarious moment of contact that was restorative in ways I had not fully recognized and protected.

Clinical illustration: whose hospitality is it?

I have seen Frieda for a very long time. She is a person often worried. She suffers impingements of all sorts so that her life feels closed up and small. During most of the therapy, she worked in a profession that offered few emotional rewards except the pleasure of using her hands. She is a general surgeon, recently retired. Over this long therapy, she's intimated that sometimes she makes things. She is very disparaging of this activity as it is of "no worth". This "no worth activity" has gained momentum nonetheless, and she submitted her work to some competitions.

Recently she's been consumed by fears of Trump and the election and, for the first time in her life, worked on getting the vote out. We met the day before the election was called, both of us in a cautiously hopeful mood. We've been working by phone, as was her preference, but that day, for whatever reason, the calls kept dropping. I tried to call her on Facetime audio, but suddenly our images appeared. After so long, we were clearly delighted to see each other's face. Then, seeing her in her home and in her studio, I was astonished by the various artistic creations that filled her space. As she saw my expression of pleasure, she said, "Let me give you a tour". This sense of my pleasure had an immediacy that easily spanned cyberspace. There ensued a slow and deliberate walk through the various rooms and outdoor spaces she uses to paint, build various structures, and make prints, and so on. The range of work and the variety of forms of visual expression were mind-blowing to me. I had never imagined the richness of visual creativity, which she had downplayed in our conversations. Seeing the various works in progress, the way her environment is a living artistic environment, was wonderful and deeply moving. Now, she had a medium to invite me literally into her world in ways not possible before COVID. To reverse Wilson's (2020) metaphor of the innkeeper, she was the hospitable innkeeper for this moment, and I, her analyst, was entering, immersing myself, in the beauty of her world.

Final thoughts (for now)

Mutuality is not only a sensibility but a reality—two contingent human beings trying to create enough of a shared experience, in which solace, peace, and shared emotions are possible. We are not insulated from the world. We never have been. Being permeated by the world is now front and center and affects all aspects of our emotional relationships with our patients. Yet, this thing called psychoanalysis is evolving. It is an open, unfinished work, a living growing thing. It is meant to be influenced and responsive to the current very difficult historical moment, containing and integrating all this within the bounds of a specialized and yet ordinary conversation that Freud invented and that we foster and protect. We are inventing new ways of being together in this specialized conversation.

Psychoanalysis is our commitment to this singular conversation, fashioned by our authenticity, our embodied presence, our emotional work to maintain it, our willingness to attune and accompany, and the reality of mutuality that opens up the opportunity for sharing the emotions of truth and beauty, even in—perhaps most importantly— during these most demanding and threatening times.

What we learn from our work in these currently adverse conditions is that what we are attached to particular aspects of our work can be just that, attachments we can let go of and mourn. There are real losses in this for the patient and analyst, definitely. But what we thought was essential may not be. This realization helps us focus on what *is* essential, no matter the situation: in a creatively engaged way, searching for the conversation to continue and for psychic emotional space to be shared—no less real than before.

References

Alexander, T. M. (1987). *John Dewey's theory of art, experience and nature: The horizons of feeling*. Albany: SUNY Press.

Aguayo, J. & Malin, B. (Eds.). (1967/2018). *Wilfred Bion: Los Angeles seminars and supervision*. London and New York: Routledge.

Alvarez, A. (1992). *Live company: Psychoanalytic therapy with autistic, borderline, deprived, and abused children*. New York: Routledge.

Armstrong, T. & Detweiler-Bedell, B. (2008). Beauty as an emotion: The exhilarating prospect of mastering a challenging world. *Review of General Psychology, 12*(4), 305–329.

Aron, L. (2000). Self-Reflexivity and the Therapeutic Action of Psychoanalysis. *Psychoanalytic Psychology, 17*(4), 667–689.

Aron, L. (2007). *A meeting of minds: Mutuality in psychoanalysis*. New York: Routledge.

Balint, M. (1950). Changing therapeutical aims and techniques in psycho-analysis. *International Journal of Psycho-Analysis, 31*, 117–124.

Balint, M. (1968). *The basic fault*. Evanston: Northwestern University Press.

Baranger, M., Baranger, W., & Mom, J. (1983). Process and non-process in analytic work. *International Journal of Psychoanalysis, 64*, 1–15.

Beckett, S. (1994). *Proust*. New York City: Grove Press.

Beebe, B., Knoblauch, S. H., Rustin, J., & Sorter, D. (2005). *Forms of intersubjectivity in infant research and adult treatment*. New York: Other Press.

Berenstein, I. (2001). The link and the other. *International Journal of Psychoanalysis, 82*(1), 141–149.

Berenstein, I. (2012). Vinculo as a relationship between others. *The Psychoanalytic Quarterly*, 81(3), 565–575.

Bion, W. R. (1957). On arrogance. In *Second thoughts*. London: Karnac Books, 1984.

Bion, W. R. (1959). Attacks on linking. In *Second thoughts*. London: Karnac Books, 1984.

Bion, W. R. (1961a). *Experience in groups and other papers*. London: Tavistock Publications.

Bion, W. R. (1961b). *Learning from experience*. London: Karnac Books, 1984.

Bion, W. R. (1963). *Elements of psycho-analysis*. London: Karnac Books.

Bion, W. R. (1967). Notes on memory and desire. In E. Bott Spillius (Ed.), *Melanie Klein today: Developments in theory and practice: Vol. 2. Mainly practice* (pp. 15–18). New York: Routledge, 1988.

Bion, W. R. (1987). *Clinical seminars and other works*. London: Karnak.

Bollas, C. (1978). The aesthetic moment and the search for transformation. *Annals of Psychoanalysis*, *6*, 385–394.

Bollas, C. (1983). Expressive uses of the countertransference—Notes to the patient from oneself. *Contemporary Psychoanalysis*, *19*, 1–33.

Borgogno, F. (2014). "Coming from afar" and "temporarily becoming the patient without knowing it": Two necessary analytic conditions according to Ferenczi's later thought. *American Journal of Psychoanalysis*, *74*, 302–312.

Boston Change Process Study Group (1998). Non-interpretive mechanisms in psychoanalytic therapy: The "something more" than interpretation. *International Journal of Psychoanalysis*, *79*, 903–921.

Buber, M. (1923). *I and thou*. New York: Scribner's, 2000.

Byers, P. (1976). Biological rhythms as information channels in interpersonal communication behavior. In P. P. G. Bateson & P. H. Klopfer (Eds.), *Perspectives in ethology*. New York: Plenum Press.

Carson, R. (1965). *The sense of wonder*. New York: Harper and Row Publishers.

Damasio, A. R. (1994). *Descartes' error: Emotion, reason, and the human brain*. New York: Putnam.

Damasio, A. R. (1999). *The feeling of what happens: Body, emotion, and the making of consciousness*. New York: Harcourt Brace.

Dewey, J. (1934). *Art as experience*. New York: Perigree Books, 1980.

Elise, D. (2017). Moving from within the maternal: The choreography of analytic eroticism. *Journal of the American Psychoanalytic Association*, *65*(1), 33–60.

Feldman, M. (1997). Projective identification: The analyst's involvement. *International Journal of Psychoanalysis*, *78*, 227–241.

Ferenczi, S. (1915). Psychogenic anomalies of voice production. In *Further contribution to the theory and technique of psychoanalysis*. New York: Brunner/Mazel, 1980.

Ferenczi, S. (1931). Child-analysis in the analysis of adults. *International Journal of Psychoanalysis, 12*, 468–482.

Ferenczi, S. (1933). Confusion of tongues between the adults and the child: Language of tenderness and of passion. (M. Balint, Ed.). *International Journal of Psychoanalysis, 30*(4), 225–230, 1949.

Ferenczi, S. (1988). *The clinical diary of Sándor Ferenczi* (J. Dupont, Ed.). (M. Balint & N. Zarday Jackson, Trans.). Cambridge and London: Harvard University Press, 1998.

Fonagy, P. & Target, M. (2007). The rooting of the mind in the body: New links between attachment theory and psychoanalysis. *Journal of the American Psychoanalytic Association, 55*, 411–456.

Freud-Jung Letters. (1988). Letter June 1909. Boston: Harvard University Press.

Freud, S. (1909). *Notes upon a case of obsessional neurosis.* Standard edition (vol. 10, pp. 151–318).

Freud, S. (1910). *The future prospects of psycho-analytic therapy.* Standard edition (vol. 11, pp. 139–152).

Freud, S. (1912). *Recommendations to physicians practicing psychoanalysis.* Standard edition (vol. 12, pp. 109–120).

Freud, S. (1923). *The ego and the id.* Standard edition (vol. 19, pp. 12–66).

Goldberg, P. (2012). Active perception and the search for sensory symbiosis. *Journal of the American Psychoanalytic Association, 60*, 791–812.

Goldberg, P. (2018). The vital dimension of the frame. Paper presented to the American Psychoanalytic Association, New York.

Grossmark, R. (2012). The flow of enactive engagement. *Contemporary Psychoanalysis, 48*(3), 287–300.

Hagman, G. (2002). The sense of beauty. *International Journal of Psychoanalysis, 83*(3), 661–674.

Hall, M. (1996). *Leaving home: A conducted tour of twentieth-century music with Simon Rattle.* London: Faber and Faber.

Harris, A. & Kuchuck, S. (Eds.). (2015). *The legacy of Sandor Ferenczi: From ghost to ancestor.* London: Routledge.

Harrison, A. M. (2014). The sandwich model: The "music and dance" of therapeutic action. *International Journal of Psychoanalysis, 95*(2), 313–340.

Isaacs, S. (1948). The nature and function of phantasy. *International Journal of Psychoanalysis, 29*, 73–97.

James, W. (1890). *The principles of psychology.* Cambridge: Harvard University Press, 1981.

James, W. (1907). *Pragmatism: a new name for some old ways of thinking*. London: Logmens, Green.

Jeffries, S. (November 30, 2002). The quest for truth: Interview with Sir Bernard Williams. *The Guardian*.

Johnson, M. (2018). *The aesthetics of meaning and thought: The bodily roots of philosophy, science, morality, and art*. Chicago: University of Chicago Press.

Joseph, B. (1975). The patient who is difficult to reach. In P. L. Giovacchini (Ed.), *Tactics and techniques in psychoanalytic therapy, Vol. 2: Countertransference*. New York: Jason Aronson.

Joseph, B. (1983). On understanding and not understanding: Some technical issues. *International Journal of Psychoanalysis, 64*, 291–298.

Keats, J. (1898). *The complete poetical works and letters of John Keats*, Cambridge Edition. Houghton, Mifflin and Company, p. 277.

Klein, M. (1957/1975). *Envy and gratitude and other works 1946–1963*. New York: The Free Press.

Knoblauch, S. H. (2000). *The musical edge of therapeutic dialogue*. London: The Analytic Press, Inc.

Knoblauch, S. H. (2005). Body rhythms and the unconscious. Toward an expanding of clinical attention. *Psychoanalytic Dialogues, 15*, 807–827.

Knoblauch, S. H. (2011). Contextualizing attunement within the poly-rhythmic weave: The psychoanalytic samba. *Psychoanalytic Dialogues, 21*, 414–427.

Langer, S. (1942). *Philosophy in a new key*. Cambridge: Harvard University Press.

Langer, S. (1956). *Feeling and form*. New York: Charles Scribner's Sons.

Levine, H. B. (2012). The colorless canvas: Representation, therapeutic action and the creation of mind. *International Journal of Psychoanalysis, 93*, 607–629.

Lipton, S. D. (1977). The advantages of Freud's technique as shown in his analysis of the Rat Man. *International Journal of Psychoanalysis, 58*, 255–273.

Lombardi, R. (2008). The body in the analytic session: Focusing on the body-mind link. *International Journal of Psychoanalysis, 89*, 89–109.

Lombardi, R. (2011). The body, feelings, and the unheard music of the senses. *Contemporary Psychoanalysis, 47*, 3–24.

Lombardi, R. (2013). Object relations and the ineffable bodily dimension. *Contemporary Psychoanalysis, 49*(1), 82–102.

Malloch, S. & Trevarthen, C. (Eds.). (2009). Musicality: Communicating the vitality and interests of life. In *Communicative musicality*. Oxford: Oxford University Press.

Marcel, G. (1928–1933). *Being and having. An existential diary* (K. Farrer, Trans.). New York: Harper Torchbooks, Harper & Row, 1965.

Marcel, G. (1933). The ontological mystery. In *The philosophy of existentialism.* New York: Citadel Press, 1956.

Marcel, G. (1940). *Du refus à l'invocation.* Paris: Gallimard.

Marcel, G. (1945). *Homo viator: Introduction to the metaphysic of hope.* London: Gollancz, 1951.

Marcel, G. (1959). *Presence and immortality.* Pittsburgh: Duquesne University Press.

Markman, H. (1997). Play in the treatment of adolescents. *Psychoanalytic Quarterly, 66,* 190–218.

Markman, H. (2006). Listening to music, listening to patients: Aesthetic experience in clinical practice. *fort da, 12*(2), 18–29.

Markman, H. (2010). "In This Room at This Time": The subtle radicalism of Michael Feldman's clinical contribution. *fort da, 16*(2), 9–21.

Markman, H. (2011). Metaphors we live by: Commentary on paper by Stephen H, Knoblauch. *Psychoanalytic Dialogues, 21,* 437–445.

Markman, H. (2015). A pragmatic approach to Bion's late work: A response to Soffer-Dudek. *Journal of the American Psychoanalytic Association, 63*(5): 947–957.

Markman, H. (2017). Presence, mourning, and beauty: Elements of analytic process. *Journal of the American Psychoanalytic Association, 65,* 979–1004.

Markman, H. (2020a). Accompaniment in jazz and psychoanalysis. *Psychoanalytic Dialogues, 30*(4), 432–447.

Markman, H. (2020b). Embodied attunement and participation. *Journal of the American Psychoanalytic Association, 68*(5), 807–834.

McCown, J. (1978). *Availability: Gabriel Marcel and the phenomenology of human openness.* Atlanta, GA: Scholars Press for the American Academy of Religion.

McLaughlin, J. T. (1987). The play of transference: Some reflections on enactment in the psychoanalytic situation. *Journal of the American Psychoanalytic Association, 35,* 557–582.

McLaughlin, J. T. (1991). Clinical and theoretical aspects of enactment. *Journal of the American Psychoanalytic Association, 39,* 595–614.

Merleau-Ponty, M. (1945). *Phenomenology of perception* (D. A. Landes, Trans.). New York: Routledge, 2012.

Milner, M. (1960). The concentration of the body. In *The suppressed madness of sane men: Forty-four years of exploring psychoanalysis.* London: Tavistock Publications, 1987.

Nacht, S. (1962). The curative factors in psycho-analysis. *International Journal of Psychoanalysis, 43,* 206–211.

Nebbiosi, G. & Federici-Nebbiosi, S. (2008). "We got rhythm": Miming and the polyphony of identity in psychoanalysis. In F. Anderson (Ed.), *Bodies in treatment.* New York and London: Analytic Press.

Neri, C. (2008). Authenticity as an aim in psychoanalysis. *Journal of the American Psychoanalytic Association, 68*(4), 325–349.

Ogden, T. H. (2019). Ontological psychoanalysis or "What do you want to be when you grow up?" *Psychoanalytic Quarterly, 88,* 661–684.

Pichon-Rivière, E. (1998). *El teoria del vinculo.* Buenos Aires: Nueva Vision.

Pichon-Rivière, E. (2017). *The linked self in psychoanalysis: The pioneering work of Enrique Pichon Rivière* (R. Losso, L. S. de Setton, & D. Scharff, Eds.). London: Karnac Books.

Racker, H. (1953). A contribution to the problem of counter-transference. *International Journal of Psycho-Analysis, 34,* 313–324.

Racker, H. (1957). The meaning and uses of countertransference. *Psychoanalytic Quarterly, 76*(3), 725–777.

Racker, H. (1968). *Transference and countertransference.* New York: IUP.

Reich, W. (1942). *Character analysis* (3rd Ed.). (V. R. Carfogno, Trans.) New York: Farrar, Straus, and Giroux, 1978.

Renik, O. (1993). Analytic interaction: Conceptualizing technique in light of the analyst's irreducible subjectivity. *Psychoanalytic Quarterly, 62,* 553–571.

Renik, O. (1999). Playing one's cards face up in analysis: An approach to the problem of self-disclosure. *Psychoanalytic Quarterly, 68*(4), 521–530.

Renik, O. (2004). Intersubjectivity in psychoanalysis. *International Journal of Psychoanalysis, 85*(5), 1053–1056.

Richter, G. (2009). *Text, writings, interviews and letters:1961-2007.* London: Thames & Hudson, Ltd.

Rose, G. (2004). *Between couch and piano: Psychoanalysis, music, art and neuroscience.* London: Bruner Routledge.

Scarry, E. (1995). *On beauty and the just.* Princeton, NJ: Princeton University Press.

Schoenberg, A. (1975). *Style and idea: Selected writings of Arnold Schoenberg.* (L., Stein, Ed.) (L. Black, Trans.). New York: St. Martin's Press; London: Faber & Faber.

Schore, A. N. (1994). *Affect regulation and the origin of the self: The neurobiology of emotional development.* Hillsdale, NJ: Erlbaum.

Schore, A. N. (2011). The right brain implicit self lies at the core of psychoanalysis. *Psychoanalytic Dialogues, 21*, 75–100.

Seligman, S. (2018). *Relationships in development: Infancy, intersubjectivity and attachment*. London: Routledge.

Shikibu, I. (1990) (c. 1004). Of this ruined house (J. Hirshfield & M. Aratani, Trans.). In *The ink dark moon*. London: Vintage Classics

Sletvold, J. (2014). *The embodied analyst: From Freud and Reich to relationality*. New York: Routledge.

Slochower, J. (1996). Holding and the fate of the analyst's subjectivity. *Psychoanalytic Dialogues, 6*(3): 323–353.

Slochower, J. (2013). *Romanian Journal of Psychoanalysis, 6*(2), 15–40.

Stern, D. N. (1985). *The interpersonal world of the infant: A view from psychoanalysis and developmental psychology*. New York: Basic Books.

Stern, Daniel N., et al. (1998). Non-interpretive mechanisms in psychoanalytic therapy: The 'something more' than interpretation. The Process of Change Study Group. *The International Journal of Psychoanalysis, 79*, 903–921.

Stern, D. N. (2004). *The present moment in psychotherapy and everyday life*. New York and London: W.W. Norton & Co.

Stern, D. N. (2010). *Forms of vitality: Exploring dynamic experience in psychology, the arts, psychotherapy and development*. Oxford: Oxford University Press.

Taylor, C. (1992). *The ethics of authenticity*. Cambridge, MA: Harvard University Press.

Trevarthen, C. (1979). Communication and cooperation in early infancy: A description of primary intersubjectivity. In M. Bullowa (Ed.), *Before speech: The beginning of human communication*. Cambridge: Cambridge University Press.

Trevarthen, C. (2008). The musical art of infant conversation: Narrating in the time of sympathetic experience, without rational interpretation, before words. *Musicae Scientiae, 12*(1) (Suppl.), 15–46.

Trevarthen, C. (2009). *SAIA Seminar: Why attachment matters in sharing meaning*. ddpnetwork.org: Glasgow.

Trevarthen, C. & Malloch, S. (2002). Musicality and music before three: Human vitality and invention shared with pride. *Zero to Three, 23*(1), 10–18.

Williams, B. (2020). (Interview in the *Guardian*).

Wilson, M. (2018). The analyst as listening-accompanist: Desire in Bion and Lacan. *Psychoanalytic Quarterly, 87*, 237–264.

Wilson, M. (2020). *The analyst's desire: The ethical foundation of clinical practice.* London: Bloomsbury Academic Press.

Winnicott, D. W. (1953). Transitional objects and transitional phenomena. *International Journal of Psychoanalysis, 34,* 89–97.

Winnicott, D. W. (1955). Metapsychological and clinical aspects of regression within the psycho-analytic set-up. *International Journal of Psycho-Analysis, 36,* 16–26.

Winnicott, D. W. (1960). The theory of the parent-child relationship *International Journal of Psycho-Analysis, 41,* 585–595.

Winnicott, D. W. (1965). *The maturational process and the facilitating environment.* Madison, CT: International University Press, Inc.

Winnicott, D. W. (1968), Playing: Its theoretical status in the clinical situation. *International Journal of Psycho-Analysis, 49,* 591–599.

Winnicott, D. W. (1971). *Playing and reality.* London: Tavistock Publications.

Winnicott, D. W. (1986). *Home is where we start from.* New York and London: Norton.

Veszy-Wagner, L. (1964). La presence du psychoanalysis: By. S. Nacht. (Presses Univ. de France 1963). *International Journal of Psychoanalysis, 45,* 128–131.

Index